STUDIES IN HISTORY, ECONOMICS AND PUBLIC LAW

EDITED BY THE FACULTY OF POLITICAL SCIENCE
OF COLUMBIA UNIVERSITY

Volume XCV]   [Number 2

Whole Number 216

AMERICAN APPRENTICESHIP AND INDUSTRIAL EDUCATION

BY

PAUL H. DOUGLAS, Ph.D.

*Assistant Professor of Labor Administration
The University of Chicago*

New York
COLUMBIA UNIVERSITY
LONGMANS, GREEN & CO., AGENTS
LONDON: P. S. KING & SON, LTD.

1921

<u>Printing Statement:</u>

To
DOROTHY W. DOUGLAS

TABLE OF CONTENTS

PAGE

PART I

AMERICAN APPRENTICESHIP: ITS BACKGROUND, DEVELOPMENT AND DECAY

CHAPTER I
Apprenticeship and its Relation to Industrial Education 11

CHAPTER II
American Apprenticeship Prior to the Factory Period 25

CHAPTER III
The Decline of Apprenticeship in the Machine Era. 53

PART II

JUVENILE LABOR AND THE EDUCATIONAL REQUIREMENTS OF MODERN INDUSTRY

CHAPTER IV
Present Conditions of Children in Industry 85

CHAPTER V
What Education is Needed for Modern Industry 109

PAGE

CHAPTER VI

The Problem of Vocational Education for Women 132

PART III

MODERN SUBSTITUTES FOR APPRENTICESHIP

CHAPTER VII

Manual Training 176

CHAPTER VIII

Trade and Industrial Schools 187

CHAPTER IX

Training of Employees by Plants 211

CHAPTER X

Evening and Correspondence Schools 229

CHAPTER XI

Coöperative and Continuation Schools 244

CHAPTER XII

Vocational Guidance 269

PART IV

SOCIAL ASPECTS

CHAPTER XIII

The Smith-Hughes Act and Federal Aid for Vocational Education. 293

CHAPTER XIV

The Economic Aspects of Industrial Education 307

PAGE

CHAPTER XV
The Attitude of Labor and Capital Towards Industrial Education . 315

CHAPTER XVI
A Program 331

Bibliographical Note 340

CHAPTER I

APPRENTICESHIP AND ITS RELATION TO INDUSTRIAL EDUCATION [1]

PERHAPS the most important educational movement of the past decade has been that of industrial education. The cause lies in the failure of the workshop to provide proper industrial training for its young employees. In order to understand the present educational situation, therefore, it is imperative to examine the roots from which is has grown, namely, the old system of apprenticeship that formerly provided broad training for the young workers of this country. The problem is not alone educational, but is economic as well and can only be understood by studying it from both aspects.

1. *Definition.* Apprenticeship is essentially a combination of education and industry. It is a process of learning by doing, under which a minor is taught the art of a trade by one who is at the moment engaged in it; the minor paying either in whole or in part for this instruction by the work done on objects destined for the master's consumption or sale.

This is a sufficient definition of an institution that was the chief means of trade education until the advent of the machine era. The apprentice differs from the ordinary child laborer in that he not only works for his master but receives instruction in his trade. Apprenticeship ceases when child labor degenerates from education to routine. Since now the shop no longer trains the child worker, other agencies must be created to assume the responsibility.

Apprenticeship can exist, either with or without a legal in-

[1] This chapter originally appeared in the *Pedagogical Seminary* for March, 1918.

denture. In its essence it is a contractual relationship between boy and master, involving an exchange of work for education. The indenture is merely the legal instrument bearing witness to this relationship. \The contract itself may be held binding in the absence of any written agreement whatsoever. For instance, a Connecticut court has held that a boy who lived to the age of twenty-one with a mechanic, learning the trade under parole agreement, was an apprentice though there were no articles of indenture existing between the two.[1] Other decisions have been made supporting this view.[2] In fact, many of the firms that now have apprenticeship systems do not have formal written indentures binding the two parties, but allow a continuance of the relation upon the pleasure of both. It goes without saying, however, that though the indenture is not synonymous with apprenticeship, it is very valuable as a means of giving needed fixity and definiteness to a relation that might otherwise become too lax.

2. *Origin and extent.* Apprenticeship originated far earlier than is commonly supposed. The popular belief is that it had its inception in the handicrafts of the medieval European town, crystallising in the regulations of the craft gilds. No writer upon economic history, in fact, has placed its beginnings further back than this period. Adam Smith declared : " Apprenticeships were altogether unknown to the ancients. I know of no Latin or Greek word (I might venture, I believe, to assert that there is none) which expresses

[1] Huntington *v.* Oxford, 4 Day, 189 (1810).

[2] State *v.* Jones, 16 Fla. 306. ` See *Niles Register*, vol. lix, p. 336 (1840), where record is made of a similar decision by which a boy was sent back to his master, though no written agreement existed. See also H. G. Wood, *A Treatise on the Law of Master and Servant*, p. 52: " When the parties to a contract are bound thereby, one to teach and the other to learn and serve at a certain trade or business, it is a quasi contract of apprenticeship, whether in writing or by parole."

the idea we annex to the word, Apprentice." [1]   This statement by Smith has been freely accepted by writers upon
economic history and industrial education.   The Encyclo-
pedia Britannica says: " So far as it can be seen, it (apprenticeship) arose in the middle ages, and formed an integral
part of the system of trade gilds and corporations." [2]   Recent works upon the subject contain similar statements.
One declares that " the modern apprenticeship system has
its origin in the medieval handicraft work; [3] another that
" the apprenticeship system took its rise in medieval handicraft work." [4]   Many similar citations could be given. [5]

As a matter of fact the history of apprenticeship does not
stop here.   Traces of it are found in the very dawn of
civilization.   The Babylonian Code of Hammurabi (2100
B. C.) recognizes and regulates apprenticeship in the following terms: " If an artisan take a son for adoption and teach
him his handicraft, one may not bring claim against him.
If he do not teach his handicraft, that adopted son may
return to his father's house." [6]   Aside from proving once
more that there is nothing new under the sun, this voice
from the past is significant in several respects.   In the first
place, the fact of codification proves that apprenticeship
was even then in an advanced state of development and had
probably already existed for a considerable period of time.
Secondly, it appears that the status of master and apprentice
was that of father and son, a blood fiction being created.
The term of apprenticeship, furthermore, lasted apparently

[1] Smith, *The Wealth of Nations* (Cannan edit.), vol. i, p. 124.

[2] 1910 edition, vol. ii, p. 229.

[3] J. L. Taylor, *A Handbook of Vocational Education*, pp. 138-139.

[4] *Bulletin 19*, U. S. Bureau of Education, 1913.

[5] Among these may be cited, Labatt's *Master and Servant*, vol. vi,
p. 6384.

[6] *The Code of Hammurabai* (Harper trans.), p. 74, rules 188-189.

for life. The apprentice leaves his father's house to go to
that of the master; if the master teaches him, he stays.
Finally, there is indication of state supervision over the relations of master and apprentice, since the master is required to teach the apprentice his trade without the right to
exploit him as boy labor.

Among the Greeks, the existence of apprenticeship is
witnessed to by references of several writers. Plato plainly
refers to it in "the Republic."[1] Xenophon says it is
" Just as necessary as when a man puts his son out to apprenticeship to be trained that a contract should be made
concerning what the son should know."[2] Thus, the existence of apprenticeship is not only established, but there is
evidence that it was regulated by agreements between the
master and the father of the apprentice. Modern classical
scholars have indeed accepted apprenticeship as an essential
factor in the economic life of Athens.[3]

Apprenticeship was furthermore present under the Roman
Empire. Lucian mentions that he was apprenticed to his
uncle to learn sculpturing, but that he broke his contract and
ran away.[4] Professor Westermann has recently translated
several indentures that give an idea of the conditions of
apprenticeship in Roman Egypt.[5] According to these con-

[1] Plato, *The Republic*, bk. iv, Spens. translates, " His sons and those
others whom he instructs "; Jowett translates, " His sons and apprentices." Jowett, *Dialogues of Plato*, vol. iii, p. 109. The word translated is demiourgos.

[2] Xenophon, *De Re Equestri*, 2.2.

[3] See for example Zimmern, *The Greek Commonwealth*, especially
the chapter on "City Economics: Craftsmen and Workmen," pp. 255-
276; also L. F. Anderson, "Some Facts Regarding Vocational Training Among the Ancient Greeks and Romans," *School Review*, vol. xx,
pp. 191-201.

[4] Lucian, *The Dream*, Dakyn's trans.

[5] W. L. Westermann, *Classical Philology* vol. xi (1914), pp. 295-315;
also an article by the same author, " Vocational Training in Antiquity "
in the *School Review*, vol. xxii, pp. 601-610.

tracts, the artisan gave trade instruction, plus other considerations, to the apprentice in return for the apprentice's labor.

Some of the masters practised the trades of weaving, shorthand writing, flute-playing, hairdressing, and nail-smithing. The time of service for these trades varied greatly. In the weaving trade, the indentures provided for a term of from one to five years, with indications that a three-year period was the one most commonly required. A boy apprenticed to a flute player had to pay a money subsidy to the master, probably because his labor would be worthless. In weaving, on the other hand, it was the master who paid the apprentice. A compensation for clothing was allowed, and money wages were paid to the guardian or parent not only during a part of the third year of service but also for such period thereafter as the apprentice might serve. The wages were progressively graduated according to the length of the contract. The apprentice, furthermore, does not appear to have lived with the master, but to have boarded at home; in return for which the master made an additional money allowance to the parent of the boy.

It is apparent that there was no fixed term of service or rate of wages, these matters being settled by individual contract. The state's interest was confined to levying taxes upon apprentices and to inflicting fines in cases of broken contracts. All the apprenticeship regulations, moreover, were confined to the provisions of the common law. None of the codes made specific inclusion of them.[1] It is undoubtedly this absence from formal Roman law that has led jurists and economic historians to deny the very existence of the apprenticeship institution.

[1] Professor Westermann states that the codes of Justinian and Theodosius seem to indicate a continuation of the apprenticeship system with governmental regulation for the purposes of taxation together with greater rigidity in the hereditary principle of choosing a trade.

But not only is the institution of apprenticeship much older than is commonly imagined it was also more universal. It was as much a part of the far eastern system of handicraft as it was of western Europe. Mr. Coomaraswamy's translation of an ancient Sinhalese potter's song describing in poetic language the operations which apprentices were to perform, reveals apprenticeship as firmly embedded in Indian handicraft,[1] while students of Chinese industry have pointed out the parallelism between oriental apprenticeship and that of medieval Europe together with the similar functions of gilds as regulatory and supervisory bodies.[2]

That apprenticeship is of ancient origin and almost universal extent should not, however, excite much surprise, for it is obviously the normal correlative of handicraft labor. Whenever industry has developed beyond the family as a self-sufficing entity, separate trades arise from which the artisan must derive the whole or a part of his living. The growth of the industry must in many cases entail more work than can be done by the sons alone. Other boys must be taught the trade, not only to insure enough skilled workmen, but also in some cases to provide continuity in its management. The inevitable result is apprenticeship.

3. *Applies to professions as well as trades.* The system of apprenticeships has been used to prepare men for all forms of industrial and professional work, not for the manual crafts alone.[3] It cannot be repeated too often

[1] *Spolai Zeylanica* (see especially vol. iv, pts. xiv and xv) translated by A. K. Coomaraswamy 1906. For an interesting description of Indian industry and the plan of apprenticeship see Mr. Coomaraswamy's *Medieval Sinalese Art.*

[2] See among others H. B. Morse, *The Gilds of China*, 1908.

[3] Among the Greeks there was no distinction between what we now designate as trades, crafts, arts, and professions. All alike were given the same name: Techne.

that apprenticeship is basically a process of learning by doing.[1] It is a higher form of the trial-and-error process, containing a large amount of imitative motion. As such, it quite naturally antedates all theoretical instruction.

The avenue of entrance to all professions formerly lay through apprenticeship. Until recent years lawyers were almost predominantly trained in law offices by practising attorneys.[2] Even to-day, despite the multiplicity of law schools, many attorneys are educated by this purely " prentice-like " practise.[3] Dentists and doctors have in the past been trained by similar methods. Indeed, as Mr. Flexner points out, English medical schools are but an outgrowth of the pooling of apprentices whom individual doctors have taken with them in their rounds through the hospitals.[4]

As medieval universities were controlled either by gilds of students or by gilds of teachers, graduation from the student ranks meant at first only entrance into the rank of teacher. Just as the medieval silversmiths, coopers, and other craftsmen were compelled to produce a " masterpiece " as evidence that they had successfully completed their appreticeship and were qualified to become full-fledged journeymen, so too was the student compelled to procure his original piece of work for graduation. The dissertation of the modern doctor of philosophy is but a vestigial remain of this custom.

[1] The educational nature of apprenticeship is seen from the French and German equivalents of the term. The French word is *apprentissage*; the German, *lehrzeit*, springing respectively from the stems, *apprendre* and *lehren*, to learn and to teach.

[2] See Redlich, *The Case Method in American Law Schools* (Carnegie Foundation), p. 7.

[3] *Ibid.*, p. 7.

[4] *The Atlantic Monthly*, Oct., 1915, p. 528.

Chivalry itself was but a species of handicraft. A boy having served seven years as page and seven years as squire was then admitted with attendant ceremony to the rank of knight. These steps were perfectly analogous to the stages of apprentice, journeyman, and master craftsman, through which the artisan passed.

In recent times pedagogy has also been taught by the method of apprenticeship. In 1846 the pupil-teacher system was introduced into the London schools to succeed the Lancastrian or monitorial system. Boys and girls were apprenticed to the head teacher, assisted him in his work, received instruction (which was generally given at the break-fast hour), and were paid a small but increasing wage for their labor. This practice was plainly nothing but apprenticeship. The teacher-apprentices were supposed to be no less than thirteen years of age; in many case they were still younger. The London County Council, in 1875, wishing to reform the situation, stipulated that no pupil-teachers would be accepted who were less than fourteen. In 1869 there were two apprentices for every teacher. This indicates that the teaching profession was not only poorly manned, but that apprentices could not be sure of final opportunity to serve as full-fledged teachers. Even in London to-day the art of teaching is imparted in this fashion. The relative number of apprentices has, however, decreased. In 1904 the ratio was one apprentice to every four masters, while the instruction formerly given by individual masters is instead given in normal schools.[1]

Though apprenticeship has been the generic form of education for all these professions, the old imitative, empirical method of education has been largely or wholly replaced by school training. Whenever a trade, craft, or profession has developed to such a stage that general principles

[1] *Final report*, London School Board, 1870-1904, pp. 138-146.

and scientific causation can be abstracted from personal contact, then apprenticeship as the sole or chief method of training for that occupation declines. That which was an art becomes a science with more or less fixed rules and a generalized method of procedure. In our day, we have seen schools of finance and administration invade the art of business management, promising to revolutionize the functions of the entrepreneur and make business a science.

Will this movement from the system of apprenticeship to school training, which has been so characteristic of the professions, take place in the manual arts as well? Will bricklaying and carpentry be taught in the schools in the future as medicine and law are now, rather than on the job? This question is indeed an open one, but as we shall see it is extremely doubtful if the school can ever replace the shop as the chief method of training manual workers. Even in the professions abstract instruction alone has been found inadequate; young lawyers must become clerks in offices; doctors must serve as internes in hospitals. In industrial pursuits the case for shop training appears even stronger. The content of the various trades cannot easily be given elsewhere than in the industry itself.

4. *Apprenticeship a preparation for life as well as for industry.* Another function of apprenticeship is the development of character and good citizenship. Originally it was a preparation for life, not a preparation for technical pursuits alone.[1] The English gilds formerly acted as the moral and educational supervisors of the apprentice—among other things, in some cases requiring church attendance,—and this

---

[1] See R. A. Bray's view of the essence of apprenticeshhip—"Originally the term apprenticeship was employed to signify not merely the practical training in the mysteries of a trade, but also that wider training of character and intelligence on which depends the real efficiency of the craftsman." *Boy Labour and Apprenticeship*, p. 1.

theory of the social nature of apprenticeship existed long
after the gild form of organization decayed.   Peel's child
labor law of 1802 was entitled, " An act for the preservation of the health and morals of the Apprentices and others
employed in cotton and other mills and cotton and other
factories." [1]   This law stipulated that educational training
should be given every day with religious instruction " one
hour every Sunday."

The apprenticeship regulations of the colonies furnish
ample proof that this conception of apprenticeship held in
America as well as in England.   The statutes of many of
the colonies provided that the apprentice should be taught
to read and write, should be given biblical instruction
(Massachusetts compelling church attendance), and that the
master must be a moral man.   Should the master violate
any of these provisions, the apprentice was to be freed from
his contract. The system was designed, in so far as the isolated life of the times permitted, to prepare the apprentice
for society, as well as for his trade. Nor should it be forgotten that the state assumed supervision over the apprentice
until he reached the age of twenty-one, in some cases, twenty-
four. At the present time the states, with few exceptions,
disclaim any responsibility for the child over fourteen. In
our far more complex life with its many dangers to adoles-
ence, we are turning children loose from seven to ten years
earlier than in colonial times.

5. *A transition stage between servitude and freedom.*
Apprenticeship has frequently resulted in a semi-servile
status which contrasts curiously with its protective features.
The relation of the apprentice is at best a dependent one,
and in primitive states of society it may readily take on some
of the aspects of slavery.   Among many of the Southern

[1] 42 Geo. III, c. 87.

colonies, notably Virginia and South Carolina, the same laws were made applicable to negro slaves and to white apprentices.[1] A study of the methods by which the various ✓ states manumitted the slaves within their jurisdiction, shows that apprenticeship was a half-way stage between slavery and complete freedom. In the slow social evolution which the Pennsylvania negro experienced, he passed through the stage of apprenticeship on his way to freedom. The abolition act of 1780 commuted slavery to a term of apprenticeship under the old masters of the former slaves.[2] New Jersey and Illinois followed a similar plan.[3]

A parallel proposal was made by the Prussian landowners when the " hereditary subjection " was about to be removed. Cuba, in freeing her slaves, pursued an identical policy.[4] When England freed her slaves in 1831, the colonial government re-committed the freedmen in the West Indies to a term of apprenticeship, owners being metamorphosed into masters. The evils that followed the creation of this new status were every whit as bad as those of the previous era. Men and women were flogged to death, and the barbarous cruelties that were practised show that slave discipline was as active and as powerful under apprenticeship as under slavery.[5]

---

[1] See Henning, *Virginia Statutes*, vol. iii, pp. 446-47, "An Act Concerning Servants and Slaves."

[2] See E. R. Turner, *The Negro in Pennsylvania*, pp. 89-108.

[3] The New Jersey act of 1846 simply substituted apprenticeship for slavery. See H. S. Cooley, *A Study of Slavery in New Jersey*, pp. 28-31. The census of 1850 enumerates several hundred New Jersey blacks who were legally "apprentices." For the process in Illinois see N. D. Harris, *The History of Negro Servitude in Illinois*, pp. 6-103.

[4] H. H. S. Aimes, "Transition from Slave to Free Labor in Cuba," *Yale Review*, vol. xv, pp. 68-84.

[5] William Bevan, *Operation of the Apprenticeship System of the British Colonies* (published in 1837), pp. 35, ff, gives a striking account of the system.

It is very interesting to note that Abraham Lincoln, during his first term in Congress, introduced a bill for the freeing of the slaves in the District of Columbia, that provided a temporary system of apprenticeship for them.[1] It was indeed the enactment of apprenticeship codes by some of the southern states after the Civil War[2] (codes which provided for a more or less permanent semi-servile status of the newly-freed negro) that was the immediate cause of the harsh measures of reprisal undertaken by the North upon the South. The leaders of the radical northern movement charged that slavery was being set up again in the South under a different guise.[3] Whether many of these nominal "apprentices" received the training necessary to continue bona-fide apprenticeship is, of course, extremely doubtful. The legal fiction of apprenticeship was however maintained.

The reasons for this curious use of apprenticeship are simple. It is dangerous for the slave to be suddenly transposed from slavery to freedom. The freedman is disposed to idle away his time. This means the disorganization of the working force of the former master. The former owners moreover feel that they are entitled to compensation. If money is denied them, they claim further service from their former slaves.

6. *Legal Theories.* The legal theories of apprenticeship have naturally changed with the successive forms of its constitution. In Babylon, as we saw, the relation of master and apprentice was that of father and son—apparently a relation of permanence. All the potential harshness of the

---

[1] Strunsky, *Abraham Lincoln*, p. 68.

[2] Notably Alabama, Louisiana, and Mississippi. For a southern account, showing the alleged necessity for a more permanent labor force, see Hilary A. Herbert's *Why the Solid South?*

[3] See, for instance, James G. Blaine's *Twenty Years in Congress*, vol. ii, pp. 94-103.

patria potestas (to use an anachronism) accompanied this relationship. By the time of Roman Egypt, apprenticeship had developed into a contractual state of fixed stipulations under which the apprentice received a money reward as well as instruction. He became, in a word, a wage-earner. This change of status weakened the concept of filiality. In the Middle Ages apprenticeship became a matter for corporate control upon the part of the gilds. The master had now become the temporary guardian, not the parent, of the apprentice. But though the apprentice is not the property of the master, his term of service is. The unexpired serving time of the apprentice is often an economic asset of the master and could, under certain conditions, be sold or bequeathed. This constitutes property in time if not in persons.

With the coming of the machine era, the length of the period of service was shortened. Industry did not now require protracted service on the part of any individual. Master and apprentice now stand more in the capacity of friends who can terminate their relation at pleasure. Two main tendencies appear in this development: (1) The movement from a personal to an impersonal basis, (2) the decrease in length of service, beginning with a lifetime and ending in some cases with but a few months.

7. *Universality of problem.* The problems presented by the decadence of apprenticeship are not peculiar to America alone. Great Britain has seen child labor robbed of its former educative qualities, and become largely routine drudgery. France, after abolishing the gilds in 1791, felt the need of skilled training, and some of the best analytical studies of modern industry have resulted from her knowledge of that need.[1] Germany as we all know, met the

[1] Some of the more important recent studies are: Charles Berteaux, *La Crise de l'Apprentissage en France* (1909); Gustav Dron, *Pro-*

problem better than any other nation. She accomplished
this through her perpetuation of the gilds as the supervisors
of trade education and through her system of compulsory
attendance in continuation schools. Italy and Switzerland
have experienced the same difficulty. Industrially backward countries, such as Austria,[1] and countries newly in-
ducted into the machine process, like Japan, face parallel
situations.

Wherever the old hand process has given way to
machinery, wherever the division of labor has been greatly
extended, there the old system of apprenticeship has broken
down. With it the training of the boy in industry, both
for the industry and for life itself, becomes more and more
difficult. The problem of the future is to devise a system
which will modernize the good features of the former
system and add to them merits which it did not formerly
possess.

*position de loi sur l'organisation de l'apprentissage, par les cours pro-
fessionel (1911) ; Constant Verlot, Rapport fait au nom de la commission
du commerce, et de l'industrie sur le projet et les propositions de lois
relatif a l'enseignement technique industriel et commercial (1912).
Also two governmental studies, Rapport de l'apprentissage dans l'industrie de l'horlogerie and L'Apprentissage industriel.*

[1] See August Letwehr, "Die Lehrlingsfrage in der Grossindustrie,"
Oesterreichische Rundschau, vol. xxxvi, pp. 199-201 (1913).

CHAPTER II

AMERICAN APPRENTICESHIP PRIOR TO THE FACTORY PERIOD

THE colonial system of apprenticeship was not indigenous to American soil. Most of the colonists were Englishmen who brought to America the ideas and the institutions of their mother country. To understand American apprenticeship, we must, therefore, understand English apprenticeship, and note the similarities and differences between the two.

1. The English Background.

The celebrated Statute of Artificers in 1562[1] which is often regarded as the real starting-point of English apprenticeship, was merely the codification of the customary guild regulations and previous enactments.[2] What had hitherto been a local affair regulated by the craft guilds[3] now became a national matter regulated by the central government according to uniform rules. Legislation concerning apprenticeship and craft regulation had been enacted for many decades before Elizabeth. It is to the credit of Elizabeth and her counsellors to have made of these scattered enactments a well-rounded system.

[1] 5 Eliz. C-4.

[2] For a good discussion of the purport and purpose of the statute, see Dunlop and Denman, *English Apprenticeship and Child Labor*, chap. iii, pp. 60-71.

[3] For a suggestive description of apprenticeship as a form of education under the guilds see L. S. Lyon, " Medieval English Apprenticeship as Business Education," *School Review*, vol. xxvii, Oct., 1920, pp. 585-99.

The Statute was modelled chiefly upon the regulations of the London guilds. It bound the apprentice formally with a written indenture that was to be kept on record; it fixed his term at seven years (with the important provision that, if he bound himself before he was 17, his term in any case should not expire until he was 24), and it granted the right to take apprentices to householderes only. It is also interesting to note that it prohibited sons of countrymen from entering most of the trades, reserving this profitable field for the townsmen.

The Statute of Artificers was also designed as a system of poor relief.[1] It gave justices of the peace and officers of towns the power to bind out any unemployed person under twenty-one as an apprentice to a trade[2] or to a husbandry, provided that in the latter case the farmer to whom he was bound owned a minimum of half a ploughland in tillage. The technical value of these two forms of apprenticeship was of course very unequal. The craftsman was taught his trade, the husbandman merely worked for his master. By the poor law of 1601[3] justices of the peace were given power to apprentice not only the children of paupers and vagrants but also the children of large families who it was thought would in the future become a burden to the state. Apprenticeship as a measure of poor relief had thus reached its widest possible scope.

[1] For a contemporary view of the state of England see John Hales, *Discourse concerning the Commonwealth of this Realm* (edited by Miss Lamond, written in 1549. Pub. under initials W. S. in 1581.)

[2] See Scott, J. F., *Historical Essays in Apprenticeship and Vocational Education*, pp. 7-26, showing that apprenticeship was not the sole means of entering a trade, but that the rank of journeyman could be also obtained by patrimony and by purchase.

[3] 43 Eliz. C. 2.

2. *Colonial Need for Cheap Labor.*

In the early days of the colonies their need for an adequate labor supply was very great. New land was being opened up, and there was a large demand for colonial products, especially tobacco. The agricultural system of Virginia was based on the plantation, which, unlike the New England farm, could not be worked by the family of the owner. A dependent class of laborers was therefore its necessary accompaniment. Later the manorial system of Maryland, and the large landed estates of New York demanded a similar class of labor.

England, on the other hand, had a surplus population. The development of the woolen industry and the sheep enclosures had dispossessed thousands of their former holdings.[1] Pauperism was on the increase, and the burden of poor support was becoming irksome to the parishes.

With such a demand for labor upon the part of the colonies and with such a supply in England, emigration to the colonies was the natural consequence. The problem was how to transport the poor, since ship passage was expensive and far beyond the means of those who desired to migrate. The simplest solution was indented servitude. This was apprenticeship divested of its educational opportunities. The servant in return for his transportation guaranteed to work for some master for a specified period of years.

Indented servitude was thus the Colonial analogue of the agricultural apprenticeship provided by the Statute of Artificers, and as such flourished chiefly in the great agricultural

[1] The number affected by the sheep enclosures is a much-mooted question. Prof. E. F. Gay, who has made a detailed study of this point, believes that the number has been over-estimated and that it did not exceed 20,000, *cf.* Tawney, *The Agrarian Problem of the Sixteenth Century.*

areas of the South. Pennsylvania too, had its share of servants,[1] and the Dutch patroons with their extensive holdings absorbed a considerable number annually. With these two exceptions, however, the cases of agricultural indentures in the upper and middle tier of colonies were not as common as in the South.[2]

3. *Apprenticeship Compared with Industrial Servitude.*

It was difficult to distinguish between an apprentice and an indentured servant. Both were under contract to serve for a period of years, both were subject to the same regulations as regards running away and breaking their contract, and the same statutes were often applied to both classes. In popular speech they frequently served as interchangeable terms.[3] The chief differences between the two classes may be summarized as follows:

(1) The apprentice was supposed to receive trade instruction, while the indentured servant was not. However, even here the popular confusion of terms was so great that we find many indentures specifying that the so-called " servant " is to be taught a trade. Obviously this is only apprenticeship in disguise.[4]

[1] K. F. Geiser, Redemptioners and Indentured Servants in the Colony and Commonwealth of Pennsylvania, Supp. *Yale Review*, vol. x, no. 2, August, 1901.

[2] Yet see in vol. xviii of *New York Historical Society Collections*, p. 571, where in 1696 Elizabeth Monis in consideration of her passage from England bound herself " to live as an apprentice with Captain Kidd for four years." Also in the *Acts of the Province of Mass. Bay*, vol. i, p. 634, an act passed Feb. 26, 1709, whereby "A bounty of forty shillings per head for male servants between 8 and 25 be given to anyone who would bring into the province one (a servant) from Great Britain."

[3] See Franklin's *Autobiography*, p. 172 (Bigelow Ed.) where he speaks of George Webb, who was being taught the trade of printing and therefore was plainly an apprentice, as a " bought servant ".

[4] See *Record of Indentures of Individuals Bound Out as Apprentices,*

(2) The Colonies, as we shall see later, prescribed the rudiments of a liberal education for the apprentice, while they required nothing of the sort for the indentured servant. The practical result of this was that, as the servant could thus work all the time while the apprentice must be taught, the servant was the more sought after, and his service-time brought a higher price.

(3) Since apprenticeship primarily involved "learning," the apprentice was generally a minor, while the indented servant was usually an adult.

(4) The apprentice was generally a child born in the Colonies, while the indentured servant almost invariably came from abroad. This meant that the apprentice made out his indenture under the immediate supervision of the Colonial Government, while the servant often brought his with him from a foreign country.[1] Consequently the working relations of the servant were far harder to control.

(5) The unexpired serving-time of the indentured servant, like that of the slave, was transferable without the consent of the servant. Theoretically at least, according to English common law, the unexpired serving-time of the apprentice could only be transferred with the consent of the apprentice himself, although in practice this provision was violated many times.

Servants, etc., in Philadelphia (between 1771-73). This contains 51 cases where an ostensible servant was to be taught a trade. A typical one is as follows: John Sherman binds himself out as "a servant to be taught the art, trade, and mystery of a spinning wheel maker and have three quarters schooling," p. 5. Despite this term, this is nothing but apprenticeship. It is characteristic in showing the hazy lines of demarcation between apprentices and servants.

Conversely, some apprentices were indentured to learn the "art and mysteries of husbandry." However, farming was not such a science then as to justify the idea that these apprentices were actually given instruction. These so-called apprentices were really indented servants.

[1] This does not apply to the redemptioners who signed their indentures after landing.

4. Classification of Indented Servants

Analyzing the status of indented servitude somewhat more closely, we may say in general that it embraced two main categories—voluntary servitude and involuntary.[1] Each of these in turn has further subdivisions.

Voluntary servitude included (a) those men and women who sold themselves to a ship-master or other persons for a term of years in return for their passage, the ship-master in turn selling them to the highest bidder upon their arrival in the colonies, (b) the redemptioners or "free-willers" who, without selling themselves to the ship master, engaged passage and upon their arrival undertook to sell themselves into servitude. This latter class conducted their sale without the aid of the middle-man, the ship master. It was provided, however, that should the redemptioner fail to dispose of himself within a specified time (generally 30 days) and thus be unable to pay for his passage, the title to his services should revert back to the ship master, who could then dispose of him.

Involuntary servitude included four classes: (a) Children bound out as apprentices by English local authorities. For example, in 1619 100 poor London boys and girls were bound out for seven years to the Virginia Company by the mayor and council of London. Some of these apprentices were in turn disposed of by the company to independent planters.[2]

(b) Children and adults forcibly seized and transported to this country against their will. This importation of ser-

---

[1] For slightly different classification see J. C. Ballagh, *White Servitude in Virginia*, pp. 33-4; (McCormack, *White Servitude in Maryland*, pp. 37-44). For a contemporary description of the kind of servants see Peter Kalm, *Travels into North America*, vol. i, pp. 387-390.

[2] J. C. Ballagh, *White Servitude in Virginia*, pp. 29-29.

vants proved such a profitable business that many traders were not satisfied with legitimate gains.   In Virginia the serving time of a male servant would bring from 40 £ to 60 £.[1]   Virginia and Maryland also gave bounties of fifty acres of land for each servant imported.   The water-front men of England were a notoriously criminal set, and, beginning in the reign of Charles I, they began to kidnap children, put them on board vessels, and ship them to America, where they were sold into servitude.   This practice was general up to 1670, and continued intermittently after that.   The "spirits" as the kidnappers were called, excited a popular terror in England comparable only to the uproar aroused a few years ago over "white slavers."[2]

(c) Debtors.   Disposing of one's person (or having it seized) to satisfy a debt had long been a common practice in England.   Now the demands of the new country gave the practice a great impetus.   Most of the indentures thus taken out were of course for servitude, but many were for apprenticeship also.   Moreover, once arrived in the Colonies, a person falling into debt was liable to fresh indenture.[3] Pennsylvania stipulated that debtors unable to pay charges against them shoud be sold into service.[4]   In Massachusetts the practice was so common and the evils so flagrant that

[1] *Ibid.*, p. 41.

[2] See P. A. Bruce, *Economic History of Virginia in the Seventeenth Century*, pp. 613-15.

[3] *N. Y. Historical Society Collections*, vol. xlii. "Indentures of Apprentices," 1718-1727. Sept. 14, 1725. "This indenture witnesseth that Mary Van der Riper of the City of New York, spinster, in consideration of her being justly indebted unto Just Looy of the same place, cooper, in the sum of fifteen pounds, and having no other way to pay or satisfy the same than by servitude, hath put herself and by these presents doth put herself a servant to the said Just Looy to serve him and his assigns during the full end and term of four years next ensuing."

[4] *Laws of Province of Pennsylvania*, 1728, p. 80.

the General Court in 1683 enacted that such pressure into service must be supervised by the proper legal authorities.[1]

(d) Convicts deported from England to the colonies. This class was a most numerous one, but not nearly so dangerous as the term would indicate. The convict class included (1) Political criminals. The latter half of the 17th century was a tumultuous one in English politics. The civil wars, Penruddock's revolt against the Commonwealth in 1655, the Scotch Insurrection in 1666, the uprising of the West under Monmouth in 1685 and its bloody suppression by Jeffries, together with the Jacobite rebellion of 1715, all furnished their quota of prisoners who were despatched to the colonies for a term of years. Most of these prisoners were, to be sure, sent to the Barbadoes, but some were sent to New England[2] and a great many to the South. Sixteen hundred and ten Scotch prisoners, according to Ballagh, were sent to Virginia in 1651 after the battle of Worcester.[3] (2) Civil Criminals. Large numbers of these were dumped upon America by the English authorities, and many sentences of death were commuted to deportation to the colonies. Though this class as a whole was not a good ingredient in the colonial population, yet it too, undoubtedly, included many decent individuals. The criminal code of England during the 17th and 18th centuries was notoriously severe, and inflicted heavy penalties

---

[1] *Records of Mass. Bay Colony,* vol. v, p. 415. During the latter half of the eighteenth century, forced service for debt was very generally changed throughout the colonies to imprisonment. Instead of selling a debtor into service, his creditor now threw him into jail. Imprisonment for debt was widely prevalent in the period 1810-1835. *Cf.* McMaster, *History of the People of the U. S.,* vol. iii, pp. 534-35. Also *Annual Reports of the Prison Discipline Society* (Boston), beginning with that of 1825.

[2] Especially those of the 1666 revolt.

[3] Ballagh, *op. cit.,* p. 35.

for offenses which we should now class as mere mis-
demeanors.

Maryland was thickly infested with these "criminals"
and one of her historians has estimated that at least 20,000
of them entered the colony before the Revolution, and that
in the period 1750-1770 the annual importation of convicts was between 400 and 500.[1]

5. *Conditions of Indented Servants*

The length of service of the indentured servant varied
from colony to colony.   In Virginia it was originally seven
years, in Maryland five years, in Rhode Island commonly
ten years.[2]   One source of trouble was that many servants
were held under verbal agreements without any written
contract.   Masters would then often allege that the agreement held for a longer period of time than it actually did.
To remedy this injustice, the Colonies passed a great deal of
legislation.   In 1654, Virginia decreed that servants over
sixteen who did not have written indentures, should serve
for six years, and that those under sixteen should serve
until they were twenty-four.   In 1661 she changed the term
of those over sixteen to five years (so that a servant might
be free as young at twenty-one) while those under sixteen
were to remain bound until they were twenty-four. In 1666
she provided that servants over nineteen were to serve for
five years but all those under nineteen until they reached the
age of twenty-four.[3]   South Carolina in 1717 provided
that an unindentured servant should have "five years service but not be freed in that time before 21,"[4] thus paral-

[1] Scharf, *History of Maryland*, vol. i, pp. 371-72.

[2] For discussion of this point see Ballagh, *White Servitude in Virginia*.
pp. 24-25.

[3] For further study of the Virginia situation, *cf.*, P. A. Bruce,
Economic History of Virginia, vol. ii, pp. 3-7.

[4] *South Carolina Statutes*, vol. iii, p. 14.

leling the Virginia Act of 1661. Maryland enacted rather complicated legislation in 1715 in order to prevent fraud and protect the servants from the danger of serving excessive time.[1] All of these colonies required masters to register their servants. The period of service could, however, legally be prolonged as a punishment for serious misbehaviour, such as running away,[2] contracting a marriage with another servant, giving birth to or begetting a child, or committing fornication with the negroes, free or slave.[3]

Running away became such a serious problem that the Colonies tried two other deterrents besides prolongation of the term of service, namely, the setting of strict bounds beyond which the servant might not go, and corporal punishment if he overstepped them. Massachusetts did not

[1] *Acts of Assembly Passed in the Province of Maryland from 1692 to 1715*, p. 144, "that whosoever shall transport any servant into this province without indenture, such servant being above the age of twenty-two, shall be obliged to serve the full time of five years; if between eighteen and twenty-two, without indenture, six years; if between fifteen and eighteen, without indenture, seven years; if under fifteen, without indenture, shall serve until he or they arrive at the full age of twenty-two years."

[2] In Virginia, the term of runaway was extended at first, 1 year, then lengthened. See Henning, *Statutes*, vol. i, p. 252. *Statutes*, vol. iii, p. 29. Act of 1686. (b) Pennsylvania stipulated (1710) that servants who ran away should serve five additional days for every day absent. Quoted from *Laws of the Province of Pennsylvania*, 1728, p. 1. (c) Maryland 1715—a runaway servant "shall make such satisfaction by servitude otherwise—not exceeding ten days service for one day's absence." *Acts of Assembly Passed in the Province of Maryland from 1692 to 1715*, p. 141.

[3] Henning, *Virginia Statutes*, vol. iii, pp. 452-53. The law of 1705 provided for one year additional service on the part of a female servant giving birth to an illegitimate child—with these exceptions: 1st, if the master was the father of the child, no additional service was required; 2nd. if a negro was the father, the mother must pay either 15£ to the county or be sold into service for five additional years.—*Laws of Province of Penn. 1728-40* (Act of 1700) imposed a maximum of two years and minimum of one year additional time.

allow the servant to leave the township without written permission.   Maryland placed the limit at ten miles from his master's home.[1]   South Carolina placed it at two miles, and decreed that if a servant were discovered beyond bounds, he was to be returned to his master and be whipped by the constable of every town through which he passed; when he finally reached home his master was to complete the good work by administering a drubbing of his own.[2]

In all cases of misdemeanor by the servants the administration of the law was in the hands of magistrates, who were, at least in the South, either the planters themselves or else their friends.   The possibility of abuse of power was therefore very great.   For a like reason, protection against actual ill-treatment by the masters was not strong.   By the terms of the indenture the master contracted to feed and clothe the servant sufficiently, not to over-work him, and to treat him kindly.   Upon complaint of the servant, the county courts could summon the master and try the case.   If found guilty, the master was fined, and if the offense was flagrant, he lost the services of his servant.   A semi-servile class, however, would obviously be slow to make any complaints, and if they did, the courts to whom they had to appeal would be apt to be prejudiced against them. All this of course is mere inference. The actual truth is so hard to discover that any definite statement would be misleading. Optimistic interpreters of the status of the indented servant, however, base their case against every probability.[3]

[1] See *South Carolina Statutes*, vol. iii, p. 710.   Act of 1744.   Virginia had a similar system of administering punishment in correspondence to distance from house.   Henning, vol. iii, pp. 456-7, 1705.   *Records of Mass. Bay Colony*, vol. i, p. 115, Act of 1634; *Acts of Assembly passed in the Province of Maryland*, 1692-1715.

[2] *South Carolina Statutes*, vol. iii, p. 627.

[3] For optimistic accounts, see McCormack, *White Servitude in Maryland*, p. 78; M. C. Tyler, *England in America*, p. 155.   For pessimistic account, see Eddis' *Letters from America*, London, 1792.

Indentured servitude was prevalent for a much longer period of time than is commonly thought, and always comprised a considerable share of the colonial population. Thus in Virginia in 1671 there were 6,000 indentured servants out of the total population of 40,000, as compared with only 2,000 negro slaves;[1] a ratio of approximately one servant to every five freemen.

The German migration from the Palatinate into Pennsylvania began about 1710, and after 1728 practically all the immigrants into the province entered as indentured servants.[2] During the years 1771-1773 nearly 5,000 indentured servants entered the port of Philadelphia alone.[3] McCormack estimates[4] that in 1660 the ratio of servants to freemen in Maryland was about 1 to 11, and that in 1752 it was approximately the same. The ratio being thus constant, though the population had increased and the original servants been freed, the only conclusion that can be drawn is that many of the freemen had either been servants themselves or were children of servants. In the North, the ratio was of course not so great. Rhode Island in 1708 had 482 servants in a total population of 7181, or a ratio of about 1 to 14.[5]

Indentured service continued through the 18th and into

---

[1] Henning, *Statutes*, vol. ii, p. 515. Gov. Berkeley's reply to interrogations of commissioners.

[2] *Cf.* Geiser, *Redemptioners and Indentured Servants in Penn.*, pp. 23-28. The earlier Germans 1710-1728 were prosperous and did not come as indentured servants, but the poorer elements sold themselves for ship-money to escape from the Rhenish provinces. Some of the Scotch-Irish immigration in this period (after 1728) entered independently.

[3] "Record of Indentures in the Office of the Mayor of Philadelphia," reprinted vol. xvi, *Proceedings of Penn.*, pp. 4-325.

[4] McCormack, *White Servitude in Maryland*, pp. 28-29.

[5] J. G. Palfrey, *Compendious History of New England*, vol. iii, p. 330.

the 19th[1] century.   In fact there was not appreciable decline in the number of German " free-willers " who entered
Maryland until after 1817, when legislation protecting the
servants made the trade unprofitable for the shipmasters.[2]
For the Colonies as a whole, Professor Commons goes so
far as to estimate that one-half of all the immigrants came
as indentured servants.[3]

With the development of slavery, however, white servitude declined.   It was not until about 1700 that slavery
became the dominant institution in Virginia, and its triumph
in the other colonies was still slower.   Negro slavery displaced white service because it was more economical.   A
master could own a white servant for a few years, and
colonial legislation was tending to decrease this period
steadily.   He could own the negro, on the other hand, for
life, and his descendants after him.   The negro was,
furthermore, more amenable to grinding labor than was the
servant; and, if a runaway, more recognizable.   Despite
his greater utility, his purchase price was at first only about
double that of the indentured servant.[4]   This was due to
the increasingly efficient organization of the slave trade by
which a small amount of rum could buy a large number of
slaves.

[1] See "Diary of John Harrower," reproduced in the *Am. Hist.
Review*, vol. vi, when he writes (1774) of " Seventy servants on board
all indented to serve for four years there at their different occupations," p. 73.

[2] Hurd's statement that " this species of servitude (indented) became
obsolete about the time of the War of the Revolution." (Hurd, *Law
of Freedom and Bondage*, vol. i, p. 218) is in consequence erroneous.

[3] J. R. Commons, *Races and Immigrants in America*, pp. 30-31.

[4] See letter from Col. Byrd of Virginia to Mr. Anchem of Rotterdam
(1739) quoted in the *Am. Hist. Rev.*, vol. i, p. 90 where Byrd states that
Palitinates selling their four year term " fetch from 6 to nine pounds,"
while negro slaves brought about twice as much.

The introduction of slavery made the lot of the servant increasingly hard.[1] He was subject to the new competition and punished severely by the master. It was common for the same legislative act to provide for both servants and slaves, and in the eyes of the law they were generally linked together.[2] A contemporary observer, William Eddis, said: "Negroes being a property for life, the death of slaves . . . is a material loss to the proprietor; they are therefore in almost every instance under more comfortable circumstances than the miserable Europeans."[3]

What happened to the servant after his term was over has seldom been satisfactorily discussed. Ballagh states that the freed servant formed " a very strong type of peasant proprietor."[4]—and that he "provided for the growth of a strong yeomanry."[5] Though the matter is shrouded in uncertainty, all the evidence points to an opposite conclusion. All that he received from his master when freed was some clothing, a few bushels of corn, a tool or two, and sometimes a gun.[6]

[1] Compare George Aldis' favorable account of the condition of indented servants in Maryland about 1670 with the pessimistic account given in 1792 by William Eddis, *Letters from America* which describes conditions after the competition with slavery had set in.

[2] *Cf. Acts of Assembly passed in the Province of Maryland*, 1715. p. 141.

[3] Eddis, William, *Letters from America*, London. 1792. (Describing conditions in America about 1770), pp. 69-70.

Ballagh, *op. cit.*, p. 87.

[5] *Ibid.*, p. 90.

[6] *Acts of Assembly of Maryland, 1692-1715.* "Every man-servant shall, at such time of expiration of his servitude—have allowed and given to him, one new hat, a good suit—; one new shift of white linen; one new pair of bench-made shoes and stockings; two hoes, and one ax; and one gun of twenty shillings price. All women-servants, at the expiration of their servitude, as aforesaid, shall have allowed and given them, a waistcoat and petticoat, a new shift of white linen,

Bruce states that the freed servant in Virginia received only a couple of suits of clothes, a few tools, and enough corn to last approximately a year, the total value of these articles not exceeding 10£.[1] Contrary to popular impression, a bonus of 50 acres of land was not given. Such an outfit was not sufficient for the freedman to set himself up in independence on any but the smallest scale, and small-scale farming was just what the agricultural system of the Southern colonies was not adapted to. The better lands were already appropriated, and the population was practically self-sufficing in so far as necessities were concerned. Towns were few and there was little call at this time for further artisans. Add to this the incoming of slavery and the consequent falling off in the demand for ordinary hired labor, and what place was left for the freed servants? From what more likely class could the landless whites, the "crackers," "poor whites" and "cove-dwellers" of the mountains have been recruited? In large part these surplus freedmen may well have been driven to the interior and to the uplands, shut out from large landed possessions, and barred from lucrative employment by slave labor.

6. *Apprenticeship in the Northern and Middle Colonies*

In the North the situation was different. Here apprenticeship, not indented service, was the rule. Since there were more towns and cities, there was consequently a greater division of labor, and it was necessary to recruit men for the handicraft industries of the time. The blacksmith, the cooper, the wheelwright, the mason, the carpenter, the

shoes and stockings; a bib apron; two caps of white linen; and three barrels of Indian corn," p. 143. Cf. *South Carolina Statutes*, Act of 1717, vol. iii, p. 14. In this colony the master gave only clothing to servant at termination of his service.

[1] P. A. Bruce, *Econ. Hist. of Va. in 17th Century*, pp. 42-44.

tailor, were necessary figures in every northern town,[1]
Many of the seaports had their shipyards, and boys were
even apprenticed to learn the " art and mysteries of navigation and mariner." [2]

Between the years 1694 and 1707, 107 indentures were
recorded in the town of New York alone, while in the period
1718-1727, 198 were filed.[3]

The length of apprenticeship varied. A statistical study
of the industries filed in New York for the years 1718-1727 [4]
shows the following results :

Period of Service	No.	Per cent
Less than 7 years	9	4.6
7 years	120	60.6
More than 7 years	69	34.8

This shows the preponderance, although not the universality of the seven-year term in New York. Of those
whose terms of service exceeded seven years, twenty were
for eight years, twenty-one for nine years, and nine for ten
years. There were two instances of sixteen-year apprenticeships and one each for seventeen and eighteen years.

Philadelphia figures for 1771-73 show different results.[5]

[1] Edward Johnson in his *Wonder-Working Providence of Sion's
Saviour in New England*, p. 248, mentions the following trades which
in 1648 were represented in Boston: "tailors, carpenters, joiners,
glaziers, painters, gun-smiths, lock-smiths, blacksmiths, naylers, cutlers,
weavers, brewers, bakers, coster-mongers, felt-makers, braziers, pen-
terers, and tinkers, rug-makers, masons, lime, brick and tile makers,
card makers, turners, pump-makers, wheelers, glowers, fell-mongers,
and furriers," p. 248 (Jamieson Edit.).

[2] Weeden, *Economic History of New England*, vol. i, p. 259. The
term of apprenticeship for the sea was generally for four years.

[3] *New York Historical Society's Collection*, vol. xviii, " Indentures
of Apprentices," vol. xlii, " Indentures of apprentices."

[4] Ref. *N. Y. Historical Society's Collections*, vol. xlii, " Indentures
of Apprentces 1718-27."

[5] *Record of Indentures of Apprentices, servants, etc.* filed in the
office of the Mayor of Philadelphia, Pa., 1771-73.

Of a total of 171 cases chosen at random from the indentures filed for these years, the following were the frequencies of the various terms of service:

Period of Service	No.	Period of Service	No.
1 year	2	11 years	7
2 years	5	12 "	6
3 "	20	13 "	9
4 "	17	14 "	3
5 "	30	15 "	4
6 "	20	16 "	1
7 "	16	17 "	4
8 "	8	18 "	1
9 "	9	19 "	1
10 "	7	20 "	1
			171

The fact that 55% of the indentures were for less than seven years in Philadelphia as compared with only 4.6% in New York is significant. This produces a corresponding reversal in the number whose terms were exactly seven years. Whereas in New York this group comprised 60.6% of the whole number, in Philadelphia it former only 9.4%. The group above seven years was comparativey constant, there being approximately 35% in each case, although there were a greater number of long term engagements in Pennsylvania.

Thus the term of service was in general shorter in Pennsylvania than in New York, although allowance must be made for the fact that New York figures are of an earlier date. In the period between New York's latest figures and Pennsylvania's earliest, New York may appreciably have shortened her term.

7. Functions of Colonial Appprenticeship

The function of Colonial apprenticeship was fourfold. It was at once a punishment for debt, a penalty for idleness, a system of poor relief, and the earliest educational institution.

(1) It was a punishment for debt. We have already seen how prominent a part binding-out for debt played in the importation of indentured servants and indeed often in their indenturing on this side of the water. Owing to the frequently undifferentiated state of apprenticeship and indented servitude and the ambiguity of the law, many of these indentures were made out for apprenticeship instead of for true servitude.

(2) It was a penalty for idleness. This, even in a child, was a sin to the Puritan. Connecticut ordered her selectmen to put out to service single persons 'who lived an idle and riotous life."[1] Massachusetts followed a similar policy and bound out those whom she deemed idlers.[2]

(3) Apprenticeship here, as in England, was a system of poor relief. Massachusetts as early as 1636 had enacted "that all towns shall take care to order and dispose of all single persons and inmates within their town to service."[3] Nor was this merely paper legislation; records exist of its enforcement.[4] In 1692 Massachusetts reenacted this law

[1] *Connecticut Colonial Records*, vol. ii, 1673, p. 66, also vol. iv. *Mass. Col. Records*, vol. ii, p. 180, where the selectmen given power to present to the court all "idle and unprofitable persons, and all children who are not diligently employed by their parents" and the courts then to bind them out. *Cf.* also vol. v, p. 373.

[2] *Cf. Records and Files of the Quarterly Courts of Essex County, Mass.*, vol. v, where in 1669 it was ordered that Joseph Turland "an idler and extravagant person" who "runs up and down, neglects his business, and is in danger of falling into mischief" should be bound out by the selectmen of Beverly, p. 160.

[3] *Records of Mass. Bay Colony*, vol. i, p. 186.

[4] *Manuscript Collections of Mass. Archives*, vol. ix, p. 5, where record is made where the children of Goodman Burril (evidently deceased) should be put out to service since their grandfather would not support them. The mother was to be shipped back to England.

with the provision that the selectmen should bind out the children and have the legal right to act for them.[1] In 1703 they made a further emendation. The previous law had been thought to apply only to children whose parents actually received alms; the new law now declared that it applied to all children whose parents were *deemed* unable to maintain them.[2] It was thus prospective, not merely retrospective. This extension of the law closely parallels that of the English Poor Law of 1601, which, as we have seen, similarly broadened the interpretation of what constituted a " poor " parent.

Virginia in 1672 had passed similar legislation. The Justices of the Peace of every country were ordered to " put the *laws of England* against vagrant, idle, and dissolute persons in strict execution."[3] The county courts must bind out " all children whose parents are not able to bring them up, apprentices, tradesmen, the males till one and twenty years of age, and the females to other necessary employments, till eighteen years and not longer."[4] South Carolina in her act of 1740 provided for the children of indigent parents in parallel fashion, while Connecticut, and indeed all the other colonies, built their poor law legislation as closely as possible upon the English model.[5]

(4) Finally, apprenticeship was a state-directed educational system. Masters were in general required by statute law, to impart not only trade training, but to give instruction in the liberal arts, and to inculcate sound mortality as well. Massachusetts in 1642, ordered that all parents and masters,

[1] *Mass. Col. Records*, not vol. iv, must be vi or vii, p. 67.
[2] *Acts of the Colony of Mass. Bay*, vol. iv, p. 538.
[3] Henning's *Statutes*, vol. ii, p. 298.
[4] *Ibid.*
[5] For review of Connecticut system, see E. W. Capen. *The Historical Evolution of the Poor Law in Connecticut.*

" should endeavor to teach, by themselves or others, their children and apprentices, so much learning, as may enable them perfectly to read the English tongue and knowledge of the capital laws," and further " do breed and bring up their children and apprentices in some honest, lawful calling, labour or employment."[1] If parents or masters neglected to give this intellectual or trade instruction, the children were to be taken away from them by the selectmen and indentured as apprentices to masters who would give it. Thus apprenticeship was made to serve as a school for children uninstructed at home. The prescribed education for every child included some instruction in the trade and some in the liberal arts. Failure on the art of the master or parent to give either was punished by the removal of the child.

Free public schools for the poor hardly existed in Massachusetts before 1700, and from then on spread but slowly.[2] In this interregnum the device of apprenticeship served as a rude substitute. It was the only guarantee that children whose parents *would not* or *could not* pay the customary tuition fees, should be instructed. It thus established the principle of universal free education.

Records exist of the enforcement of this Massachusetts Act of 1642. The selectmen of Dorchester, Brookline, and Watertown haled delinquent parents before them and carried out the provisions of the law.[3] In 1668, however, the legislature stated that it had not been well observed, but that the selectmen should enforce it more stringently in

[1] *Colonial Laws of Mass.* (edit. by Whitman), p. 136.
[2] G. L. Jackson, *The Development of School Support in Colonial Massachusetts*, pp. 34-74, gives an analysis of the early school records of 21 Massachusetts towns. Dedham had a free public school in 1646, but it was an isolated instance for several decades.
[3] For detailed discussion, see Jackson, *op. cit.*, pp. 29-31.

the future.   The Essex county court in the following year ordered the selectmen of Topfield to enforce the act and to make out a " list of all those young persons who do live from under family government." [1]

Professor Jernegan holds that the act of 1642 was nullified in 1695 by the refusal of the English Privy Council to allow the act passed by the Massachusetts legislature upon the merging of the colonies of New Plymouth and Massachusetts which continued all legislation hitherto enacted by either colony.[2]   Thereafter all new legislation concerning apprentices save for a special act in 1735 for Boston, applied only to poor children and not to all children.   With the exception of Boston, therefore, apprenticeship could not be legally resorted to after 1695 as a method of educating children whose parents had neglected their duty.

Both the Connecticut and New Haven colonies passed acts almost identical with the Massachusetts act of 1642.[3]   Thus the New Haven act of 1656 provided that if parents and masters did not teach children and apprentices " to read the Scriptures and other good and profitable printed works in the English tongue and to understand the main grounds and principles of Christian religion necessary to salvation," the children were to be taken from them and placed as apprentices " with such others who shall better both for publick convenience and for the particular good of said children of apprentices." [4]

In New York, on the other hand, apprenticeship was not

[1] *Records and Files of the Quarterly Courts of Essex County, Massachusetts*, vol. iv, p. 212.

[2] M. W. Jernegan, *Compulsory Education in the American Colonies*, School Review, vol. xxvii, pp. 24-43.

[3] R. F. Seybold, *Apprenticeship and Apprenticeship Education in Colonial New England and New York*, pp. 52-60.

[4] *New Haven's Settling in New England and some Laws for Government*, published in 1656.

used as a means of compelling parents to educate their children. · Indeed it was not until 1788 that it was required that poor children bound out as apprentices be taught reading and writing.[1]   Despite the absence of legal requirement, however, approximately one half of the indentures filed between 1694 and 1707 specified that the master should teach, or have the apprentice taught, reading and writing, while from 1718 to 1727 the percentage was still greater.[2]   A large number of the indentures provided that the master should send the apprentice to school during the winter, or during the evenings.   This is a clear indication of the use of agencies other than the master himself to give liberal training to the apprentice.

By 1770 in Pennsylvania as well, although legal enactment was lacking, the indentures almost invariably required the master to give schooling to the apprentice.[3]

In Virginia, the apprenticeship regulations took a slightly different turn.   A law of 1646 provided for the apprenticing of poor children " to tradesmen or husbandmen to be brought up in some good and lawful calling."[4]   So far it is merely the application of the Elizabethan poor law.   But it also commanded the commissioners of every county to choose two poor children, whose parents were unable to support them and send them " to James City "—to be employed in the public flax houses under such masters and mistresses as shall then be appointed, in carding, knotting, and spinning.[5]   It was prescribed that the children should be

[1] Seybold, *op. cit.*, p. 87.

[2] New York Historical Society's Collections. *Vol. xviii, Indentures of Apprentices, 1694-1707. Vol. xlii, Indentures of Apprentices, 1718-1727.*

[3] Record of the Indentures of Individuals Bound as Apprentices, Servants, etc., Philadelphia, 1771-1773.

[4] Henning, *Statutes*, vol. i, pp. 336-37.

[5] *Ibid.*

furnished from their home county with sufficient clothing and provisions to maintain them.[1]   An appropriation of 10,000 lbs. of tobacco was made to house these children, and two buildings were ordered to be erected for them.

It does not require much perspicacity to perceive that this was a trade-school for poor children, state-built and county-supported.   No mention is made of teaching the children reading or writing.   The act, unlike that of Massachusetts, provided for industrial training only.   It was not till 1705, in an act applying apprenticeship to orphans, that it was ordered "that the master. . . . shall be obliged to teach him to read and write."[2]   This educational provision was extended in 1769 to illegitimates, when it was provided that they should be indentured as apprentices under the protection of the County Court.   So long as the aristocratic landholders were in power in Virginia, free public education was impossible.[3]   Apprenticeship was therefore the only means of education that the poorer classes possessed.

In all the colonies with the possible exception of the South, therefore, trade training was not the only educational feature of apprenticeship.   Instruction was required in the liberal arts as well, while in New England, the colonies required that the apprentices be educated in the Christian religion and sound ethics.   Apprenticeship was thus not a mere means of acquiring trade efficiency, but it was a preparation for citizenship and for life.

[1] To wit—"Six barrels of corne, two coverletes or one rugg and one blanket, one bed, one wooden bowle or tray, two pewter spoons, a sow shote of six months old, two laying hens, with convenient apparell both linen and woolen with hose and shoes"—certainly a quaint provision. Henning, vol. viii, p. 376.

Henning, *Statutes*, vol. iii, pp. 375-76.

[3] For an account of Virginia's early education system see E. W. Knight, *The Evolution of Public Education in Virginia, Suwanee Review*, January, 1916, pp. 24-41.

8. Other Features of Colonial Apprenticeship

While in theory the consent of the apprentice was necessary before he could legally be transferred from one master
to another, in practice this provision was often disregarded
or deemed a mere technicality. Apprentices were often listed
among the assets of bankrupts, and were either taken personally by the creditors as payment for debt or sold to satisfy the
obligation.[1] Upon the death of the master, the apprentice
was often sold with the rest of the estate by the heirs.[2]
Often indeed the sale of apprentice's unexpired serving-time
was resorted to by thriving and solvent masters. The
papers of the colonial period frequently contained advertisements listing apprentices for sale.[3]

Again, colonies, in order to protect the apprentices provided that they should not be sold out of the colony.[4]
Such a measure was necessary since it would otherwise have
been possible for a Massachusetts cobbler to have sold his
boy apprentice to a Virginian tobacco planter. Since the
apprentice would be out of Massachusetts jurisdiction, he
could be exploited as cheap labor.

Female apprentices served longer and were given fewer
educational opportunites than were boys. (a) They served

[1] *Records and Files of Quarterly Court, Essex County, Mass.*, vol.
iv, p. 445, *ibid.*, vol. iii, p. 174.

[2] *New York Historical Society Collections*, vol. xlii, Indentures of
App. 1718-1727, p. 121, where 20£ was paid to Peter Colwell by William
Dugdale and John Leach " for 11 years 3 months of unexpired serving
time of John Galloway, Apprentice." Also *Mass. Archives*, vol. ix
(Domestic Relations), p. 6064 where the unexpired term of an ap-
prentice was transferred in payment of debt.

[3] *Boston News Letter*, April 15, 1774, *ibid.*, April 25.

[4] *Laws of Province of Penn.*, 1721, pp. 9-10. South Carolina provided that not only should the apprentice not be sent out of the colony
but that he must be transferred only to those persons engaged in the
same trade. Cf. *South Carolina Statutes*, vol. iii, p. 544.

longer. Of 125 cases selected as random from the Philadelphia record books, 41, or 32.8% were for less than 7
years, 13, or 10.4% were for 7 years, and 71, or 56.8%
were for more than seven years, whereas only 35.6% of the
indentures of men were for more than seven years.[1]
(b) They were given fewer educational opportunities.
Though there are instances of girls entering the trades,[2]
such cases were too rare to affect their general status.
Woman's career was in the home, and formal education
was deemed unnecessary for it. Though bound out to a
tradesman, female apprentices were really not workshop
assistants but rather household servants. The technical
educational provisions in their indentures were generally
confined to specifying that they should be taught " to sew
plainly." [3]

Their liberal education was also less than that of the boys.
The Massachusetts law of 1642, as we have seen, specified
that while all male apprentices should be taught to read and
write, female apprentices were only required to be taught
reading.[4] In 1771 " ciphering " was added to the educational requirements of the male apprentice, and writing, but
not " ciphering," to that of the female apprentice. The
privileges of the girl apprentice thus always lagged a step
behind those of her brother.[5]

9. *An Appraisal of Colonial Apprenticeship*

In summing up our survey of Colonial apprenticeship, we
may say that it was true to its English prototype in two

[1] See *Record of Indentures* of Individuals Bound Out as Apprentices
in Philadelphia, Penn., 1771, 1773, p. 21325.

[2] See Abott, Edith, *Women in Industry*, pp. 13-171.

[3] See *N. Y. Historical Society Collection*, vols. xviii and xlii.

[4] *Acts of Col. of Mass. Bay*, vol. i, pp. 654-55.

[5] An exception should be made as regards Virginia in respect to the
apprenticing of illegitimates, *cf.* Henning, *Statutes*, vol. viii, p. 376.

particulars. It was a system of poor relief and a penalty for idleness. It differed, however, from the English system in that (a) the seven-year term was not as universal, (b) apprenticeship became a means of acquiring a liberal education, (c) practically all apprenticeship regulations were administered, not by guilds,[1] but by the town and county officers.

In appraising apprenticeship, we must be on our guard against wrapping it in the vague glamour of the past. The close filial relationship of master and apprentice, the certainty of a trade, the supervision over morals and education, have all excited encomiums that are more enthusiastic than critical, and many novels have praised the idyllic conditions of the " prentice-boy." [2]

The dark side of the shield has been seen less readily. The apprentice did not work solely at his trade, but was also compelled to assist with the family " chores." Often he worked at jobs that bore no relation to the trade in which

[1] Gilds, while infrequent, were not absent in colonial handicrafts. See *Collected Records Mass. Bay Colony*, vol. iii, pp. 132-33, when in 1648, Richard Webb, James Everill, Robert Turner, Edmund Jackson " and the rest of the shoemakers" were incorporated and given power to elect officers and to, "have power to make orders for the well governinge of their company, in the manageing of their trade and all the affayres thereunto belonging, and to change and reform the same as occasion shall require and to annex reasonable penalties for the breach of the same." It was provided that " any person or persons who shall use the art of a shoemaker or any part thereof, not beinge approved of by any of the officers of ye sed shoemakers to be a sufficient workman, the s'd court shall have power to send for such persons and suppresse them "—This latter is a delegation to the guild of power to suppress or to supervise its workmanship which would naturally involve apprenticeship. A similar grant was made to Thomas Venner and others for a cooper's guild " for preventing abuses in theire trade," *ibid.*, p. 133. For the part played by English gilds in the enforcement of the Statute of Apprentices, see Dunlop and Denman, *English Apprenticeship and Child Labor*, pp. 75-81.

[2] Especially those of Elijah Kellogg.

he was supposed to be trained. In order to be a black-smith's apprentice, he had to hoe his master's garden. In order to master the "mysteries" of metal work, he had to take care of the stock—the horses and the cattle, assist in the weaving, and help out at harvest time. In a word, he was "hired man" as well as apprentice. His work at these household tasks was a complete waste of time so far as learning a trade was concerned.

Another real fault of the old apprenticeship system was that the period of apprenticeship was too long. The rough handicraft trades of that day could ordinarily be mastered in much less than seven or even five years. This extra period constituted an exploitation of the boy, for we must remember that the apprentice earned no wages, being supposed to be paid for his labor by the trade instruction he received. If he learned the trade before his period of service expired, this added labor was an outlay for which bare maintenance did not compensate. If this lengthy term of service was an injustice to the average boy, it was certainly a particular cause for grievance to the superior boy. It did not matter whether he learned quickly or not, he must serve the same term in any case. The inelasticity of the indenture could but incite dissatisfaction among the more capable apprentices and engender a tendency to "soldier" since there were not any rewards for skill and ability.[1]

It is not true, however, that the long term of apprenticeship was made hazardous by inventions, which obviated processes in which boys had been working for years and made unnecessary their accumulated experience. Inventions were few in the colonial handicraft period. Industry passed on from one generation to another in almost identical form.

[1] *Cf.* on this point. Testimony of Carrol D. Wright, *Report of Industrial Commission*, vol. vii, p. 18.

Doubtless also many of the masters were men of the sort who abused the confidence reposed in them, and many injustices and cruelties were practiced which the isolation of the court, the looseness of government, and the scantiness of the records obscure.

The good features of apprenticeship were, however, real. The state supervised the training of the child until he came to maturity. The master was compelled to teach the apprentice his trade, to give him the rudiments of a liberal education, and to impart sound morals. Neglect to perform any of these tasks entitled either a fine or the loss of the apprentice.[1] The whole youth of the child in industry, not merely his working day, was supervised and directed.

This system continued practically unchanged through the turmoil of the American Revolution, and indeed wherever hand production prevailed, well down into the 19th Century.

[1] For instances of enforcement see, *Mass. Coll. Records*, vol. iii, p. 310.

CHAPTER III

The Decline of Apprenticeship in the Machine Era

1. The Development of the Factory System.

It is difficult to fix a definite date for the advent of the American Industrial Revolution. The transition from a hand to a machine basis and from the domestic and the " putting out system " to the factory system, is necessarily a slow and long-drawn-out process. It progresses more swiftly in some industries and in some sections of the country than in others. The cotton and woolen industries were in the factory stage long before shoe-making and brewing.[1] The South, with the exception of such cities as Atlanta, remained on a handicraft basis long after the Civil War, and the frontier of course indefinitely longer. Even now there are hamlets off the beaten track of communication in which life goes on much as in the days before the machine.

It might be said that the opening of Slater's cotton mill in 1794 marks the initial step of the movement. But the manufactures of that day, as shown by Hamilton's reports, were comparatively few and cumbrously managed.[2] It was not until the Embargo and Non-Intercourse Acts, followed by the war of 1812, that there came, in some lines,

[1] *Cf.* Blanche E. Hazard, " The Organization of the Boot and Shoe Industry in Mass. before 1875," *Quarterly Journal of Economics*, vol. xxvii, pp. 237-262. Also J. R. Commons, "American Shoe Makers, 1848-1895," *ibid.*, vol. xxiv, pp. 39-85. For the brewing industry see Schlüter, *History of the Brewing Industry and Brewery Workers Organisation*, pp. 24-85.

[2] Hamilton's Report on Manufactures in *State Papers on the Tariff* (edited by Taussig), pp. 79-107.

the necessity as well as the opportunity of providing for
home needs by domestic industry. Manufactures of cotton
and wool, and a few other staples, were established by the
conclusion of the war, and fostered by a series of tariffs
beginning in 1816. But certainly down to the twenties
the major part of our industries were still organized essentially as they had been during the colonial period. "The
master worked side by side with his journey-man and his
apprentice, and was not sharply distinguished from them
by either his earnings or his social position." [1] It was not
until the booming industry of the 20's and the 30's and the
springing up of such mill towns as Pawtucket, Lowell and
Lawrence, that America experienced her first taste of the
real factory system. The suddenness of the change is indicated by the chorus of protests in the late twenties. That
period witnessed for the first time regularly organized workingmen's parties, a labor press, and such well-known leaders
as Fanny Wright, Robert Dale Owen, the Evans brothers,
and Seth Luther. But while the movement of the twenties
was very real and while the factory system steadily gained
ground in the North, especially in Southern New England
from 1840 to 1860, it was not until after the Civil War that
its period of greatest growth began. [2]

2. Effect Upon Status of Apprentices

The effects of the industrial revolution upon children
should be most carefully noted. It is quite clear that it de-
based the conditions of the children in industry in two ways:
—(a) It divested apprenticeship proper of its educational
features both trade and civic, (b) it added children to in-

[1] E. L. Bogart, *Economic History of the United States* 2nd. ed., p. 252.
[2] See P. W. Bidwell, "Population Growth in Southern New England,
1810-1860," *Publications American Statistical Association*, vol. xv, pp.
813-39. For the state of manufactures prior to 1860 see Victor S. Clark,
History of Manufactures in the United States.

dustry who were not even nominally apprentices at all, but merely child laborers. Apprenticeship and child labor had been synonymous terms; they now became separate and distinct.

If the ordinary craftsman was deeply affected by the substitution of power-driven machinery for his hand-tools, much more deeply and more subtly was the apprentice. For him it meant a revolutionizing not only of his methods of work but of his entire social status as well, both at home and in the shop.

His home had formerly been at his master's. He had lived and worked familiarly with him, receiving his board and clothing in return for his services. Now, with the growth of industry, the master could no longer house all of his apprentices. He had to let them find their own shelter, and commute their former benefits into a cash allowance. The apprentice thus found himself a wage-earner, with greater freedom, greater opportunity, and greater danger as his lot.

Within the shop the change was equally great. The master was no longer literally a " master-workman," in close personal touch with each boy. The very nature of machine production had fixed a gulf between the two. The tasks of the employer were becoming more and more exclusively those of the business man, his immediate concern was buying and marketing rather than craftsmanship. His contact with his apprentices grew rapidly infrequent and impersonal. In brief, master and apprentice had stood in the relation of father and son; they now stood in the relation of employer and employee.

The training the apprentice received changed no less than his station. Machine production does not require the all-round skilled workman because it increases the division of labor and splits a trade into many different jobs. There

is less opportunity to exercise general skill should it
be acquired, and the mastery of the whole gamut of
machines within a trade becomes well-nigh impossible.
One man, one machine is the rule. Apprenticeship accordingly became specialized.

The purely cultural training of the apprentice fared of
course even worse. The master who did not see him from
one week's end to the other could hardly be expected to
teach him his letters or his catechism. Accordingly we
find the period of the early Industrial Revolution from 1810
to 1830 characterized by a rapid rise in day-schools. The
earliest schools in Pennsylvania were for the pauper children who could no longer get cultural training from their
employer. Is it a mere coincidence, then, that the wide-
spread development of secular Sunday schools where working children could be taught the rude elements of reading,
writing, *etc.*, coincided with the rise of the new impersonal
factory system? In the same period, to serve as a substitute for the loss of the personal touch, came the founding
of societies for the improvement of apprentices and the
establishment of libraries for their education.[1]

3. Child Labor Under the Factory System

The new system, however, not only divested apprenticeship of its educational and personal opportunities, but it
brought into industry large numbers of children who were
set at routine jobs under conditions that were often exceedingly bad.

In the cotton and woolen mills, women and children
furnished the majority of the operatives. Tench Coxe,
Hamilton, Niles, Clay and Mathew Carey advanced as one
of their chief arguments for the protective tariff, the fact

[1] Such as the Apprentices Free Library in Philadelphia.

that manufactures could be run by the surplus labor of women and children who would otherwise be idle.   Even Gallatin in his Free Trade Memorial of 1831, admitted that protection might be justified on this count.[1]   The general reasoning involved was very simple.   Puritan morality had regarded idleness as a sin and had forced chilren to work at an early age.   At first it therefore welcomed the wider opportunities of manufacture, since if it was proper for women and children to be kept busy in the handicrafts and agriculture, it was also proper that they should work in the mills.

Statistics are scanty for this early period, but the Digest of Manufactures in the Census of 1820 gives complete statistics for the textile mills of Massachusetts, Rhode Island and Connecticut.   In Massachusetts boys and girls constituted 43% of the laboring force, in Connecticut 45% and in Rhode Island 55%.   What age-group is included under the heading "boys" and "girls" is not specified, but it probably comprised those under 16.   The Friends of American Industry in 1832 said that there were 3472 children under 12 years working in the cotton mills of Rhode Island, or 40% of the entire force.   According to the report of their committee, child labor under 12 in this industry was non-existent in Virginia, Maryland, Maine, Massachusetts, Pennsylvania, and Delaware, and existed but slightly in Vermont, New Hampshire, Connecticut, New York, and New Jersey.   Miss Otey has shown that this was not so and that children were often employed where it was claimed that they were not.[2]

The hours of work in these mills were generally from

---

[1] "Free Trade Memorial of 1831." (Taussig, *State Papers and Speeches on the Tariff*, p. 129).

[2] Otey, "Beginnings of Child Labor Legislation in Certain States," vol. vi of the *Report on Conditions of Woman and Child Wage-earners*.

sunup to sundown. Manufacture, in other words, had taken over the working day of the handicrafts, ignoring the newer and more severe strains imposed by machinery and the bad conditions of heat, light and ventilation.

Nor was corporal punishment of the child worker unknown. Seth Luther gives instances of such cruelty as the use of the whip, the breaking of a girl's leg by throwing a stick of wood at her, and hitting a child over the head with a board.[1] In Pennsylvania conditions were especially bad. In 1870, an overseer testified that the Rhode Island overseers generally used a strap with tacks inserted with which to punish the children employed[2] while in Massachusetts, whipping persisted even as late as 1870.[3]

Apprenticeship had paved the way for much of this juvenile labor. A child was expected to work. When a father contracted to furnish the labor of his children to a manufacturer, he was but carrying out a precedent which apprenticeship had furnished.

There were two systems of hiring labor: the family and the boarding-house system. Under the first, the manufacturer contracted for the services of a family. By the second, he secured the services of individuals who were to board at company houses. Children were included in the first class, but not in the second, as their board would be too expensive to justify hiring. The family system prevailed chiefly in Rhode Island, Connecticut, and the middle and southern states, while the boarding-house system was characteristic of the Northern tier of the New England states, including Massachusetts.[4]

[1] Seth Luther, *Address to the Workingmen of New England*, p. 20; and *Penn. Sen. Journal, 1837-8*, vol. ii.

[2] *Report of Mass. Bureau of Labor 1870*, p. 107.

[3] *Ibid., Report 1871*, p. 489.

[4] Edith Abbott, *Women in Industry*, pp. 338-340.

Nevertheless, the introduction of the factory system in America did not produce as grave abuses as in England. (a) In the first place, the number of pauper children under public control here was small. While it would be wrong to say that we had no Poor Law System, since a number of pauper children were apprenticed to factories in Baltimore, New York and Connecticut,[1] their importance was comparatively slight. (b) Secondly, the development of the West gave an opportunity for the working population to migrate. This in turn compelled the manufacturer to offer better conditions in order to retain his working force.[2] In England the conditions had been exactly the opposite, the enclosures driving the population from the country into the manufacturing towns and there producing a glut of labor. (c) Finally, the natural spirit of the American people was more independent. The American child was not so amenable to the restrictions of apprenticeship as was his English cousin. Slater tried in vain to introduce the English system of apprenticeship into his cotton mills. The reaction of the American temperament is well shown by the boy who advised his rebellious friend, " Well, cut up like the devil, and Slater will let you off."[3]

[1] See *Niles Register*, vol. xv, p. 419 (1819) ; Bagnall, *History of the Textile Industry in the U. S.*, vol. i, p. 185; Orcutt, *History of the Old Town of Derby, Connecticut*, p. 45. Orcutt mentions a mill which employed 73 apprentices hired from neighboring almshousees. In New York City in 1839, 349 pauper children were apprenticed—chiefly to mechanics and tradesmen. See Homer Folks, *Care of Dependent, Defective and Delinquent Children*, p. 41.

[2] Though absolute free land did not exist till the passage of the Homestead Act in 1862, yet the western movement of population was tremendous and this depleted the labor force in the east. For influence of the frontier, see F. J. Turner, *Rise of the New West*, pp. 10-134 and *The Significance of the Frontier in American History*. *Report of American Historical Association*, 1898.

[3] A reminiscence of Samuel Slater by his son, quoted by Weeden, *Economic and Social History of New England*, vol. ii, p. 913.

4. Use of Apprentices as Cheap Labor

The introduction of machines precipitated an endless quarrel between employer and workmen over the number of apprentices that should be employed. Industry could now be carried on with the majority of the workers doing specialized tasks and with a minimum of all-round craftsmen. It was early complained that manufacturers were taking large numbers of boys into their service, promising to teach them the whole trade, but in reality teaching them only one or two processes. It was cheaper to hire these boys than regular journeymen, as their wages were small. Full-fledged journeymen were in consequence displaced by these "learners," who, upon terminating their apprenticeship, would demand journeyman's wages. They were incapable of doing all-round skilled work because their training had been so specialized that they did not know the trade. Even had they been more skillful, a fresh crop of boys would have been cheaper to the employer.

Such a process could but produce a constantly increasing number of half-trained men who were thrown out of employment by a fresh batch about to go through the mill from which they had just emerged. Many apprentices, moreover, would run away before they had finished their term and would pass themselves off as journeymen. The workmen felt therefore that restriction of some sort was necessary. This could be accomplished in two ways: (a) By limiting the number of apprentices at any one time in proportion to the number of journeymen; (b) by lengthening their customary term of service—thus decreasing their rate of transformation into journeymen.

A letter to the Mechanics Free Press in 1828, stated that " there are many men in this city (Philadelphia) who have from fifteen to twenty apprentices, who never, or very seldom, have a journeyman in their shops but . . . . as one

apprentice becomes free, another is taken up to fill the ranks
The boys are unable to find work after their apprenticeship, as they have ceased to be of value, as the manufacturers
only want apprentices.   A hat manufacturer was asked
how he could sell hats at such a low price.   He answered
' By using apprentices.' "

As early as 1811, the New York Typographical Society
complained of the overstocking of the trade with apprentices and the consequent forcing out of full-fledged journeymen.[2]   In 1831, a reorganization of the Society was affected, and in the constitution of the new association it
is declared, " the practice of runaway or dismissed apprentices working for small compensation has proved a great
pest to the profession.   By the poor training which is given
to them, many who have spent three to seven years of the
flower of their lives in acquiring a knowledge of their professions are left without employment, or obliged to resort
to some business with which they are unacquainted, and
thus serve a second apprenticeship." [3]   General Duff
Green, the printer for the national government, dismissed
many journeymen from his shop and hired in their stead
fifty boys.   He proposed to institute a school to train 200
boys and to educate them by their own labor.   Through this
use of apprenticeship he aimed to do away with the journeymen who were attempting to control the trade.   The few
men that he did have working for him received only two-
thirds of the pay of journeymen.[4]   There is little doubt

[1] Letter signed Candidus, *Mechanics Free Press*, Nov. 29, 1825, quoted
in Commons—*Documentary History of American Industrial Society*,
vol. iii, p. 70.

[2] N. Y. Bureau of Labor Statistics 1911, *History of Typographical
Union No. 6*, p. 69.

[3] *Ibid.*, p. 108.

[4] *Ibid.*, pp. 192-193.

that more men were trained in the printing trades than could find employment.[1] The residue were forced to travel about for positions—hence the historic figure of the tramp printer.

The coachmakers also complained that their profession was overcrowded with cheap apprentices.[2] The shoe-makers had similar grievances. A Lynn, Mass, union speaks of " the injurious practice of taking apprentices for a few weeks or months, letting them make one part of a shoe, and then turning them out so-called shoemakers, thereby multiplying poor workmen and filling our market with miserable goods."[3] The cigarmakers also suffered from this surplus of apprentices. Overcrowding existed as well in the blacksmiths' and machinists' trades.[4]

5. Attempts by Unions to Regulate Apprenticeship

Labor's belief in the " right to a trade," and the desire of the workmen to lessen competition, though much weaker here than in England, may well have played a part in the general opposition to the use of apprentices. In the main, however, the opposition was based upon the plain fact that these boys who were hired in large numbers, were used merely as a substitute for adult labor.

The desire to regulate apprenticeship was indeed one of the prime causes for the creation and growth of our early trade-unions. By 1806 the Philadelphia Cordwainers were regulating apprenticeship and requiring all apprentices to join

[1] For instance the printers of Charleston, S. C. in 1860 objected to the use of apprentice labor in competition with that of journeymen on the part of Col. Cunningham, editor of the *Charlestown Evening News*. Snowden, *Notes on Labor organization in South Carolina 1742-1861*, pp. 30-32.

[2] Commons, *Doc. Hist. of American Industrial Society*, vol. vi, p. 167.

[3] *Ibid.*, vol. viii, p. 232.

[4] J. M. Motley, *Apprenticeship in American Trade Unions*, p. 26.

the union upon the termination of their services.   In 1836,
the National Typographers' Convention resolved that "every
beginner shall serve until he is 21, at the time of entering
he shall not be more than 15, and every boy taken as apprentice shall be bound to the employer in due form of
law." [1]   The apprentice was to be taught all the trade processes, not merely one or two.   In 1838, a second convention
was held which lowered the length of apprenticeship to five
years.   This was the prescribed time till 1869, when it was
made 4 years.

While the workingmen's movement of the late 20's and
the early 30's started as a political movement, it crystallized
after a few years in the form of a number of organizations
existing principally for the purpose of collective bargaining.
In these scattered unions regulations concerning apprenticeship were common.   The Troy coachmakers, for instance, enacted that only one apprentice should be hired for
every four journeymen. [2]

The International Typographical Union in 1850 declared
that the regulation of apprentices was one of its most important purposes. [3]   The National Association of Hat
Finishers which was organized in 1854 had as its basic
purpose the limitation of apprentices. [4]   The Iron Molders'
Union of North America was directly caused by the excess
of apprentices. [5]   Since the average in some sections was
two apprentices to one journeyman, the union was anxious
to prevent overcrowding of its labor market.   The consti-

[1] N. Y. Bureau of Labor Statistics, 1911—*History of Typographical*
Union No. 6, p. 156.

[2] Commons, *op. cit.*, vol. vi, p. 167.

[3] *Tenth Census of United States*, vol. xx, "Report on Trade Societies."

[4] *Ibid.*, p. 10.

[5] See *Third Report of California Bureau of Labor Statistics*, 1887-88,
pp. 215-16.

tution of the National Builders' Union stated that "one of the objects is to devise and suggest plans for the preservation of mechanical skill through a more complete and practical apprenticeship system." [1]

It was the control of apprenticeship that was the paramount reason for the organization of the Green Glass Blowers in 1857, and for their reorganization in 1866.[2] So also with the German-American Typographical Union, the Brotherhood of Carpenters and Joiners, the Painters and Decorators Union[3] and the union of shoe-makers known as the Knights of St. Crispin.[4]

With the Civil War, the question of apprenticeship became even more serious. Military life withdrew so many men from industry that a free use of apprentice labor seemed absolutely necessary. Manufacturers, moreover, fostered it as the one ready means of staving off a wage increase.[5] The expansion of the factory system following the civil war brought with it an increased division of labor and specialization of tasks. All-round apprenticeship consequently became still less common: boys were kept at specific operations and not taught the trade as a whole. This inevitable development caused a fresh outburst of protests from the workmen.

Thus the Chicago Conference of Working Men in 1867 passed resolutions declaring that "a great difficulty exists in many mechanical branches from their being over-stocked

[1] Founded in 1887. For discussion see G. C. Sikes, "Apprenticeship in the Building Trades," *Journal Political Economy*, vol. ii, pp. 397 ff.

[2] *New Jersey Bureau of Statistics of Labor and Industries*, 1887, pp. 77-84.

[3] *Ibid.*, pp. 89-94.

[4] See Don D. Lescohier, *The Knights of St. Crispin.*

[5] Fite, *Social and Industrial Conditions During the Civil War*, pp. 187-88.

with apprentices and as the time has come when the apprentice system is being more extensively used to the detriment of those who have spent years in making themselves proficient in their different trades." [1]   The unions in certain trades, moreover, continued sporadically to protest against alleged abuses of the apprentice system and against an excess amount of juvenile labor.   For a long time after the Civil War the Iron-moulders complained that the trade was suffering from a surfeit of half-trained apprentices or "berkshires" as they were called; in many plants it was stated that there were as many as four apprentices to one journeyman. [2]   Other trades to complain from time to time of being overcrowded with apprentices and learners were the leather workers, [3] the bakers [4] (1885), the table-knife grinders, [5] the wall-paper workers, [6] the gold-beaters in Philadelphia; [7] the plumbers and printers in New York [8] (1885), the cigar-makers, [9] the carpenters in Chicago, [10] and the musicians [11] (1890-96).

The employers verbally at least stood out for the right to hire an unlimited number of apprentices.   The attitude which the employers generally assumed is well

[1] *Documentary History of American Industrial Society*, vol. ix, p. 192.

[2] *Iron Moulders Journal*, August, 1896, p. 1.

[3] *Leather Workers Journal*, 1904, pp. 521-22.

[4] *American Federationist*, Sept., 1912, p. 597.

[5] *Ibid.*, p. 561.

[6] *Ibid.*, Sept., 1903, p. 847.

[7] *Ibid.*, Sept., 1903, p. 897.

[8] *Fourth Annual Report N. Y. Bureau of Labor Statistics* (1886), pp. 113-16.

[9] Motley, *Apprenticeship in American Trade Unions*, p. 23.

[10] *The Carpenter*, vol. xxx, no. 5, May, 1910, pp. 9 ff.

[11] Owen Miller in the *American Federationist*, November, 1912, pp. 871, *et seq.* Also John R. Commons, "The Musicians of New York and St. Louis," *Quarterly Journal of Economics*, vol. xx, pp. 419-22.

illustrated by a statement of an Albany moulding firm to the employees whom they had locked out: " We claim the right to employ any such number of boys as we may find advantageous, and also expect each molder to employ a helper," [1]   The pamphlet went on to say that some western firms encouraged the journeymen to have " four, five, six or even seven helpers apiece." [2]   The helpers were to do the heavy work and enable the molders to earn $8 to $10 a day.   The fact that these same helpers would later menace the journeyman's job was not mentioned.

The unions sought to regulate apprenticeship both, (a) by legislative enactment and (b) by trade-union regulation.

The movement for state legislation to control apprenticeship began in the late 60's and reached its climax in 1870-71. Thus the Chicago Conference of Workingmen in 1867 resolved " that it is the opinion of this body that it is highly important that the legislatures of each state should use their influence to secure such laws as will protect employers, apprentices, and journeymen."   The unions of machinists, blacksmiths, stovemolders, shoemakers, cigar-makers, printers, brick-layers, plasterers, and stone-cutters all made similar demands, including a definite time limit and the limitation of numbers, while the machinists, blacksmiths, and stove-molders advocated state legislation, as well.

The labor movement of the 60's accordingly tried to effect the full legal recrudescence of apprenticeship.   It advocated in general (a) that the apprenticeship period should be not less than 5 years; (b) that the number of apprentices be strictly limited, (c) that the employer be compelled to teach his apprentices the whole trade, not merely specialized parts of it; (d) that the employer should

[1] Perry, J. S., *Some Considerations Presented to the Molders Lately Employed by Perry & Co.*, Albany, N. Y., p 7.
[2] *Ibid.*

be responsible as formerly for his apprentices' moral education, (e) that a legal system of indenturing be re-established.

6. *The New York Apprenticeship Law and its Enforcement*

As a result of this agitation, Massachusetts, Illinois and New York actually passed apprenticeship laws, while similar measures were nearly enacted in Pennsylvania and Ohio. The New York law of 1871 provided:[1] (1) A written indenture must be drawn up and signed by both parties before an apprentice could be taken. (2) This indenture must be based upon the following terms: (a) the term of apprenticeship was to be not less than three and not more than five years; (b) the employer must provide the apprentice with suitable board, lodging and medical attention; (c) the employer must teach or have the apprentice taught "every branch of his or their business;" (d) the employer must give the apprentice a certificate upon the satisfactory conclusion of his service. (3) Penalties for violation of indentures: (a) On the part of the apprentice.—If the apprentice would not try to learn his trade or serve faithfully, he was to forfeit his back pay and the indenture would be cancelled. If he ran away before his term of service expired, he was liable to a jail sentence; (b) On the part of the employer.—If the employer did not care for the apprentice suitably according to the terms of the indenture and the provisions of the law, he could be sued by the apprentice or by his parents. If it could be shown that the employer had neglected his duty, the court was to cancel the indenture and impose a fine of not less than $100 and not more than $1000, which was to be paid to the apprentice or to his parent or guardian.

[1] For text of the Act see *Laws of New York, 94th Session*, vol. ii, pp. 2147-2150, chapter 934. For recommendation for apprentice legislation see Message of Governor Hoffman in *Messages of the Governors.* (Lincoln edit.), vol. vi, p. 123.

It will be noticed that the act did not attempt to limit the number of apprentices although in other respects it embodied the demands of the unions. As, however, it depended for its enforcement upon the complaint of the parties interested to the courts, it was seldom enforced at all and did not better the situation. In 1888 the enforcement of the Act of 1871 was made a duty of the factory inspectors,[1] but their work in this direction was almost fatally crippled by an opinion in that year by the State Attorney-General. He ruled that the law did not apply in the case of a minor for whom there was no written indenture binding the employer to teach the youth a trade. The opinion read in part as follows:[2] "It does not appear that this act was intended to affect the right of a parent or guardian to procure general employment for a minor. Minors might be employed for the purpose of learning the art or mystery of a trade without having attached to them all the incidents connected with apprenticeship." This definition therefore not only excluded the general mass of juvenile labor, but even drew a distinction between learning a trade and apprenticeship, and declared that the former was not proof of the latter.

This ruling made the law almost impossible to enforce, for as the factory inspectors stated: "In but few instances would the employer acknowledge that he employed his minors as apprentices to teach them a trade, but almost invariably asserted that he employed them " generally " or in sub-divisions of the trade in which they were most apt or familiar.[3]

[1] Chapter 437, Laws of 1888, see also *Seventh Annual Report of the Factory Inspectors*, pp. 52-54.

[2] See *Fourth Annual Report Factory Inspectors*, Assembly Documents 113th Session, vol. iii, pp. 33-42 (1890).

[3] *Ibid.*, p. 36.

It is significant to note that no demand for enforcement of the law was made to the factory inspectors by labor unions, parents, minors or employers, and few cases came up under it. The laws in the other states met the similar fate of non-enforcement and became virtually dead-letters.

7. *The Nationalization of Trade Union Restrictions upon Apprenticeship*

Contemporaneous with the attempt to regulate apprenticeship by legislation went the attempt to regulate it by trade-union enactment and collective bargaining. At first the formulation of the rules governing apprenticeship was left largely to the local unions. This of course proved inadequate. A national problem could not be regulated by the uncoördinated rules of local bodies. In those cities where the unions were weak or non-existent, large numbers of apprentices or juvenile workers could be employed and taught only a fraction of their trade. Many of these, upon completing their service and failing to secure a journeyman's position, would go to other cities and menace the position of union workmen there. Often, moreover, a weak union would prefer to admit men as full-fledged journeymen even though they had served no apprenticeship, believing that these men menaced them less inside the organization than without.[1] These entrants could then go to other cities, present their union card, and be treated as master workmen. Impotent as the locals proved to be, the national bodies were nevertheless slow in shouldering the responsibility for regulation.[2] As late as 1890, only seventeen of forty-eight trades unions, comprising 16½% of the total membership, regulated or

---

[1] The unions of Louisville, Kentucky, followed this policy, see *Leather Workers Journal*, April, 1904, pp. 521-22.

[2] See T. W. Glocker, *The Government of American Trade Unions*, pp. 35-36.

attempted to regulate apprenticeship through their national bodies. Ten had general policies of restriction but surrendered to the local unions the power to enact the concrete regulations and to enforce them while twenty-one made no mention of apprenticeship whatsoever.[1] By 1904, however, as Professor Motley points out in his able monograph, 70 out of 120 national unions, comprising 900,000 members out of a total of 1,675,000, had enacted apprenticeship regulations. This means an increase in 14 years from 16½% to 54%.[2]

8. The Effect of Trade Union Restrictions

This much vexed question of apprenticeship regulation was however wellnigh negligible as a cause of strikes. From 1881 to 1886 inclusive, strikes affected as many as 22,300

[1] See E. W. Bemis, "Relation of Trades Unions to Apprentices," *Quarterly Journal of Economics*, vol. vi, pp. 76-93.

[2] Interesting features of apprenticeship are the age of entrance and the wage as compared with that of a full fledged worker. The age of entrance varied. A New Jersey study shows the trades with an early entrance and those with a comparatively later age of entrance. *Report New Jersey Bureau of Statistics of Labor and Industries*, 1891, pp. 185-186.

Those having a comparatively small per cent of their numbers who began their apprenticeship before 16 were:

Plumbers	3.6%	Painters	11.7%
Bricklayers & Masons	6.6%	Potters (Kilnmen)	18.8%
Glass Blowers		Printers	30.0%
a. Green bottle	10.0%	Carpenters	18.8%
b. Flint	12.6%	Hat Makers	28.0%
c. Window	2.7%		

The following statistics from Ohio for 1885 (*Report of Ohio Bureau of Labor Statistics 1885*, pp. 45-47), indicate the relative wage which the apprentice received in comparison with the journeyman.

Trades	Av. yearly wage of Journeyman	Av. yearly wage of Apprentice	Per cent Apprentice to Journeyman wage
Iron Molders	$497.61	$232.36	46.6%
Cigar-Makers	$413.59	$142.55	34.4%
Typographers	$623.68	$154.85	24.8%

The wage of the apprentice ranged then from one-quarter to one-half that of the journeyman.

establishments, yet in only 213 or about 1% of the total, was the question of apprenticeship paramount.   In the period of 1885-1893 there were strikes involving over 22,000 establishments, of which only 161 or less than 1% were caused by disputes over apprenticeship.[1]

As a cause of lockouts, apprenticeship restrictions were of course much more prominent.   From 1881 to 1886, 2214 establishments locked out their employees and[2] in 169 or 7.7% of these cases, opposition to union restriction of apprentices was assigned as the principal cause.   167 of these cases occurred in the single year of 1886.

The opposition to apprenticeship regulations found expression in the claim that they " prevented the American boy from learning a trade."   It was alleged that the unions, by limiting the number of apprentices, deprived boys of the opportunity of becoming skilled workers.   A Boston paper voiced this view when it said, " A liberal apprenticeship will do as much as anything else to put a wholesome restraint upon trade-union tyranny and to make the mechanic arts again desirable and serviceable to the sons of American citizens."[3]   Exponents of this view have been both numerous and insistent.[4]   A confusion of ideas, however, lies at the bottom of it.   It assumes that an increase of apprentices is all that is needed to teach boys a trade, that mere numbers will ensure training.   It ignores the fact that just because of the former surplus of apprentice labor, boys were not taught the whole trade, but only a few detailed processes.   The more boys there are free to enter

[1] *Report of Bureau of Labor Statistics of Minn.*, pp. 312-314.
[2] *Ibid.*, p. 316.
[3] *Boston Journal*, July 15, 1890.
[4] In the decade 1900-1910, Mr. Anthony Ittner, chairman of the committee on Industrial Education of the National Association of Manufacturers, became the chief defender of the so-called "American Boy."

a trade, the less incentive the manufacturer is likely to feel to give any one of them a thorough training.

In any case, however, the actual burden of restriction appears to have been very slight.   In the first place the unions were relatively weak. Moreover, had they really. prevented boys from learning a trade in those industries in which they were strong. we should at least expect to find that both boys and employers would take advantage of what opportunities remained to them.   If, for instance, the allotted ratio was one apprentice to four journeymen, we should expect to find at least that proportion of apprentices actually at work.   As a matter of fact. taking the country as a whole, *there were not as many apprentices as the unions. allowed.*

Apprenticeship therefore decayed primarily because of other forces than trade union regulation. As early as 1869, a Massachusetts investigation showed that employers were realizing that it was unprofitable for them to employ apprentices.   Forty-six out of fifty-two employers stated that they had served an apprenticeship in their business, but only twenty-seven were now employing apprentices. Only 19 believed apprenticeship to be valuable.[1]   A Philadelphia study of the following year shows that there were but 3,500 apprentices in 8,000 establishments in that city with a total working force of 92,000 men.[2]   This was a ratio of approximately one apprentice to twenty-five journeymen, a number not sufficient to keep a trade alive were apprenticeship the sole means of recruiting workers. A comparison of the number of apprentices to journeymen permitted by eight national unions with the number actually

[1] *Report of Committee of Massachusetts Charitable Association,* " Relation of Apprentices of their Employers," pp. 3-6.

[2] Whitney, James, *Apprenticeship,* 1872 (published in the *Philadelphia Social Science Series*), pp. 12-13.

employed in Massachusetts in 1890 shows some interesting results.[1]

Name of Union	Ratio of Apprentices to Journeymen (union regulation)	Actual Ratio in Mass.
1. Pattern Makers Union	1 to 4	1 to 48
2. Journeymen Tailors Union	1 to 1	1 to 12
3. Silk & Fur Hat Trimmers	1 to 10	1 to 288
4. Wood Carvers Association	1 to 5	1 to 25.5
5. Form Makers Union	1 to a shop and 1 extra for every 8	1 to 51
6. Typographical	1 to 5	1 to 9
7. Carpenters	1 to 6	1 to 62
8. Plumbers	1 to 4	1 to 44

In Ohio, however, there was apparently no such paucity of apprentices. In 1884, an investigation[2] of 74 plants in the machinists, molders, blacksmiths, wood-carvers, pattern-makers, coopers, cigar-makers, carpenters, brick-masons and compositors trades showed a total of 275 apprentices to 1385 journeymen or a ratio of 1 to 5. The case of the cigarmakers, typographers, and iron-molders was even more striking. In the cigar industry there were 609 apprentices and 809 journeymen, or a ratio of 1 to 1⅓; in the iron molders there were 521 apprentices and 1451 journeymen or a ratio of 1 to 3; in the typographical plants there were 211 apprentices and 791 journeymen or a ratio of 1 to 3¾. Here quite evidently the trades unions did not effectively restrict opportunities to learn the trade, for the number employed was far in excess of the number set by the union.

9. The Decline of Apprenticeship

Taking industry throughout the country as the standard, however, apprenticeship was rapidly decreasing in impor-

[1] Bemis, E. W., "Relation of Trades Union to Apprentices," *Quarterly Journal of Economics*, vol. vi, pp. 83-84.

[2] *Report of Ohio Bureau of Statistics of Labor 1884*, p. 261.

tance. The Census statistics show a steady decline in the ratio of apprentices in the manufacturing industries as a whole.[1]

Year	Number of Apprentices	Total number Employed in Manufacturing and Mining	Ratio
1860	55,326	1,850,034	1 to 33
1880	44,170	3,837,112	1 to 87
1890	82,057	5,091,293	1 to 62
1900	81,603	7,112,987	1 to 88
1910	118,964	11,623,605	1 to 98

The figures for 1870 are worthless. In the census although apprentices were counted as a special class, they were enumerated under their particular trade without definition. While it is possible that there were some apprentices who were not listed as such by the Census, it is probable that their number was not appreciable.

An apparent paradox now confronts us. If the number of apprentices was actually decreasing, why did so many of the unions still insist that their trades were being over-crowded with apprentices? The answer is twofold: In the first place, though the general decline in the number of apprentices was genuine, overcrowding did still exist locally in some trades. such as plumbing, cigar-making, and typography.

In the second place, we must remember that " apprenticeship " was a term often employed loosely by the unions to designate juvenile labor. Boy labor was on the increase, and the laboring men were really enveighing against this when they spoke of apprentices. The old idea was that no child should be in industry unless he was actually learning a trade. When the numbers of employed children were

[1] 8th Census, 1860, pp. 565-677. 10th Census, 1880, vol. i, " Population," p. 746. 11th Census, 1890, vol. iii, p. 397. 12th Census, 1900, vol. ii, pp. 566-7 (this includes helpers as well, so number of Apprentices was probably less). 13th Census, 1910, vol. iv, p. 91.

observed, it was thought that they must be in this class. And when it was discovered that they were not being taught as apprentices should be, the cry was immediately raised that apprenticeship was being abused. The fact was not clearly grasped that a new class of workers was being created: namely, children who were valued for their immediate labor, not for their ultimate productivity.

During the eighties unions sought recourse again in legislative enactment. The Federation of Organized Trades and Labor Unions, the precursor to the American Federation of Labor, at its inception in 1881 resolved as one of its fundamental principles "that necessity demands the enactment of uniform apprentice laws throughout the country: that the apprentice to a mechanical trade may be made to serve a sufficient term of apprenticeship from three to five years. and that he be provided by his employer with proper and sufficient facilities to finish him as a competent workman."[1] Laws which should regulate the term of service and the conditions of employment and compel the master to teach the whole trade, were specifically advocated both in California and New York.[2] The states, however, refused to take action.

The manufacturers of the day were not particularly concerned with the fact that the decadence of apprenticeship had destroyed the only means of recruiting skilled workers. Down to 1885, the country had not seriously faced the problem of machine technology, even though manufacturing was becoming predominant. Though plunged into large scale production, America retained the ideas of handicraft and agriculture. Unconsciously, however, American industry

[1] *Report of First Annual Session of the Federation of Organized Trades and Labor Unions of the United States and Canada,* p. 3.

[2] See *Fourth Annual Report of Statistics of Labor,* pp. 197-203. *California Bureau of Labor Statistics,* 1887-88, pp. 94-97.

was taking that turn which now renders it characteristically
American.   High wages plus an abundance of raw materials
forced the manufacturers to resort to quantitive, mass production.   Qualitive standards of workmanship were impossible in the face of the high wage schedules.   The
machine process became more automatic, the subdivision of
labor more extended, the workmen more nearly reduced to
the status of machine tenders.   All-round trade training
ceased to be necessary for many.

One of the theories advanced for this lack of interest
upon the part of the employers is that we were then recruiting our skilled workers from abroad and therefore did not
need to train them at home.   Many of the contemporary
pamphleteers were of this opinion.[1]   The theory explains
the awakening of interest in industrial education during
the decade which followed 1900 by the fact that the " new "
immigration from southeastern Europe was far more unskilled than the " old " immigration from northwestern
Europe and that in consequence, the United States was compelled to recruit her skilled workmen from her own population.

Though this view is endorsed by practically all recent
works on immigration,[2] it is not borne out by a careful
statistical study of immigration in the two periods.   Thus
skilled laborers formed but 11.5 per cent of the total immigration into the country for the period 1871-82 inclusive
while 15.0% of the total immigration for the years 1899-

[1] See James Whitney, *Apprenticeship*, Philadelphia, 1872, Mr. J. S.
Perry, *Some Considerations Presented to the Molders lately Employed
by Perry & Co.*, p. 7.

[2] Jenks and Lauck, *The Immigration Problem*, p. 31, express the
orthodox view. Hourwich, I. A., *Immigration and Labor*, pp. 67-68,
dissents from this. His book is in general so polemic and so permeated
with the *post hoc ergo propter hoc* fallacy that his views on this point
have not received the attention that they merit.

1910 inclusive were skilled.[1]   If we eliminate all these without occupations (chiefly women and children), the percentage of skilled of those with occupations in the early period was 23.2 and 20.3 in the later period.   When the immigration from Northwestern Europe and from Southeastern Europe is compared for the respective periods when each was dominant, it will be seen that immigrants from Northwestern Europe in the 70's and early 80's were as unskilled as the immigrants from Southeastern Europe in the decades preceding and following 1900.   Popular confusion has arisen on this point because the two immigrations were compared by the Immigration Commission for the same period of time (1899-1910), when they should have been compared for the periods when each was in turn dominant.[2]

It should not be inferred from the foregoing discussion that apprenticeship is, as so many have claimed, dead.   As we shall see, many plants have apprenticeship systems to train high-grade mechanics, but in general the system can be said to be declining as industry becomes more and more

[1] The statistics for 1871-82 were compiled from the *Annual Reports of the Bureau of Commerce and Navigation*.   Those for 1899-1910 were taken from *Report of United States Immigration Commission*, vol. i. p. 100.   The definition of skilled has been made coterminous for the two periods.   See my article, " Is the New Immigration more Unskilled than the Old "? *Quarterly Publications American Statistical Association*, June, 1919, esp. pp. 396-97.

[2] In my article, "Is the New Immigration more Unskilled than the Old," *op. cit.*, pp. 393-403, I have pointed out the fallacy of the Immigration Commission and Messrs. Jenks & Lauck in drawing conclusions as to the relative skill of the " new " and the " old " immigration on the basis of a comparison for the same period.   These terms should include (1) a space relationship to differentiate between the peoples of Northwestern and Southeastern Europe but also (2) a time relationship to compare the immigration of one period with a previous one.   The article shows that if the immigration from Northwestern Europe for 1871-82 is compared with that of Southeastern Europe for 1899-1910, it will be seen that it did not possess a larger number of skilled workmen, if indeed it possessed as many.

specialized and automatic. It is not at present of great actual importance as a method of trade training.

10. *The Recrudescence of Apprenticeship in Wisconsin*

As the author has pointed out elsewhere,[1] despite this general decline, the apprenticeship system in Wisconsin has, during the last few years, shown unmistakeable signs of growth. The industrial education law of 1911 began the regulation of apprenticeship by prescribing that every apprentice should receive not less than five hours a week of instruction in English, citizenship, business practise, physiology, hygiene, the use of safety devices, and such other branches as might be approved by the state board of industrial education. This law also provided for the registration of all apprenticeship indentures.

In 1915, the apprenticeship laws were amended so that they included: (1) Compulsory indenture. Every apprenticeship contract was to be made in writing and a copy filed with the state industrial commission. (2) Time for instruction in the continuation school. A minimum of five hours a week was required to be devoted to instruction and the employers were required to pay the apprentice for this time. (3) Regulation of hours and wages. Every indenture was to state the number of hours to be spent in work. Not more than fifty-five hours a week (including instruction) was, however, permissible. Apprentices over eighteen years could work overtime not to exceed thirty hours a month, and were to receive for this one and one half ordinary wage rates. (4) Specification of the particular processes to be taught the workmen and the approximate time to be spent on each. (5) Supervision and direction of the system by the state industrial commission. The

[1] " The Recrudescence of Apprenticeship in Wisconsin," *School and Society*, vol. vii, pp. 22-23, Jan. 5, 1918.

commission was given the power to classify trade and industries; to construct and supervise the contracts, and to act as the mediator for differences between apprentices and employers.

The commission was wise enough to create a state apprenticeship board to administer the act, composed of representatives of the employers, of the unions, and of the state continuation schools. Perhaps most important of all was the appointment of a full-time supervisor of apprentices who was also to act as the secretary of the board.

The board has succeeded in enlisting the confidence and cooperation of both employers and employees. Its most important accomplishment has been the formation of proper standards of apprenticeship in different trades and industries. Under the old relation of apprenticeship, the duties of apprentice and master were loosely defined. With the coming of the machine era, it became impossible to determine what processes must be taught the apprentice and what might be omitted. The clear definition of what is to be included under apprentice training removes much ambiguity and its attendant opportunity for abuse.

The board has also worked out a uniform indenture blank and has issued diplomas to boys who have successfully completed their apprenticeship. These measures help both in standardizing conditions and in offering an incentive for the apprentices to do their best and to complete their apprenticeship.

Statistics show that the results of this system have been most satisfactory. Under the law of 1911, the following number of apprentice contracts were entered into: 1912, 142; 1913, 260; 1914, 220, and 1915, 163. The 1915 law first became fully operative for the year 1916, and in that year a total number of 468 new contracts were filed. This was an increase over the previous year of approximately

200 per cent. and an increase of 80 per cent, over the highest mark in the four previous years. The distribution, by trades and localities, of the total number of apprentices is very interesting. Five hundred and sixty-six, or 58 per cent., of the 969 apprentices registered, were in the machinist trade; 121, or an additional 12 per cent., were pattern-makers. The number of apprentices in such trades as tool-making, carpentering, plastering and painting was very meager. Seven hundred and forty-four, or 77 per cent. of the total for the state, were concentrated in Milwaukee. The number of supervised apprentices has steadily grown until it now includes several thousand. Wisconsin, however, is the only state to show such a development.

11. *Causes for the Decline of Apprenticeship*

Why has this system of apprenticeship once so prevalent, now decayed? For two main reasons: (1) Because there is no longer the need for as large a proportion of skilled workers in industry as formerly. The development of machinery and the fast increasing specialization of labor has rendered it unnecessary for the vast majority of factory operatives to know more than one, or at most a few, processes. Only a few need to have the all-round knowledge formerly required and which apprenticeship was designed to give. The very reason for apprenticeship, in its former sense of a thorough mastery of a trade, is thus largely removed.[1] (2) Because it has come to be thought unprofitable by individual employers, workmen, parents, and the boys themselves to train even those all-round workmen that are needed.

[1] It should not be inferred that this removes the necessity for training. Not only is some training required for the specific occupations but the broader civic, intellectual, and moral functions of apprenticeship need, not only to be carried out in the modern situation, but to be improved.

(a) First, apprenticeship was unprofitable to the indivi-dual manufacturer. To his mind it confused the function of the shop with that of the school. The apprentice's aim was to learn as much as possible: the employer's aim was to produce as cheaply as possible. These two ideas are generally anta-gonistic. The manufacturer under competitive conditions must run his machines at the highest possible efficiency. That cannot be accomplished by transferring a worker as soon as he has mastered any given process. The initial ex-pense of " breaking in " a man or boy is too great for that. Once the employee has mastered the workings of a particular machine, it is more profitable for the employer to keep him there than to move him on. This means that the appren-tice is not taught the whole process, but merely a specialized part. His position is divested of its trade educational features. While ostensibly an apprentice, he is actually a mere worker devoid of training.

Apprenticeship is moreover rendered still more unprofit-able for the employer by the fact that once he has trained an apprentice, there is no guarantee that he can permaner'.y enjoy his services. The apprentice costs more at first because of the disarrangement of the plant, time spent in training, and spoiled products. While learning he is gener-ally unprofitable. The only opportunity for the employer to recoup is to enjoy his increased productivity when he is once trained. Once the apprentice is trained, however, other firms who did not go to the expense of teaching the boys themselves can hire him away. The first employer cannot afford to pay as high wages as the second, because he already has more invested in the boy, for which he must get a return. A premium is thereby placed upon not train-ing apprentices. Firms rely upon stealing rather than training hands. Though it would be a benefit to the in-

dustry as a whole to have a supply of well-trained apprentices, to the *individual firm* it usually spells a loss.[1]

(b) In the second place the workmen already in the shop
dislikes apprenticeship. The boy is his potential rival. He
is afraid that the learner may ultimately supplant him. In
consequence, he does not show him all of the tricks of the
trade. Painters' apprentices say that it is practically impossible to get a master who will teach them thoroughly.
"Let the kid pick it up for himself" is the general sentiment
towards the novice.

Every moment the workman spends in teaching the apprentice moreover is a moment withdrawn from his own
task. He is valued by his employer as a producer, not as
a teacher of others. Furthermore, machinery, unlike
hand-work is not susceptible of interruption; it demands
constant attention, and there is little leisure in which to instruct one's neighbor. This concentration upon the immediate machine and its product is especially intense where
piece-work is the rule. Here a direct pecuniary loss will
follow any attention to others. In the clothing trades,
where piece-work prevails, the novice is given but little
instruction, although she may be operating dangerous high-
power machines.

Finally, even if the workman should be willing to give
instruction, he is generally incapable of doing so. He has
little all-round training himself and his trade knowledge is
generally confined to but a few operations. Nor is the foreman much better adapted to act as a teacher. His chief function is to speed up the operatives. He is not necessarily a
highly-skilled workman himself, and he tends to be hostile
or at best indifferent to an operative primarily learning

---

[1] This is merely another instance of the falsity of the laissez-faire
doctrine that each man by pursuing his own interest thereby pursues the
interest of the whole.

rather than producing. Indeed the whole spirit of the modern work-shop is unfriendly to the conception of it as a place for the development of skilled craftsmen. Skill is a matter of time, and modern production is in a hurry.

(c) Nor is apprenticeship a system that finds favor with many parents. The ambitious among them are discouraged by the uncertainty of the training offered; and what is more important, the poor are held back by the financial sacrifice it involves. To apprentice a boy instead of setting him to work means a very considerable immediate loss in wages. That this loss will be more than made up in the future is small comfort when the present is heavy with want. The superior initial wage of the unskilled worker looms large in such cases, and it is only the unusual parent who will stand out against it.

(d) Finally, even the boy himself is hostile to apprenticeship. Like his parents, he sees the larger wage which the unskilled worker gets. He does not see that this wage will not increase. Moreover he relishes his independence. He does not wish to bind himself legally or even verbally for a prescribed period of time. He is restless and wishes to change. The prospect stretching out before him of years of steady work at one industry bores him sadly.

Apprenticeship, moreover, presents itself as an opening into the manual trades alone. It spells overalls and greasy hands. These are associated in his mind with foreign labor and the jokes of his schoolfellows. Ten to one he prefers the social prestige of any sort of "clean-collar" occupation, so he becomes errand-boy, messenger-boy, office-boy,—and skilled craftsmanship goes by the board.[1]

---

[1] For descriptions and accounts of the causes for the downfall of the apprenticeship system, see: *Mass. Committee on Relationship of Apprentices to Employers* (1869), pp. 7-11. Sykes, G. C., "Old and New

To the extent therefore that the decline in apprenticeship has been due to faulty organization and to indifference, the Wisconsin method offers hope for a rehabilitation of the old system. To the extent, however, that it has been caused by the inevitable specialization of the machine era and by the individualistic conduct of industry, it presents no real remedy.

Conditions of Apprenticeship in the Buildings Trades," *Journal Pol. Econ.*, vol. ii, pp. 408 ff. Wright, *Bulletin Bureau of Education*, 1908, no. 6, pp. 84-86. Stevens, G. A., "Influence of Trade Education upon Wages," *Journal of Pol. Econ.*, vol. xix, pp. 19-24. Weyl and Sakolsky, "Conditions of Entrance to the Principal Trades," *Bull. Bureau of Labor Statistics*, no. 67.

CHAPTER IV

PRESENT CONDITIONS OF CHILDREN IN INDUSTRY

For the average child of from fourteen to sixteen, school life is over and industrial life has begun. Whatever his reasons for leaving school, whether poverty or apathy towards the school itself, he has little idea what particular trade he wishes to follow. He does not know which occupations need boys nor which will afford him a future. He takes the first job that he finds, an unskilled job; works for some time, perhaps a few weeks or a few months; finds that there is no opportunity to learn the trade, that the pay involved does not loom as large as it did at first; he is tired by the monotony of the task, and quits. He runs about the streets and casually looks for another position. After a while he finds it. It is another unskilled job. He works a short time at this task, and then leaves it as he did the first. And so he drifts from job to job, from industry to industry, still unskilled, and exposed to all the social and industrial evils which threaten adolescence. Once grown, he is crowded out of his job forever by another younger crop of workers, and finds himself one of the class of the permanently unskilled with the attendant low wages and unemployment of his class. He had nothing to sell but his youth; he sold it, and received nothing in return.

1. *Early age at which children leave school.* Children leave school early. How early and in what numbers it is not easy definitely to determine. The census figures for

291

85

1910[1] on the proportion of children in school afford one source of information.

Years	Number attending school	Percentage of total number of children of that age
11–12	1,555,301	91.2
12–13	1,716,310	89.8
13–14	1,574,253	88.8
14–15	1,501,456	81.2
15–16	1,175,009	68.3
16–17	943,511	50.6
17–18	629,866	35.3

It is important to notice that nearly one-third of the 15-year-olds and approximately one-half of the 16-year-olds were not in school. The National Committee on Vocational Education in 1914 found that there were 345,666 children of 14 and 546,216 children of 15, who were not attending school, making a total of 892,882 children, or nearly 900,000 between 14 and 16 out of school.[3] Doctor L. P. Ayres, after a study of 58 cities, estimated that in the United States 250,000 children of 14 years fail of graduation from the grammar grades and leave school forever. He also declared that of the 200,000 children of 14 who do graduate, a large proportion also leave school.

Probably the most satisfactory study of all is that made by Professor E. L. Thorndike in 1908. His conclusions, for American cities of 25,000 and over, were that for every 100 entering pupils, the schools retained

[1] *13th Census*, vol. i, p. 1099.

[2] *Report of the Commission on National Aid to Vocational Education.* House Doc. 1004, 63rd Congress, 2nd Session, vol. i, p. 104.

[3] Gulick and Ayres, *Why 250,000 Children Leave School*, Russell Sage Foundation, Department of Child Hygiene, *Bulletin 77*, p. 1.

[4] Bureau of Education, 1908, *Bulletin No. 4*, p. 11.

```
90 to grade 4
81  "    "   5
68  "    "   6
54  "    "   7
40  "    "   8 (Usually last grammar grade)
27  "    "   1st Year High School
17  "    "   2nd  "     "     "
12  "    "   3rd  "     "     "
 8  "    "   4th  "     "     "
```

On an age calculation taking as its base 100 school pupils at the age of eight, the school retained:[1]

Years	Per cent
10–11	100
11–12	98
12–13	97
13–14	78
14–15	70
15–16	47
16–17	30
17–18	16.5
18–19	8.6

Several interesting facts emerge from these statistics: (1) that only 40 percent of the children finish the grammar school: (2) that 19% drop out in the 13th year, while only 8% drop out in the 14th year. This seems to indicate that children often withdraw from school before they are legally allowed to do so. This is a commentary upon our method of enforcing school attendance, and permits us to surmise as to the actual enforcement of child-labor laws. (3) it is noticeable that only 47% of the children are still in school during their 15th year. During the four years from 12-15 inclusive, an even 50% of the children leave school.

These statistics of Thorndike for cities undoubtedly present a more favorable picture than would similar data from

[1] *Ibid.*, p. 23.

the country districts.   These latter, the draft statistics have shown to give inferior educational opportunities.[1]

Criticism of the statistical method which Thorndike followed has been offered,[2] but similar investigations have tended rather to confirm than to disprove Thorndike's investigation. Thus, Dr. George D. Strayer after compiling in 1911 the school censuses of 318 cities, declared that " in our cities considerably *more than half* of the children are eliminated between the ages of 13 and 15 inclusive." [3]

From these statistics it is safe to conclude (a) that there are approximately 1,100,000 children from 13 to 16 who have left school permanently, (b) that the school mortality during these years is at least 50% of those who began school before 13, (c) that only 40% of the children ever finish the grammar grades, (d) that approximately only 8% finish their high school education.[4]   It is quite possible that this latter percentage is now somewhat higher and may increase still more.

2. *Reasons for leaving school.*   Why do these children leave school and go to work? This is not easy to determine because the reasons assigned both by parents and by

---

[1] Thus 21 per cent of the white men and 51 per cent of the negroes in the national army were illiterate. Henry Wembridge, *The Southern Illiterates in the U. S. Army, School and Society*, Nov. 6, 1920, p. 424.

[2] L. P. Ayres, *Laggards in Our Schools*, pp. 66-72.

[3] G. D. Strayer, *Age and Grade Census of Schools and Colleges in the U. S.*, p. 11, Bureau of Educ., 1911, *Bul. No. 5.*

[4] Interesting figures are given in Parsons, *Choosing a Vocation*, 1909, pp. 100-6, on the percentage who complete their high school course. The enrollment in Boston High Schools was but 6% of that in the first room grade; in Washington 7%; while in Philadelphia it was but 3%. Parsons makes the mistake however of regarding these percentages as accurate indications of the elimination of school pupils. The classes that were then graduating from high school were in all probability smaller when they began in the primary grades than those then beginning. In other words, Parsons did not allow for the increase of school population in the intervening period.

the children themselves are generally not the real ones. The parent is reluctant to admit that poverty has forced him to withdraw his child from school, while the child is loath to confess that failure in his studies has discouraged him. Moreover, there are generally a complex of causes which operate together, making it almost impossible to determine the exact importance of each.

(a) The Federal Investigation into the Condition of Women and Child Wage-Earners, after a careful study of selected cases in different parts of the country, constructed the following table of causes :[1]

Primary Causes	Number	Per cent
Earnings necessary to family support	177	29.3
Child help desired though not necessary	172	28.4
Child's dissatisfaction with school	161	26.6
Child's preference for work	60	9.9
Other causes	35	5.8
Total	606	100.0

The investigation chose as its criterion for deciding whether the labor of the child was economically necessary, a family income of $1.50 a week for each member of the family, excluding rent and the child's wages. In those families which had an income below this amount, the investigation judged the child's contribution to be actually necessary. On this basis, in only 29.3% of the cases was the cause declared to be predominantly economic.

A study conducted under the auspices of the Public Education Association of New York City in 1912 by Miss Alice Barrows, employed the same standard of necessity, that had been used by the Federal Government. After

[1] *Report on Conditions of Women and Child Wage-Earners in the United States*, vol. vii (Senate Document 645, 61st Congress, 2nd Session,, p. 46.

studying 327 typical cases, Miss Barrows found that in only 20%of the cases was the weekly income of the family (exclusive of child's wages) less than $1.50 per capita, and consequently decided that poverty was the predominant factor in only 20% of the cases.[1]

The Douglas Commission[2] which in 1906 investigated vocational education in Massachusetts, declared that in only 24% of the cases were the wages of the children necessary for the family support.

But is not the standard set by the federal investigation and followed by Miss Barrows much too low? A per capita weekly income of $1.50 per week would total for the normal family of five but $7.50 per week, and if no time or money were lost by unemployment, accidents, or sickness, would thus amount to $390 for the year plus an allowance for rent. This latter under the most liberal estimate for families of that wage group could not be more than 20% of the family income or $97.50. This would make the $1.50 per week per capita allowance roughly equal $490 a year.

Now this sum was plainly inadequate for the needs of a family of five at the time these studies were made. Chapin in his classic study, estimated that to maintain a physical existence, a family of five in New York City in 1907 require an income of between $800 and $900 a year.[3] Mrs. Louise B. More, in a similar, though smaller, investigation fixed the absolute physical minimum for a New York City family at $728 in 1906, but added that to make any provision

[1] Alice P. Barrows. *Report of Vocational Guidance Survey, Bulletin No. 9*, Public Education Association of the City of New York, 1912, p. 8.

[2] *Report of Douglas Commission on Industrial and Technical Training*, 1906, p. 92.

[3] Chapin, R. C., *The Standard of Living in New York City*, pp. 245-248.

for the future the family would require $800-$900.[1]   F. H. Streightoff, after a detailed study in 1914 declared $876[2] to be the minimum upon which the normal family could exist.   In 1915, the Bureau of Personal Service of the Board of Estimate and Apportionment made a minimum budget estimate for unskilled laborers of $845.   Streightoff, after a very careful study, concluded that in 1914, $772 was necessary for the average family of five in Buffalo, New York; excluding rent, the amount necessary would be $620.[3] Kennedy in his study of the cost of living in Chicago, concluded that: " The minimum amount necessary to support a family efficiently in the stock-yards district is $800 per year, $15.40 per week." [4]

The federal investigation itself, in its monograph on " Family Budgets of Typical Cotton Mill Workers," fixed a minimum for barely physical needs for a family of five in Fall River, Massachusetts in 1909 at $484.41 a year and stated that it would require from $691 to $732 to maintain a fair standard of life.[5]   The same investigation fixed $408 as the absolute minimum which Southern Cotton Mill operative could subsist upon although only $45 was allowed annually for rent.[6]

Some idea of the rigors of this subsistence budget for the South may be obtained from the following statement of the

[1] More, L. B., *Wage-Earners Budgets*, pp. 269-270.

[2] F. H. Streightoff, *Report on Cost of Living*, Fourth Annual Report (New York) State Factory Investigating Committee, p. 1668.

[3] See F. H. Streightoff, *Report on Cost of Living*, Fourth Annual Report (New York) State Factory Investigation.

[4] Kennedy, J. C. and others, *Wages and Family Budgets in the Chicago Stock Yards District*, p. 80.

[5] *Report on Conditions of Woman and Child Wage-Earners in the United States* (Senate Doc. No. 645, 61st Congress, 2nd Session), vol. xvi, pp. 233-45.

[6] *Ibid.*, p. 143.

report: "If the family live within this sum without suffering, wisdom to properly apportion the income is necessary. No tobacco can be used. No newspapers can be purchased. *The children cannot go to school,*[1] because there will be no money to buy their books. Household articles that are worn or destroyed cannot be replaced. The above sum provides for neither birth or death nor any illness that demands a doctor's attention or calls for medicine. Even though all these things are eliminated, if the family is not to suffer, the mother must be a woman of rare ability. She must know how to make her own and children's clothing; she must be physically able to do all of the household work, including the washing. And she must know enough to purchase with her allowance food that has the proper nutrition value."

It is small wonder that the Report states[2] that the "minimum standard of living is so low that one would expect few families to live on it." The Report concludes that $600 a year is necessary to maintain a "fair standard" in the South but will permit the children to attend school.[3]

From the above budgetary it appears evident that the allowance made by the investigation and Miss Barrows of $1.50 per week per capita exclusive of rent was far too low even for the period 1907-12. The total yearly income was as we saw only $490 on this basis, and the gap between it and the proper yearly income necessary even for subsistence is thus seen to be very wide.

An estimate of $2.00 per week per capita exclusive of rent as the "necessity line" for this period, below which children were forced to go to work, seems most conservative. This would be equivalent to a yearly income of $520 a year

[1] Italics mine.
[2] *Ibid.*, p. 142.
[3] *Ibid.*, p. 152.

plus rent.   Again allowing 20% for rent, this would give a
yearly income of $650.   Even this income would have been
insufficient to maintain physical efficiency in New York City,
Chicago, Buffalo and probably in New England in this
period, although it might have sufficed in the South.

Adopting this new criterion of an income of $2.00 a week
per member of the family, we find that of the 605 cases
of children who were studied by the Federal Investigation
that 250 or 41.3% came from families with incomes of less
than this amount.[1]   Miss Atherton, in her stimulating investigation in 1913-14 of employed girls in Wilkes-Barre,
Pennsylvania showed that 44.9% of the girls between 14
and 16 at work came from families with weekly incomes of
less than $2.00 per capita.[2]   This was clearly insufficient
for the year in which the study was made because prices
had risen appreciably since 1909.

It seems clear therefore, despite opinions to the contrary,
that poverty was the primary cause for children leaving
school and going to work five or more years ago.   Have
conditions changed since then and if so, in which direction?
Definite information is lacking since there have been no
studies recently to determine the economic pressure forcing
children to leave school.   In June 1918 Dr. W. F. Ogburn
brought Chapin's budget and that of the New York State
Factory Investigation Commission up to date by the use
of the prices then prevailing.   Dr. Ogburn found that the
Chapin budget would have cost at that time $1390 and that
of the Factory Commission $1360.   Independent investiga-
tions at the same time by the United States Bureau of
Labor Statistics set the minimum of subsistence budget at

[1] *Report on Conditions of Women and Child Wage-Earners*, vol. xvii,
p. 57.

[2] Sarah Atherton, *Survey of Wage-Earning Girls Below 16 years of
Age in Wilkes-Barre, Pennsylvania*, p. 48.

$1380.[1] It therefore appears that from $1350 to $1400 was necessary physically to maintain a family of five in New York City in June 1918. The cost of living for ship builder's families increased 22.5% in New York City from December 1, 1917 to December 1, 1918 and 23.6% from December 1917 to June 1919.[2]

On the supposition that the increase from December 1, 1917 to December 1, 1918 was evenly distributed, this would indicate an increase of 11.2% from June 1918 to June 1919.

On the average, money wages of workmen have probably not increased as fast as the cost of living and consequently in general real wages have fallen although for a few groups. they have increased. Rubinow[3] and Jones[4] have shown that from 1900 to 1913 real wages for union workmen fell appreciably while from 1913 to 1918, according to Professor Irving Fisher's computations real hourly wages decreased at least 20 percent.[5] If poverty therefore was the primary cause of 40 percent of the children leaving school in 1910, it is possible that it may be the primary cause for an even larger percentage at the present day.

(b) Even in those cases where the earnings of the child are not needed to maintain a physical basis for life, the desire on the part of both parents and child to at-

[1] W. F. Ogburn, "Standard of Living as a Basis for Wage Adjustments," *Proceedings Academy of Political Science*, vol. viii, no. 2, pp. 107-108.

[2] *Monthly Labor Review*, September, 1919, p. 108. Using December, 1914 as a base or 100, December, 1917 showed an index of 144.68. December, 1918, 177.28 and June, 1919, 179.22.

[3] I. M. Rubinow, "The Recent Trend of Real Wages," *American Economic Review*, December, 1914, pp. 798-817.

[4] Jones, "Real Wages in Recent Years," *American Economic Review*, June, 1917, pp. 318-330.

[5] Irving Fisher, *Stabilizing the Dollar*, p. 56.

tain a comfort level operates to force children out of school into industry. Dr. Ogburn placed $1760 as the amount necessary to maintain a family in a large eastern city in June 1918 on this comfort level,[1] and he fixed $2200 as necessary to maintain a family of five on this level in August 1919 in Washington, D. C.[2]   When we realize how small a percentage of workingmen's families have incomes of this size, some idea is gained of the economic pressure upon children to leave school.

(c) The present system of school administration is moreover undoubtedly at fault.   The teaching is so dull, scholastic discipline so severe, and above all the curriculum has so little connection with life, that the child is discouraged.   If he is clever and ambitious, he wants to make his way in the real world at once; if he is dull or in ill health, he is glad to escape from his own apparent failure.   He is apt to become either impatient or disheartened and to leave even when there is no pressing financial need.

(d) The sub-normal child is especially apt to leave early. A fourteen-year-old boy in a class of ten-year-olds feels embarrassed and wants to be with those of his own age. Work will allow him to do this, while our modern school does not.   Quite naturally he chooses work.

(e) Parents too are often responsible.   Many who could afford to keep their children in school, take them out to get the benefit of their earnings.   Many parents regard their children as their property and consider it obvious that they should either get the child's wages or have him help at home.[3]

[1] Ogburn, *op. cit.*, p. 107.

[2] *Tentative Cost and Quantity Basis Necessary to Support Family of Five in Washington, D. C. in August, 1919*, published by U. S. Bureau of Labor Statistics.

[3] *Report on Conditions of Women and Child Wage-Earners*, vol. vii, pp. 50-57.

3. *No guidance given to children.* Little or no attention
is paid by parent, child or school, to the work the child
should take up.[1] "It was found that in a large number of
cases neither the children nor the parents had any definite
ambition. To both it seemed the natural thing for the child
to go to work as soon as the law allowed, and as for what
would come after that, time would show."[2]

4. *Children predominantly enter unskilled and routine
positions.* The jobs that these young people under 16 get are
almost all unskilled. They are openings that offer little or no
possibility for future advance. The children of that age
rarely desire to learn a trade, and seldom have the patience
to stick to it. Their carelessness makes the manufacturer
and craftsmen refuse to train them. There are, however,
numerous unskilled jobs where adult labor is too expensive
but where it is profitable to employ children. The Massachusetts Commission on Industrial and Technical Education reported that "the fourteen year old child enters unskilled industry and remains there."[3] This commission examined the
records of 8057 children in industry between the age of 14
and 16. It classified them on the basis of skill required in
their particular trade as follows:

Character of Industry	Number	Per cent
Completely unskilled	3509	43.6
Low grade skilled (giving practically no training)	3648	45.3
Skilled	900	11.1
Total	8057	100.0

Thus only 11% or one-ninth were in industries where
they were receiving training.[4]

[1] The movement for vocational guidance to remedy this situation will
be discussed in a later chapter.

[2] *Report on Women and Child Wage-Earners*, vol. vii, p. 188.

[3] *Report of Massachusetts Commission on Industrial and Technical
Education*, 1906, p. 57.

[4] *Ibid.*, pp. 31-34, note: The classification of industries as unskilled,

Miss Barrows, after a study of 406 jobs held by 14-16 year old New York children found that in 314 or 71.3% of the cases, absolutely no training was given; that in 41 or 10% of the cases there was a slight chance of " picking up " training; that in 30 jobs, or 7.4%, one process was taught, while in only 21, or 5.2%, was any real supervision or direction given by the employer.   A Chicago investigation found that, of 560 boys and girls between 14 and 17 at work, only 35, or less than 7%, were in skilled occupations where they received any training.[1]

In Hartford, Connecticut, only 5% of the boys and girls at work under 16 were in skilled employments.[2]   As the Hartford report says " The skilled trades are almost entirely closed to a child of that age (14-16 years).   The majority of these children are taking up unskilled odd jobs in factories and stores.   In the metal factories, which as a group employ more children than any other type of factory in the city, the younger workers do errand and truck work, stock-boxing, odd jobs about the office, inspecting, assorting, as-

low grade skilled, or skilled was based on the following principles: (1) Work which consisted in a repetition of a single or a few simple operations which one easily and quickly learned and in which one particular operation was not coördinated with other operations was rated as unskilled. (2) A low grade skilled industry was said to be one where a good workman need not know all the operations and where the process did not require much skill or time to master. (3) A skilled occupation was listed as one that required some degree of training before it might be said to be mastered. (4) An unskilled occupation would be learned in a few hours or in a day or two. A low grade skilled occupation requires a few days, a highly skilled job a few months.

Any such classification is of course not wholly capable of being applied as a test with surety to every job. There are always cases in the " twilight zone " that baffle classification. This system is as workable however as any that has been devised.

[1] E. L. Talbert, *Opportunities in School and Industry for Children of the Stockyards District,* 1912, pp. 23-24.

[2] *Vocational Guidance in Hartford, Connecticut,* Report of General Committee, 1914, p. 5.

sembling, light grinding, polishing, feed automatic machines, drilling, testing chains, foot-press work, wiring, unwiring, transferring, cutting out transfers and cleaning type in typewriter factories." [1]

A St. Louis investigation [2] using the three-fold classification of the Massachusetts Commission, found that of 4,335 children, 3842 or approximately 88% entered unskilled occupations; such as bell and hall-boy service, cash, messenger, errand, delivery and wagon service. The most comprehensive survey of this question, undertaken in Philadelphia, examined the industrial records of 13,740 children, and found that only 422 or 3% were in skilled trades. [3] That this condition is even more strikingly true of girls is shown by Miss Anna Davis of Chicago, [4] and by a federal investigation in Worcester, Mass. [5]

It should be borne in mind, however, that all these studies, save that of the Massachusetts Commission, deal with city children exclusively. Conditions in the country communities have not as yet been analysed. Those localities numbering less than 8000 people, contain approximately 58% of the children from 14 to 16. [6] Whether the percent-

[1] *Ibid.*, pp. 4-5.

[2] E. E. Lewis, " Studies in Vocational Education," *School and Home Education*, March, 1913, p. 249.

[3] J. S. Hiatt, *The Child, The School, and The Job*, p. 5. It is probable that the number actually receiving training was greater than Mr. Hiatt indicates. In his study all children employed in factories were rated as unskilled. The great majority certainly are, but not all. This would increase the percentage of those given trade education.

[4] Anne Davis, *Finding Employment for Children who Leave the Grade Schools to go to Work*, pp. 19-41.

[5] Of over 700 girls who left school in Worcester, Massachusetts, during the years 1909-10 only 1% entered the skilled trades. *Bulletin U. S. Bureau of Education*, 1913, No. 17, "A Trade School for Girls, pp. 58-59.

[6] I have computed this percentage from the raw data given in the *Hand Book f Federal Statistics of Children* (issued by the Children's Bureau), pt. i, pp. 9-43.

age in skilled trades would here be as low as in the urban localities is doubtful. There are fewer street trades, and proportionately more small-scale skilled handicrafts. Even so, however, it seems undeniable that the vast majority of children are in unskilled trades.[1] In Michigan, a somewhat typical state in its distribution of rural and urban population, it was found in 1910 that few children entered the skilled trades.[2]

5. *Wages of Children are low.* Since child labor is unskilled, and since children have, practically speaking, no independent standard of living, and little or no bargaining power, their wages are low. The 1900 census and the 1905 census of manufactures give only the average wage for children under 16, while the 1910 census fails to make any separate classification of children's earnings whatever. The relative insignificance of the average annual earnings of children under 16 in manufacturing establishments is shown by the following table.

This shows that the wages of children at this period averaged only from $3.00 to $3.50 a week and were on the average only one-third that of men.

[1] The smallest percentage of 14-16 year old children in unskilled industries that has been disclosed by any investigation is 68% as found in a study of 41 children in Springfield, Illinois. (See Odencrantz and Potter, *Industrial Conditions in Springfield, Illinois*, p. 127. Even these figures indicate an unhealthy condition while the overwhelming mass of evidence indicates that they are an understatement of the true situation. A survey of Hammond, Indiana, a town of 20,000 inhabitants, shows that of 94 boys to whom working permits were issued in 1913-14 only 6 could be said to be in position requiring skill, and that of 65 girls, only three were so placed. R. S. Leonard, *Some Facts Concerning the People, Industries, and Schools of Hammond*, pp. 37-42.

[2] *Report of Michigan Commission on Industrial and Agricultural Education*, 1910, p. 15.

AVERAGE ANNUAL EARNINGS OF WOMEN AND CHILDREN IN MANUFACTUR-
ING IN 1900 AND 1905 IN RELATION TO THOSE OF MEN [1]

Class	1900		1905	
	Ave. Annual Earnings	Relative Wage	Ave. Annual Earnings	Relative Wage
Males over 16	$477	100	$534	100
Females over 16.....	271	57	298	56
Children under 16..	152	32	176	33

The Investigation into the Condition of Woman and Child Wage-Earners in 1909 showed that in the cotton industry 29.8% of the boys and 37.4% of the girls from 14 to 16 earned less than $4.00 per week; 56.8% of the boys and 58% of the girls received less than $5.00, while 76.4% of the boys and 76.1% of the girls received less than $6.00 weekly.[2] In the glass industry, 17% of the boys under 16 received less than $3.00 a week; 32.4% less than $4.00 a week; 58.6% less than $5.00; and 81.2% less than $6.00.[3] 38% of the girls in the same industry received less than $4.00 a week and 80% received less than $5.[4] 59% of the boys under 16 and 53% of the girls in the silk industry of New Jersey received less than $4.00 a week, while in Pennsylvania 86% of the boys and 87% of the girls fell in this class.[5] Finally 98% of the female workers under 16 in miscellaneous industries were found to be earning less than $6.00 a week.

6. *" Turnover " of juvenile labor exceedingly high.* Not only is the typical child's job unskilled and pitiably ill-

[1] Compiled from *Census Report on Manufactures*, 1905, p. lxxi.
[2] *U. S. Bureau of Labor Statistics*, Bulletin *175*, p. 62.
[3] *Ibid.*, p. 129.   [4] *Ibid.*, p. 151.
[5] *Ibid.*, p. 186.   [6] *Ibid.*, p. 407.

paid, but it is extremely short-lived. The importance of
" labor turnover " has only recently come to public notice
in the case of adult labor;[1] in the case of the child it is even
more significant.   In Rochester, New York, the Board of
Education found that the boys who leave school between 14
and 16 change their jobs every 17 weeks during their first
year at work, or over three times a year.[2]   In Richmond,
Virginia, there is apparently a much greater permanence, but
even there children occupied on the average 1.4 jobs during
their first year at work.[3]   An investigation of one thousand
tenement children in New York who entered industry at
fourteen, disclosed that one-third of them averaged during
this first working year six places apiece.[4]   Significant testimony comes from the employment records of Swift & Company of Chicago where the average term of employment for
boys in their service was only 3½ months.[5]   This is at the
rate of three boys a half a year per position or a labor turnover of 342%.   In Hartford, Conn., 57 children occupied
on the average two and a quarter jobs per year.[6]

So far as is known, Maryland is the only state which has
anything approaching complete data on this question.   By

[1] See Slichter, *The Turnover of Factory Labor*, also an article by the
author, " The Problem of Labor Turnover, *Am. Econ. Rev.*, June, 1918,
pp. 306-16.

[2] *56th Annual Report of the Board of Education*, Rochester, N. Y.,
1913, p. 142.   (A study of 696 boys.)

[3] *Report of Survey Committee of Richmond*, p. 22, also *Bull. 162*,
Bureau of Labor Statistics, p. 20.   It is interesting to notice that white
boys and negro boys change positions more frequently than white and
negro girls, respectively; but that the whites both male and female,
change much more frequently than the negroes.

[4] Jane Addams, *The Spirit of Youth and City Streets*, pp. 115-6.

[5] *Bulletin of the National Association of Corporation Schools*, April,
1916, p. 13.

[6] *Vocational Guidance in Hartford, Conn.*, pp. 10-12.   These were
children who had benefited by the advice of a vocational counsellor.

a law of 1913, not only must the child receive a permit to enable him to go to work, but he must apply for a new permit for every new position entered.   This affords a means of following the working history of children under 16, the result is a clear picture of the transitory nature of their work.[1]

For the year 1913, 6,571 children took out their initial permit.   Since those who took out permits at some time during the year were counted, this figure does not represent 6,571 "working years."   It seems safe to estimate that the number of "working years" was approximately one-half this amount, or roughly 3300.   This is probably correct on the assumption that most of the permits were granted in June and July and for the rest distributed evenly throughout the year.   There were issued however during the year a total of 10,161 permits, or additional permits to the number of 3,590.   This means that on the average the number of permits issued later during the first year of employment was something over 100 percent. 1511 of these permits, or 15%, were issued for the third or more time. The following table shows the length of time that 4,132 children reported that they had been employed on their last job.[2]

Time	Number	Percentage
Less than 2 months	2,132	51.3%
More than 2 months	2,000	48.7%
Total	4,132	100.0%

Of these who worked less than 2 months at their position, 633 or 15.2% of the total, were employed for less than two weeks.

In the two years 1913-14, 228 children held as many as 1,686 jobs.[3]   Twenty-one had ten or more jobs during

[1] *Report of Maryland Bureau of Statistics and Information*, 1914, p. 49.
[2] *Ibid.*, p. 51.   [3] *Ibid.*, p. 93.

this time.   Of these, two had been employed at 15 different positions, two at sixteen, two at seventeen, and one at eighteen.[1]

Indianapolis, Indiana, also requires the granting of a new permit upon changing a job or leaving work. The following statistics for the period April 15, 1915 to July 31, 1916 show a high juvenile ternover.[2]

LENGTH OF TIME CHILDREN WERE EMPLOYED, PER JOB IN INDIANAPOLIS, INDIANA: DURATION OF TERMINATED PERMITS

Less than	Cumulative Number	Cumulative Per cent
15 days	467	7.0
1 month.	1034	15.8
2 months	2043	30.3
3 months	3234	48.0
6 months	4746	70.7
9 months	5582	81.7
1 year	5982	87.7
Over one year	728	12.3
Total	6710	100.0

Thus 7% of these positions were held for less than 2 weeks, 15% for less than a month, 30% for less than 2 months, 48%, or practically one half, for less than three months.

In Evansville, Indiana, 212 children from 14-16 worked a total of 1269 months during the year May 1, 1915 and

[1] *Ibid.*, p. 97.

[2] Adapted from figures given in *Bulletin 21*, Indiana State Board of Education, "Indianapolis Vocational Survey," vol. i, p. 119. These figures are something of an overstatement. (1) They include only those permits which had been terminated and were not then in force which numbered 2690, (2) They include vacation permits as well as permits for work during school year. The former have, necessarily, only a brief duration. These, however, were not many. Despite these inadequacies the net result still shows a vast amount of shifting from position to position.

May 1, 1916, and held during this time 379 jobs. This is an average length of 3.4 months per job or over 3½ jobs a year.[1] Dr. R. M. Woodbury's exhaustive study of the working history of 7000 Connecticut children from 14 to 16, showed that for the boys "a position was terminated, on the average, every 9.6 months of actual work while for the girls a position was terminated, on the average for every 13.3 months of work."[2] The labor turnover for boys (on the separations basis) would be approximately 125 percent, and for girls 90%. The boys therefore, show a distinctly greater tendency towards instability than the girls.

The children, if we may believe that Maryland Report to be typical, seem to leave chiefly upon their own initative, and not because they are "fired." In 75 percent of the cases reported by the employers to the Maryland Board, the employers stated that the children left voluntarily.[3]

A detailed examination of the reasons given by the children as to why they left voluntarily is given below.[4]

[1] *Educational Bulletin 19*, Indiana State Board of Education. *Report of Evansville, Indiana Survey for Vocational Education*, pp. 417-430. An allowance must be made in these figures covering the number of jobs held, not terminated. Hence, some who were at their first job would not leave for sometime and therefore cannot be accurately classed as having "held one job."

[2] R. M. Woodbury, *Industrial Instability of Child Workers*, Publications Children's Bureau, No. 74, U. S. Department of Labor, p. 25.

[3] Compiled from data given on page 55 of this report.

[4] (Table compiled from p. 60 of the Maryland Report.) Thus less than 1% of the children left because they wanted to learn a trade and only 1.6% left to go back to school. Mrs. Helen T. Wooley's investigation of 700 working children in Cincinnati, disclosed that 40% left their jobs because of economic reasons, i. e., low pay, unemployment, etc.; 20% because of dissatisfaction with the work itself; 11% due to physical inability to continue at the work; 11% to failure of child to get along with fellow-workmen or to incompetence; 9% to home difficulties; and 8% because of conflict with the child labor law. See Mrs. Wooley's "Charting Childhood in Cincinnati," p. 5. (Reprint from *Survey*, Aug. 9, 1913.)

(a)	Dissatisfaction with the position	Number	Position
1.	Did not like the position	667	24.9
2.	Excessive physical demands	633	23.3
3.	Insufficient wages	599	21.9
4.	Long Hours	132	4.8
5.	Required to do other work than specified	68	2.4
6.	Too far from home	127	4.7
7.	No opportunity to learn a trade at work	15	4
	Total	2278	83.5
(b) 1.	Personal reasons	136	4.9
2.	Temporarily employed in the country	92	3.4
3.	Needed at home	45	1.6
4.	Returned to school	45	1.6
5.	Miscellaneous	180	6.6
	Total	453	16.5
	Grand total	2731	100.0

7. Much time lost between jobs. The children do not find new work immediately. There is an intermediate period of considerable length between the old and the new job. The following data from Maryland illustrates this point.[1]

This table deserves careful analysis. While 58.6% of the children lost less than two weeks' time, 14.8% lost between 2 weeks and a month, and 26.7% over a month, while 7.2% spent over four months between positions in idleness. A rough average of the time lost between positions amounts to approximately one month per child.

The Chicago City Club found that over one-half of the 23,000 children between 14 and 16 who were not in school in Chicago in 1909, were unemployed[2] If this was typical of conditions, it is fair to conclude that in Chicago, children

[1] Compiled from data given on page 54 of the 1914 Report of Maryland Bureau of Statistics and Information.

[2] *A Report on Vocational Training in Chicago* by a Committee of the City Club, p. 34.

TIME IDLE BETWEEN POSITIONS

Time lost	Number	Percentage
Less than 1 week	976	25.3
1 week to 2 weeks	1289	33.3
2 weeks to 1 month	575	14.8
1–2 months	419	10.8
2–3 "	224	5.9
3–4 "	105	2.7
4–5 "	68	1.8
5–6 "	65	1.7
6–7 "	28	.7
7–8 "	29	.8
8–9 "	30	.8
9–10 "	21	.5
10–11 "	9	.2
11–12 "	12	.3
Over 12 months	16	.4
Total	3866	100.0

between 14 and 16 years work but half the time, and spend one of the two years in idleness. Dr. Woodbury's investigation of the 7000 Connecticut children showed that " 10.2 percent of the total work histories of these children was spent in unemployment." [1]

Many believe that such changing from job to job is good for a child, and that by trying various trades he acquires experience; that by learning what he cannot do, he finds what he can do, and that the hard school of experience teaches him resourcefulness. Such people approve Emerson's laudation of the lad " who teams it, farms it, peddles, keeps a school, preaches, edits a newspaper, goes to Congress, buys a township, and always, like a cat, falls on his feet." When they speak of the advantages of changing positions, they are really thinking, however, of tasks under the open sky or beside the work-bench; of positions which develop man-

[1] Woodbury, *op. cit.*, p. 34.

liness-and resourcefulness, even if some of them are lacking in technical training.   Such work but rarely exists today for urban or even for village boys.

8. *Summary*.   Today the child works largely at jobs that are enervating rather than energising.[1]   Emerson himself would not have put much faith in the quality of self-reliance caused by carrying parcels, tending a cotton loom, stitching button holes, canning oysters, rolling cigarettes, and opening doors. A change of jobs is rarely a change upward, merely a change to another unskilled and routine task.

This constant shifting causes a considerable economic loss to the employer.   It takes time and money to " break in " a boy even to unskilled work.   And where there are three or four sets a year it becomes practically burdensome. This in turn makes the employer refuse to admit children of this age to the skilled trades, and fastens them more securely to " blind-alley trades " as the only industrial opening for them.   These changes, moreover, breed irresponsibility in the child himself.   His thought is, " If I don't like it, I'll get another job.".   This prevents him from looking into the prospects of a position before he takes it, since he feels that he can always leave.   He consequently tends to substitute hindsight for foresight in choosing a position.   Similarly discontent, rather than sober choice, causes him to choose new jobs.

[1] This distinction between juvenile position was first made by Dean Hermann Schneider. See his *Education for Industrial Workers*, pp. 5-17. The elements of energizing work are (a) out of doors or in well-ventilated work-rooms, (b) provides a well-rounded physical development, (c) requires continuous mental development, (d) mental alertness required for emergencies, (e) comprehensive grasp of the interdependence of occupations within an industry, (f) conditions of work never exactly the same, (g) work that breeds readiness for self-sacrifice. The elements of enervating work are (a) vitiated air, (b) standing in a strained position, (c) monotonous repetition of simple tasks, (d) hours of work so long that fatigue poisons accumulate.

The period of idleness between positions, which has been
shown to be so large, is another evil factor in the child's industrial life. He is neither at work nor in school; he
is industrially adrift. Unemployment for adults is bad
enough; for children it is positively vicious. It breaks
down habits of industry which are slowly forming, and
exposes them to all sorts of positive dangers. Loafing
about "waiting for something to turn-up" does not make
strong men and women. For the city child, such idleness
is especially dangerous.[1] The "gang spirit" seizes the
unemployed boy, and he seeks satisfaction in his group,
generally to anti-social ends.

Now it was the function of apprenticeship to protect
this adolescent child. It gave him moral oversight and a
steadiness of employment. It was a recognition by the
state of guardianship over the child. Today with the
breakdown of apprenticeship we allow the child to shift
for himself. We allow him to drift into employments that
are socially and individually harmful. We wash our hands
of responsibility, and in consequence both the child and the
nation suffer.

[1] Children in street trades in which the employment is irregular and
intermittent are particularly injured by this. A study of juvenile
delinquency of boys by the federal investigation into the conditions of
woman and child-wage earners, shows the following occupational
distribution:

Trade	Per cent
Newsboys	21.83
Errand boys	17.80
Drivers and helpers wagons	7.30
Messengers (telegraph, etc.)	2.39
Bootblacks	1.77
Peddlers	1.71
Total	53.00%

These trades therefore furnish one-half the cases of juvenile delinquency, they certainly do not contain 50% of the boy workers. See
Report on Conditions of Women and Child Wage-earners, Senate Doc.
645, 61st Congress, 2nd Session, vol. viii, p. 69.

CHAPTER V

WHAT EDUCATION IS NEEDED FOR MODERN INDUSTRY

As we have seen, the division of labor was the real destroyer of apprenticeship. Industry developed so many subdivisions that all-round training was both expensive and useless. This same obstacle confronts any scheme for industrial education today. Many loose-thinking advocates of vocational education have ignored this fact and have assumed that there is a limitless demand for skilled workers. Such is not the case. Modern industry does not require a large percentage of all-round skilled workmen. The vast majority of jobs can be learned in the space of a few days or at the most, in a few weeks.

The division of labor wthin an industry is not a consequence of machinery alone. Specialization existed in the days of handwork. One is apt to forget that Adam Smith illustrated the division of labor, with his famous example of pin-making, before the machine era had opened.[1] The report of the United States Bureau of Labor[2] on hand and machine labor shows very clearly that considerable specialization existed even in the days of the handicraft and the domestic systems. The eighteenth-century watchmaker did not make every part of the time-piece himself. Other helpers and fellowcraftsmen worked on particular parts which were later combined.

Machinery has, however, increased and extended the division of labor. The possibility of reviving apprenticeship or of devising an adequate substitute for it, depends

[1] Adam Smith, *Wealth of Nations* (Cannan Edition), vol. i, pp. 6-7.
[2] *13th Annual Report*, U. S. Bureau of Labor, 1899, 2 vols.

therefore upon a number of factors. First, how great a degree of specialization exists today in the various industries? Second, has this specialization, by limiting the number of diverse operations performed by one workman, increased the difficulty of the work required for a particular task? Phrased more briefly, has specialization increased or decreased the amount of skill required?[1] What kind of training is needed to fit men for modern industrial life?

It is exceedingly difficult to generalize on this point. Specialization varies not only from industry to industry, but also from plant to plant and from locality to locality. The larger the plant, of course, the greater is the division of labor. The Ford automobile works in Detroit is an example of a highly specialized plant, with such an extreme division of labor that little or no skill is required of its workers. Another plant in the same city. however, employs skilled workmen almost entirely who understand all branches of automobile manufacture. Country plants are generally smaller than urban; consequently they do not have as great a division of labor.[2] Where wages are low and labor cheap, there is little inducement for the introduction of machinery and increased specialization. Due to this fact, cigarette, and cigar-making is far less specialized in the south than in the north.

Any sweeping statement about industries would therefore be inadequate, and in many respects false. It is difficult if not impossible to establish a modal type for each industry. The general trend of specialization and skill is, however, shown by the following table.

For the purpose of convenience, we have classified the in-

[1] It is obvious that this question is different from that which is commonly put; "has the division of labor decreased the amount of skill *exercised.*" We are here concerned with possibilities, not merely with what are the present conditions.

[2] *Report of the Industrial Commission,* 1901, vol. vii, p. 265.

dustries into three groups: (1) machine-building, (2) machine using, and (3) machine repairing.

I. Machine-Building Industries

Industry	Number of different processes
1. Plow manufacture [1]	52
2. Car building [2]	13
3. Machinist	27
4. Automobile	250 (Ford)
5. Gas engine [3]	50

In modern industry, machines produce other machines, Steel gives birth to steel.[4] The system of interchangeable parts necessitates standardized construction and absolute accuracy, and this in itself prevents machinery from being hand-manufactured. Large-scale production, moreover, prevails in the industry, and this in turn leads to the utilization of the advantages afforded by machine construction.

In consequence there is a sharp differentiation in the skill required of the working force. A large number of highly-trained and competent engineers are needed in the drafting room. For the other workmen, however, muscle and endurance rather than skill and dexterity are required.[5]

[1] *13th Annual Report*, United States Bureau of Labor, 1899, vol. i, p. 96.

[2] *Bulletin No. 163*, Bureau of Labor Statistics, 1914, p. 6.

[3] *Educational Bulletin 19*, of Indiana State Board of Education, "Evansville Vocational Survey," pp. 265-66. "Comparatively few all-round machinists are employed," *ibid.*, p. 264.

[4] The evolution of American machine-making is well described in J. W. Roe's *English and American Tool Builders*, where a series of biographical sketches of important tool builders and their contributions is given.

It is especially significant that the system of scientific management with its differentiation of the task, has chiefly flourished in industries which build machines. In 15 of these industries scientific management had been introduced by 1915. See *Report of Committee American Society of Mechanical Engineers*, 1912; H. B. Drury, *Scientific Management*, 1915, p. 146. C. Bertrand Thompson, "Scientific Management in Practice," *Quarterly Journal of Economics* (Feb., 1915), vol. xxix, pp. 256-66.

II. Machine-Using Industries

Industry	Number of different processes
A. Clothing and Textile Industries.	
1. Hosiery [1]	47
2. Underwear [1]	37
3. White-goods [2]	23
4. Dress and Waist [4]	24
5.	22
6.	28
7. (coats)	39
8.	52
9. [9]	90
:	98
B.	
. ...	34
2. Plaining Mill.	
a. Doors [13]	21
b. Sashes [13]	22
3. Furniture. [14]	
a. Bed-steads	52
b. Chairs	26
c. Lounges	34
d. Side Boards	22
e. Tables	20
C. Food.	
....	42
[16]	23
....	17
D.	
1. Pins [18]	12
2. Bolts [19]	13
3.	22
4. [21]	25
5. Cutlery	25
6. Needles [22]	30
7. Pottery [24]	44
8. Hardware [25]	133
9. Blast Furnaces [26]	123
E. Miscellaneous.	
1. Cigarette [17]	12
2. [28]	17
3.	120
4.	43–62
5.	80
6. [31]	90

[1] *13th Annual Report Bureau of Labor*, vol. i, p. 53.

[2] *Report on Condition of Women and Child Wage-Earners*, vol. xviii, pp. 200-201.

Specialization in these trades is therefore minute.   When

[3] *Bulletin No. 159*, U. S. Bureau of Labor Statistics, pp. 88-91.

[4] *Bulletin No. 145*, U. S. Bureau of Labor Statistics, p. 158.

[5] *13th Annual Report Bureau of Labor*, 1899, vol. i, p. 50. From investigation at Troy, N. Y.

[7] Pope, *The Clothing Industry in New York*, pp. 70-71. The number of sub-divisions within this industry varies greatly from shop to shop and has since greatly increased. In one case a coat was worked upon by 62 different persons. See *Bulletin No. 135*, U. S. Bureau of Labor Statistics, p. 31.

[8] Report on *Condition of Women and Child Wage-Earners*, vol. xviii, pp. 150-151.

[9] *13th Annual Report*, Bureau of Labor, vol. i, pp. 220.

[10] *Ibid.*, vol. ii, pp. 572-576.

[11] *Bull. No. 153*, "Wages and Hours in Lumber Manufacturing, Mill Work, and Furniture Manufacturing," Bureau of Labor Statistics, pp. 24-31.

[12] *13th Annual Report Bureau of Labor*, vol. ii, pp. 1364-65.

[13] *Ibid.*, vol. ii, pp. 1385-86.

[14] *Ibid.*, vol. i, pp. 49-50.

[15] J. R. Commons, *Trade Unionism and Labor Problems*, p. 226.

[16] *13th Annual Report*, U. S. Bureau of Labor, vol. ii, pp. 1064-65.

[17] *Report on Conditions of Women and Child Wage-Earners*, vol. xviii, pp. 167-172.

[18] *Ibid.*, vol. xviii, pp. 222-224. In the pin-making industry the effect of machinery has been to reduce the number of operation. The number of different workmen has been reduced and specialization consequently lessened. Most of the 12 operations cited are concerned with the marketing rather than with the manufacturing of pins.

[19] *13th Annual Report*, Bureau of Labor, vol. ii, p. 1214.

[20] *Ibid.*, vol. ii, pp. 1229-1231.

[21] *Bulletin No. 162*, U. S. Bureau of Labor Statistics, 1914, "Vocational Education Survey of Richmond, Va.," pp. 106-140.

[22] *13th Annual Report*, U. S. Bureau of Labor, vol. ii, pp. 981-83.

[23] *Report on Conditions of Women and Child Wage-Earners*, vol. xviii, pp. 224-225.

[24] Bureau of Foreign and Domestic Commerce, *Report on the Pottery Industry* (Dept. of Commerce, Miscell. Series 21), p. 385.

it has been carried to great length, skill is not a requisite. Steel mills[1] and shoe factories, where the division of labor has been widely extended, employ few trained operatives. The silk, cotton, and worsted industries have also reduced the quality of labor needed to run their machines to simple automatic operations.[2] Collars are manufactured by automatic processes for which unskilled labor suffices; while the clothing trades are manned by employees who, with the exception of the cutters, are specialized and unskilled.[3] Hosiery, underwear and corset factories are also characterized by a predominance of routine work requiring little or no technical

[25] *Report on Conditions of Women and Child Wage-Earners*, vol. xviii, p. 183.

[26] *Report on Conditions of Labor in Iron and Steel Industry*, Senate Doc. 110, 62nd Congress, 1st Session, vol. i, pp. 19-23.

[27] *Report on Conditions of Women and Child Wage-Earners*, vol. xviii, pp. 79-55.

[28] *Ibid.*, pp. 89-102.

[29] *Bulletin No. 19*, Indiana State Board of Education, "Evansville Vocational Survey," pp. 396-99.

[30] *Bulletin No. 124*, U. S. Bureau of Labor Statistics, "Conciliation and Arbitration in the Building Trades of Greater N. Y.", pp. 27-28.

[31] *Shipyard Occupations*, published by Emergency Fleet Corporation, 1918.

[1] *Report on Conditions of Labor in the Iron and Steel Industry*, Senate Doc. 110, 62nd Congress, 1st Session, vol. i, p. xvii. "Great as is the proportion of unskilled labor in the iron and steel industry, the tendency of recent years has been constantly toward the reduction of the number of highly skilled men employed and the establishment of the general wage upon the basis of common, unskilled labor. Each year sees a larger use of mechanical appliances which unskilled labor is usually competent to control."

[2] For a keen and thorough analysis of the process of manufacture of these goods see F. W. Taussig, *Some Aspects of the Tariff Question*, see pp. 229-233, 272-276, 456.

[3] For description of sub-divisions see, *Bulletin 135*, U. S. Bureau of Labor Statistics, pp. 31-36.

skill.[1] Wood-working plants have similarly witnessed the rapid extension of the machine process: whereas formerly furniture factories employed all-round cabinet makers, to-day such an artisan is the exception rather than the rule. In practically all operations, untrained workers are said to be as competent as trained.[2] The manufacture of food articles has also undergone specialization.   Meat-packing is of course a notorious example, while the milling industry is conducted by automatic machinery, and all employees save the grinders and bolters are absolutely unskilled.[3]   The baking trades are tending to become more and more concentrated in larger plants with a consequent greater division of labor.   Thus 92% of the employees in cracker factories are unskilled.[4] Canning and preserving, is also a variety of work that demands little training.

Similar conditions of specialization prevail in the manufacture of hardware.[5]   Pin and needle manufacturing plants likewise require little skill from their employees. An exception to the general tendency must be noticed in the case of the pottery industry, for although this industry is sub-divided into 44 occupations, only 38% of its workers are said to be unskilled.[6]   The tobacco trades have become

---

[1] *Report on Conditions of Women and Child Wage-Earners*, vol. xviii, p. 197. An exception to this rule must be noted in the case of the so-called "Full-fashioned" knitting machines which demand highly skilled operations.

[2] *Bulletin No. 129*, U. S. Bureau of Statistics, "Wages and Hours in the Lumber, Mill-work, and Furniture Industries, 1890-1912, p. 135.

[3] National Society Promotion Industrial Education, *Bulletin 21, Report of the Minneapolis Survey for Vocational Education*, pp. 321-23.

[4] *Report on Conditions of Women and Child Wage-Earners*, vol. xviii, p. 165.

[5] *Ibid.*, p. 182.

[6] Bureau of Foreign and Domestic Commerce, *Report on the Pottery Industry* (Dept. of Commerce, Miscellaneous Series, no. 21, p. 242).

more routinized with every passing year. Skill has largely ceased to be necessary, and a monotonous repetition of simple movements characterizes nearly every stage.[1] The building trades have lost much of their former skill because of the invasion of their field by mill work. Sashes, blinds, doors, mantles, stair material and the like are now made, not by hand but by machinery in factories. In consequence a carpenter does not need to be as adept as formerly. Moreover in large construction the tendency is to sub-divide the task and confine the work of the skilled men to specific operations, while utilizing lower-grade labor for the remaining.[2]

The wartime experience of the Emergency Fleet Corporation in training workmen for the shipyard trades furnishes interesting proof of how little time is required to master the main principles of a modern trade. Training courses were established in seventy-one yards under the direction of the Fleet Corporation. The men who were thus taught trades were drawn principally from unskilled work and from manufacturing. When the learners left their training course they were able in the main to hold their own with experienced journeymen, while in certain cases they even excelled the journeymen in the latter part of their training period. Yet the average training period for all men in the seventy-one yards for which statistics were available, was only nineteen days! A detailed summary by trades is given below:

[1] *Bulletin No. 162*, U. S. Bureau of Labor Statistics, Vocational Education Survey of Richmond, Va., pp. 278-279. Also *Bulletin No. 19*, of Indiana State Board of Education, "Evansville Vocational Survey." pp. 205-211.

[2] F. B. Gilbreth's accomplishments in bricklaying where he attained a large output by training low-skilled men to perform most of the preliminary motions by which skilled bricklayers were enabled to devote themselves exclusively to the laying itself, is but a logical conclusion to a tendency that has been steadily developing.

LENGTH OF TRAINING PERIOD FOR TWENTY TRADES IN TWENTY-ONE YARDS, COVERING 9,700 MEN [1]

Trade	Average Days for Each Trade	Trade	Average Days for Each Trade
Riveters	28	Machinists	39
Holders-on	14	Pipe fitters	39
Heaters	10	Regulators	12
Ship fitters	51	Gas welders	30
Chippers	28	Electric welders	28
Drillers	13	Burners	23
Reamers	12	Punchmen	21
Bolters	10	Ship carpenters	48.
Linermen	8	Hand caulkers	34
Erectors	20	Tank testers	33

3. Machine Repairing

It is here that skill is required. To repair one part of a machine requires a knowledge of the whole mechanism. Modern industry has made repair work a trade in itself. The man who runs the machine does not know how to put it into working order. This is left to a separate force. These men must be thoroughly competent, for a variety of problems face them every day. They must have more all-round skill than the old craftsman ever dreamed of.

In both cotton and woolen mills, the loom fixer is the most skilled worker in the plant.[2] In saw mills it is the filer or repair man who is the most important employee.[3] The United Shoe Machinery Company repairs the machines

[1] Table taken from P. H. Douglas and F. E. Wolfe, "Labor Administration in the Shipbuilding Industry During the War," "II" *Journal Political Economy*, May, 1919, p. 379 (vol. xxvii.)

[2] The loom-fixer on the average has supervision over 85 automatic looms. *Bulletin U. S. Bureau of Labor Statistics No. 143*, pp. 19-24.

[3] *Ibid., Bulletin No. 153*, "Wages and Hours of Labor in the Lumber, Mill-Work, and Furniture Industries," p. 30.

which it has leased to shoe factories, and maintains a staff of highly skilled mechanics for this service. This has the dual effect of tightening the monopoly of the company and lessening the amount of skill required in the factory force. The telephone industry requires a large corps of skilled electricians who can make rapid yet accurate repairs. Railroad repair shops must have experts able to detect the trouble with damaged engines and possessed with the skill to repair them.[1]

The predominance of skill in the repair end of industry is shown by the fact that in the corporation schools over four-fifths of the students are in the machinists trade and are being trained to understand repair work. The following figures were collected in 1914 and cover the returns from over 50 plants.[2]

	Number of Students	*Percentage*
Machinists Trade	4202	80.8
All others	997	19.2
Total	5199	100.0

These figures are especially significant since they are from corporation schools. Modern business concerns will train

[1] The repair of passenger and freight cars does not require as much skill but there is specialization even in repairing cars; a government investigation showed that this branch of work had 13 sub-divisions. See *Bulletin No. 163*, U. S. Bureau of Labor Statistics, "Wages and Hours of Labor in the Building and Repairing of Steam Railroad Cars," p. 6.

[2] This table was compiled from raw material contained in a report by the sub-committee on manufacturing and transportation, and published in the *Proceedings of the Second Annual Con. of the Nat. Assn. Corporation Schools*, pp. 408-415.

employees only for those tasks for which they are needed. The great predominance of men equipped for repair work is therefore strong proof of the fact that it is chiefly in repair work that skill is needed. The skill which was formerly spread out thin over the whole mass of workers has been concentrated in these men. They are distinctly the aristocracy of the labor-force. And in order to equip them for their work, they need a thorough technical and practical training.

Since repair work claims but a small proportion of the laboring force in industry, we should therefore expect the percentage of skilled operatives to be relatively low.

An investigation by the Chicago City Club of 189 plants in twenty industries disclosed the following distribution of skill:[1]

	Number	*Percentage*
Unskilled employees.....	27,750	31.1
Low-grade skilled employees.........	36,773	41.2
High-grade skilled employees	24,810	27.7
Total	89,333	100.0

The low-grade skilled employees were those who could pick up their work in a few days. Over two-thirds of the workers could, therefore, be regarded as practically unskilled.

After all allowance is made, it seems clear that skilled workmen are distinctly in the minority. The amount of

[1] *A Report on Vocational Training in Chicago* by a Committee of the City Club of Chicago, p. 45. The employees were grouped in the various classes according to the classification of the Douglas Commission on Vocational Education.

skill which the average worker must posses is still further decreased by the system of scientific management. The various constituent parts of the system,[1] motion study, the standardization of tools and equipment, the setting of the standard task, routing, and functional foremanship, all divest the individual operative of much of the skill and judgment formerly required, and concentrate it in the office and supervisory force. Under the ordinary system of shop management the workman must take care of the machine, make adjustments, care for the belting and to some degree determine the rate of speed with which the work is to be done. This is completely altered by functional foremanship. These sub-jobs are now handled by specialists. One specialist attends to the belting, another to the hand tools which the operator may need, one will superintend the speed at which the machine is driven, while still another will make the minor repairs. The system of routing and scheduling together with the use of instruction cards prescribes the manner in which the work is to be done, and standardizes the task. The work of the machine hand is thereby reduced to more automatic processes, and the necessity for appreciable skill is taken from the individual workman.

Time and motion study, moreover, tend to reduce each job to its simplest elements. This in turn gives an opportunity for the introduction of still more machinery which will take over much of the routinized hand work. Professor Hoxie corroborates this when he says:[2] " the preponderancy of time-study is to split up the work into smaller and simpler operations and tasks." Professor Hoxie's conclusion that, " Scientific management furthers

---

[1] For description of each of these methods see F. W. Taylor, *Shop Management* and H. B. Drury, *Scientific Management*, pp. 69-86.

[2] R. F. Hoxie, *Scientific Management and Labor*, p. 125.

the modern tendency towards the specialization of the workers "[1] seems therefore to be justified.[2]

But if the labor of the rank and file has been rendered less skilled by scientific management, the skill required of the office and supervisory force has been enormously increased by it. The standardization of the task, together with the routing and the planning, make larger demands upon the planning room. What was formerly left to the initiative of the workman must now be cared for, in a scientific manner, by a central body.[3] In like manner the functional foreman must be capable of greater trade ability than that which the average worker formerly required.

In consequence of the added burdens under scientific management, the planning and supervising force must comprise a larger percentage of the working staff than under the old rule-of-thumb methods. The office force of the Tabor Manufacturing Company before the introduction of scientific management numbered only 4% of the total number employed, while afterwards the percentage had risen to 20.[4] One plant in which scientific management has been introduced actually has more men in the planning room and in supervisory positions than as common artisans. The effect of both the machine process and scientific manage-

[1] *Ibid.*, p. 123.

[2] F. W. Taylor, the father of the system, in his *Principles of Scientific Management* clearly indicates that such is the effect of the movement when he says, " The man in the planning room, whose specialty under scientific management is looking ahead, invariably finds the work can be done better and more economically by a subdivision of the labor; each act of each mechanic for example should be preceded by various preparatory acts done by other men," p. 38.

[3] F. W. Taylor, *op. cit.*, " Under the management of initiative practically the whole problem is up to the workman, while under scientific management fully one-half of the problem is up to the management," p. 38.

[4] H. B. Drury, *op. cit.*, p. 82.

ment upon the skill of the workman may be compared to the working of a cream separator in which milk is divided into two sections, one consisting of skim milk with no fats, the other of thick cream. The extension of machinery has had similar results. The skill which was formerly spread but thinly over the great mass of workers is concentrated. The large mass of machine builders and machine users are divested of it: they are the skin milk. A small minority, the repairmen and the designers and planners, possess a great deal more skill than ever before: they are the cream. Scientific management extends and amplifies this tendency. It squeezes out from the machine operation the little skill that is left and gives it to the planning and repairing force. This process was hastened by the dilution of labor during the war caused by the labor shortage. Particularly in England, was the division of labor carried to a hitherto unthought-of degree.[1]

Ruskin and William Morris battled against this tendency of machine industry. They tried to lead the way back to the days of handicraft, to restore to the craftsmen some of the wholeness which specialization prohibits. Their belief in the joyousness of the medieval craftsman was doubtless exaggerated. Work under hand-production was probably more laborious than now, and the mass of mechanics never sang so loudly or continuously as modern admirers of the middle ages such as Mr. G. K. Chesterton and Mr. Arthur J. Penty seem to believe. Much as we may honor the idealism which lies behind the Arts and Crafts movement, we must admit that it has not proved to be a business success. Some of the material produced by hand may be intrinsically superior to the machine production, but part of it undoubtedly derives its value from the very fact that it is costly.

[1] See Sidney Webb, *The Restoration of Trade Union Conditions.*

Its very cost, moreover, prohibits it from meeting the demand of the vast majority of people. A standardized product produced in large amount with low-unit cost is the one which gives the greatest utility to them, and such a standardized product must necessarily be machine-made.

Since then no substitute for the machine process seems to be available, advocates of industrial education should recognize that mechanical production does not require many skilled workers, and that consequently the old handicraft ideal of giving each workman all-round technical skill is impossible of fulfilment.

The leaders in the vocational education movement have hitherto been reluctant to face the facts of modern large-scale production with its specialization of labor. They have been trying to equip the boy with an education that he does not need and cannot utilize. The sooner they cease to think in terms of the handicraft era, the greater will be the chance of creating an educational system that is worth while.

However, one should beware of jumping to the opposite extreme and concluding that the modern worker needs no education. This would be an even greater error. The worker and more especially the juvenile worker, needs perhaps more education that he ever did before; but its nature is far different from that which the old apprentice boy required. The education which the worker needs to-day is at once broader and narrower; broader in that it should include more training in industrial life, in hygiene, civics and so forth; narrower in that trade training in the specific trade processes need not be so prolonged.

In the days of handicraft and in the early stages of manufacturing, specialization in a profession was impossible; to learn one branch, an apprentice must learn all. Once a man learned a trade, he must practise it for life. He had given a hostage to fortune in the form of a prolonged technical education. His industrial career was specialized and confined within the trade he had mastered; mobility of labor in the sense of being able to transfer from one industry to another, was absent.

The extension of machinery broke the trades up into many parts. Learning a trade was no longer a difficult affair. The mastery of a process in one industry gave the worker a basis for learning a similar process in another, should occasion arise. The artisan was no longer confined to one industry, but could work in several. The very process of machinery which made work more specialized, made the worker less specialized. He was now transferable. The working history of the typical artisan illustrates this. He moves from shoe factory to cotton mill, from cotton mill to machine shop, and so on. A machine-tender who has learned the general principle of caring for a machine can tend ribbon-weaving machinery as well as shoemaking. He is really an interchangeable part in the industrial mechanism.[1] The effects of this increase in mobility have been numerous: (a) it enabled an industry rapidly to meet an increased demand whereas it was formerly difficult for an industry to expand rapidly because of the lack of workmen; (b) it broke down the isolation hitherto existing between crafts, and promoted a treatment of the problems of labor as an organic whole.[2]

---

[1] Of all industries, this is probably least true of the printing, building and metal trades, yet in Richmond, Va. a city of stable working conditions where industrial change is minimized, 35% of the workers in these industries had practiced other trades. See *U. S. Bureau of Labor Statistics Bulletin No. 162*, p. 79. 179 of 507 workmen engaged in occupations had transferred from other work.

[2] It is in the ranks of this floating mass of labor which transfers from one industry to another that the theories of syndicalism have found their chief support.

Craft-unionism begins to give way before industrial union-ism and the demand for " one big union." (c) We are especially concerned with its influence upon the training re-quired of the worker. It obviates the necessity for general trade training, but if the worker is to move around from industry to industry he must be equipped for his transitions.[1]

In order to effect complete mobility of labor the factory worker must, however, have a general knowledge of machine methods and management. Though men move from in-dustry to industry, preference is always given to a man who has been in the same industry before. It takes a few days " to get the swing " of the new machine, and during this time the plant loses on the new employee. There is thus a bar-rier which prevents men from being completely inter-change-able. This serves to increase unemployment because one job is not immediately replaced by another. General instruction in the care of machinery, ability to re-gulate its speed, together with a working knowledge of mathematics and mechanics, would enable the machine-tender to shift from one industry to another with less effort and would shorten the intermediate period of unemployment.

Moreover, the workman must be taught more than one set of operations in order to protect him from mental monotony, and from physical malformation and fatigue.[2]

The workman, furthermore, needs thorough instruction in safety methods. Miss Eastman in her classic study of accidents in Pittsburgh found that in 132 of 410 fatalities studied, the workman was partially or wholly responsible.[3]

---

[1] A somewhat similar conclusion may be found in Paul de Rousiers, *The Labor Question in Britain*, pp. 288, *et seq.*

[2] See Josephine Goldmark, *Fatigue and Efficiency*, pp. 9-39, where the physiological nature of fatigue together with its causes is analyzed. The effect of monotony is ably studied in pp. 58-68.

[3] Crystal Eastman, *Work-accident and the Law*, pp. 86-87.

Most of these 132 deaths were due to ignorance. Nearly all were foreigners, unable to understand English or appreciate their danger, while in 22 cases the workman was " green," and unaccustomed to his job. Several had been at work only a few days while 13 more were only boys from 14-16.[1] An English investigation has declared that [2] " the unskilled worker is more liable to accident than the trained mechanic. The greater use made of unskilled labor during the introduction of automatic machinery in the brass trades was the cause of the increased accident risk, also an increase in risk in engineering, shipbuilding, smeltering, general building and joinery *is due to the decay of the apprenticeship system.*" [3]

If operatives were trained how to care for their machines, were drilled in safety regulations, and given instruction in accident prevention, the number of accidents would decrease. Such instruction should be part of every system of industrial education that is offered. The operation of workmen's compensation laws has forced many corporations to undertake educational work but this is largely confined to large firms and is voluntary. It should apply to small plants as well and be compulsory for all. To be thus effective, it must be a part of a general system of education supervised by the state.

Education in health protection is even more necessary. Competent investigators have estimated that " each of the 30,000,000 workers in the United States loses on the average about nine days every year on account of sickness alone." [4] If the loss of wages is reckoned at $4.00 per day

---

[1] Eastman, *op. cit.*, p. 88.

[2] Great Britain, *Report of the Departmental Committee on Accidents,* p. 19 quoted in G. M. Price, *The Modern Factory*, pp. 142-143.

[3] *Italics mine.*

[4] B. S. Warren and E. Sydenstricker, " Health Insurance," *Public*

and the expense for medical attention at $1.00, the total
loss would then total over $1,350,000,000 annually.   This
estimate given after an investigation covering approximately
1,000,000 workers does not seem to be an exaggeration.

Health insurance will do much towards the alleviation
and prevention of this gigantic amount of ill-health but
education must play its part.   Sanitation and hygiene should
be taught to all entering an industrial career but they should
be furnished an opportunity to live a real healthy, vigorous
life.   Individual care can do much to prevent illness and
instruction along this line should be part of the new apprenticeship that the workers in industry must serve.[1]

The reasons why the employer should want industrial
education for his employees are just as cogent.

In the first place, it pays him to have his factory tenders
understand the use of machinery.   The more trained they
are in the care of a machine, the less will the machines need
repairing.   This is a dual economy.   It diminishes the
number of repairmen and lessens the loss which results
when the capital goods of a plant lie idle.   General training of the workmen in machine principles would then be
productive from the standpoint of the employer.

Secondly, every plant must have many " general utility "
men.   Accidents and illness leave gaps in the factory force
that must be filled, while men are also discharged or leave.

Health Bull. No. 76, p. 6.   The German and English figures indicate an
average annual loss of about 8-9 days caused by sickness.   It is corroborated by recent investigations made in Rochester, N. Y. and in
Trenton, N. J. and is closely similar in its results to a federal investigation in 1901.   For further figures and enumeration of diseases see
American Labor Legislation Review, June, 1916, pp 155-162.

[1] A syllabus that might well serve as a model is that issued by the
Joint Board of Sanitary Control in the Cloak, Suit and the Dress and
Waist Industries of N. Y. City, entitled, *Workers Health Bulletin*,
22 pp., 1915.

New men cannot be found immediately to take the place of the old. In consequence every employer must have a reserve force of handy men who can fit into those jobs which are temporarily vacant.[1]   These employees must know several branches of the industry and be able to run many machines. To have them simply "pick up" the requisite knowledge would be an exceedingly risky affair.   They must be trained for their utility work.   They approximate the old-time apprentice more closely than any other class of factory operatives.

Finally, if health education and accident prevention are important to the workers, they are equally vital to the employer.   Fewer accidents will spell lower accident premiums, while a diminution of illness means an increased output per man.[2]

Moreover, society as a whole, as well as the employer and employee, needs to have the worker given further training. Good citizenship, with all that the word implies, is a necessity for all.   The division of labor has progressed so far that the worker on a specialized machine is likely to forget that he is a part of the complicated structure of industrial society. He needs to know the industrial process and to see the interrelation of industries and their co-operation towards the production of goods.   A history of manual labor, tools and of machinery would make the factory-hand more interested in his task.   Every worker moreover should be ac-

---

[1] The Goodyear Rubber Co. has a gang of 130 men (called the Flying Squadron) who are made expert in all the production processes of the shop. They are able to take any place and keep production moving smoothly.   See *Proceedings, 3rd Annual Convention Nat. Assn. Corps. Schools*, p. 254.

[2] For a recognition of this fact by a manufacturer, see W. C. Redfield, *The New Industrial Day*. The National Association of Corporation Schools has recognized this necessity and its Secretary, F. C. Henderschot, has repeatedly declared that one of the fundamental purposes of the Association was to conserve and deepen the health of the employees in the plants.

quainted with the significance of his particular industry. Thus, if he is a shoe operative, the course might include: a sketch of the history of shoe-making; a description of the present system of manufacture; an examination of the sources of the raw material; the main stages in manufacturing, and the system of marketing. All these would make the specialized employee more conscious of the importance of his particular niche, and would allay much of the dissatisfaction which necessarily arises from the isolated and minute nature of our tasks. The relation of the worker to the state should be discussed and, if it is possible to secure fair and impartial treatment, the subject of unionism should not be ignored.

It is furthermore of vital importance that those best fitted should reach the upper rungs of the industrial ladder. To-day, however, we have huge noncompeting groups between which there is little competition.[1] The children of the poorer classes leave school, as we saw, at 14 or shortly after, to enter unskilled jobs. They are given no training that will fit them for the more highly skilled work for which many of them have natural talents. In consequence nearly all, save the truly exceptional, are confined to the lower grades of work. The better positions are filled from a restricted economic class and there is, consequently not as rigid a selection as there would be if there were a larger number to choose from. A system of education that would allow all an equal opportunity to try for the better positions would partially remedy this. Many who are now confined to unskilled labor would then rise to more responsible positions.

[1] For a discussion of the economic and social significance of non-competing groups see J. E. Cairnes, *Some Leading Principles of Political Economy*, pp. 66-68, where a suggestion of Mill's is expanded without due credit being given, *cf.* J. S. Mill, *Principles of Political Economy*, pp. 248-49 and pp. 257-260. A more expanded treatment is given by F. W. Taussig, *Principles of Economics*, vol. ii, pp. 129-142.

The least efficient of the present occupants of the high positions (who now hold their jobs because of the lack of competition) would be weeded out. The consequent increase of national efficiency would be great and would in itself justify a more prolonged education than is now given.[1]

So far we have been speaking of the rank and file of labor. We have seen that even for them, more training is required than is now given; in making them better men, we make them at the same time better workmen.

There remains, however, the so-called aristocracy of labor, including the higher-grade machinists, repairmen, subbosses, foremen, and superintendents. This group is by no means homogeneous as respects the amount of skill required. Repairmen and the machinists need technical skill while on the other hand, foremen and sub-bosses must primarily have the ability to lead or to drive men. Every industrial plant must have all these men. Its success will largely depend on how capable they are.

The training therefore of these non-commissioned officers of industry is of great importance. To make them efficient in their respective tasks, a thorough system of technical education must be super-imposed upon that given those in the lower grades. The repairmen and high-grade machinists should know shop arithmetic, mensuration and how to determine the weight of a material from its density. Instruction should be given in plane geometry, in the use and interpretation of blue-prints and in rough sketching. A study of the principles associated with the level and inclined plane would be another essential, and also the principles of mechanics as exemplified by every-day shop experience.

[1] Such a system would not of course obviate the comparative advantage of the very rich as compared with the very poor. It would merely smooth out some of the barriers between intermediate classes, more especially between unskilled labor and the upper-class mechanics.

The foreman and sub-bosses need a somewhat different kind of instruction.   They are the employer's immediate representatives and the personal attitude of the employees to the employer is chiefly determined by their conduct.   Too often they are bullies and try to rule through fear.   In such cases they alienate the sympathy of the workers and lower the efficiency of the plant.   Employers should see to it not only that the rougher element is not given these supervisory jobs, but that those men who are chosen should be trained to handle men.

Psychology is a much-abused term yet it is a requisite for all foremen.   The various bosses in a factory should meet together and discuss, under instruction, methods of shop management and, what is more important, problems of human management.   This system might be extended to include classes comprising foremen from different plants who would meet to exchange ideas, and pursue common studies.

These men, foremen and machinists, alike, are now chosen from the ranks of labor.   It is important that the best-fitted men should be so selected and trained.   At present, a firm has the alternative of either training its own non-commissioned officers, or of hiring them from some other plant.   In the latter case they are merely shifting the burden of training on to someone else.   The necessity for education and selection must still be met.   To recruit the upper grades most efficiently, there should be an opportunity for competition on the part of the lower.   Classes in shop management might be held whereby the managers might pick out the ablest members and try them out when a vacancy in one of the more responsible positions occurs.

CHAPTER VI

THE PROBLEM OF VOCATIONAL EDUCATION FOR WOMEN

I. Introduction.

WOMAN's work is not a new phenomenon. Women have always worked. What is new is the fact that women now work for wages. Formerly women were unpaid servants, performing their household duties not because of economic choice but because of family ties. Today a considerable percentage work in industries upon the basis of business contract. Any study of working conditions and educational needs is therefore incomplete which neglects the peculiar problems caused by the presence of women in competitive industry. The problem of vocational education for women differs sufficiently from the problem for men to justify a separate treatment. Unlike the preceding chapter, this chapter will include a discussion of domestic and personal service, trade and transportion, as well as manufacturing. Consequently it will treat of vocational education as a whole, rather than the narrower field of industrial education.

The statement is often made that " women follow their occupations out of the home into industry." By this it is meant that as weaving and spinning, the making of clothing and the preparation of food are constantly tending to be performed in factories rather than in homes, women have followed their old tasks into these new surroundings.[1]

[1] For statement of this viewpoint, see J. Adams Puffer, *Vocational Guidance*, p. 157, and David Snedden, *The Problem of Vocational Education*, pp. 51-52.

In this explanation, the transition of occupations from the home to the factory is made the dynamic, while the movement of women is the passive factor. This statement must be modified in at least two respects: (1) whereas formerly women worked at all these tasks, nowdays the factory woman works at only a part of one. The division of labor has narrowed women's work as well as men's. (2) It is furthermore as true of men as of women, since all industry has proceeded from the home. The male artisan, whether under the domestic or handicraft system, was a home-worker. The factory and the home were, in fact, undifferentiated. It would be equally correct therefore, to say that men have followed their occupation from the house to the mill.

What has caused so much emphasis to be placed on this tendency in the case of women has been the fact that on the whole they have been slower than men to go through the process. Cooking, the making of clothing, and laundry work have but recently been organized upon the factory basis. Their disappearance in a large measure from the household has necessarily lightened the toil of the house wife. The evolution of these industries has released the energy of millions of women for other tasks. Naturally they have entered in general the occupations for which they fancy their customary training has equipped them.

The recent movement of women into industry is shown by the fact that while in 1880 only 14.7% of the females over 10 years of age were gainfully employed, this percentage had risen to 17.4 by 1890, to 18.8 in 1900 and by 1910 it had reached 23.4.[1]

Some of the effects of this entrance of women into industrial life should be noted. Perhaps first in importance

---

[1] *13th Census,* vol. iv, "Occupations," p. 26.

is the fact that the industrial life of the average female worker is relatively brief. Thus, 30.8% of all women employed in 1910 were under 20 years, as contrasted with 16.5% of the men. Only 16% of the women gainfully employed were over 45, while 26.1% of the men were above this age.[1] Professor Persons computed that in 1900, 49.14% or practically one-half of all women workers were under 25 and 71.4% or over seven tenths were under 35.[2]

The early age at which women leave industry is indicated by the fact that, whereas approximately 40% of all girls between 16 and 20 were employed in 1900, that only 26% of those between 21-44 were so employed; while 96% of men between 21-44 were employed as against only 80% from 16 to 20 years. Had this 21-44 group been separated into five-year age groups, it would have undoubtedly shown a great falling off in the percentage of women at work above thirty.

The cause for the sudden drop in the percentage of women who are at work is of course marriage. In the 21-44 year period nearly all who are ever to be married, become so. This makes them leave industry for the home. They have definitely forsaken the factory or the store and few will return. Thus what is for men a life-long career, is for women but a temporary occupation. Five or at the most ten years is the average length of time a woman spends in industry.

This transient nature of woman's work has a dual effect: (a) It prevents them from doing skilled work in the industry in which they are engaged, and (b) it tends to unfit them for housekeeping which most of them must later enter.

[1] *13th Census*, vol. iv, p. 69.
[2] C. E. Persons, "Women's Work and Wages," *Quarterly Journal of Economics*, vol. xxix, p. 215.

It takes time to acquire skill in modern industry. While learning, wages are necessarily lower than they would be if the worker did not need to be instructed. Learning is therefore an investment, which depends for its profitableness upon long service. It is hard enough for a boy with a whole lifetime in industry before him to realize that it might be a good thing to learn a skilled trade. For a girl who sees marriage before her as a probability, it is almost an impossibility. She believes that she will no sooner master the trade that she is studying than she will marry and turn from the mill or shop to the household. Of what avail then will be her ability as a skilled buyer or cutter? Her inevitable thought is, "Isn't it better to work at a job with a higher starting wage, even though it affords no opportunity for trade education?"

Such considerations discourage all girls, not merely those who ultimately marry. The prospect of marriage looms before them all, and each sub-consciously feels that she is destined for the home, not for the factory. Thus women enter industry regarding it as a place where they can kill time and assist their families until Thomas, Richard, or Henry "turns up." Naturally therefore, they flock into the unskilled positions in every industry they enter. They are essentially youthful, unskilled, low-paid and transient workers.

Once at work, they have little incentive to become interested in their trade. The positions at which they are employed are, as we shall see, in the main uninteresting and mechanical. This tends to extinguish any instinct of workmanship that might be dormant within them. Marriage is still the probable career and prevents them from taking their work seriously. By the age of 25 most of the girls have married and have left industry; by 30 practically all have done so, and a fresh batch of girls has taken the place of those who have departed.

There are left, however, those women who have not found a husband; who, like their sisters, neglected to prepare at the outset for a prolonged industrial career. They find themselves at 30 somewhat fatigued by the pace which modern industry has set, and since it is now too late to start in training for the higher positions, they continue to work along at the unskilled jobs and remain, on the whole, at the foot of the industrial ladder.

This modern situation, however, not only prevents the woman worker from acquiring industrial skill, but it also operates to lessen her training in home-making. The period of woman's life which she now devotes to industry was formerly devoted to learning how to manage a home. Through the instructions of her mother she learned how to become a fairly competent housewife. Much of the training was of course given by the rule-of-thumb method, but the period from 16-25 was distinctly one of preparation for her future work of housekeeping. Nowadays, the woman in industry has little opportunity to get this education. Her days are spent elsewhere, and her work leaves her so tired that she does not want to study at night but quite naturally she instead craves amusement.

Moreover, she is necessarily more concerned with getting married, than with fitting herself for marriage, since the qualities that men desire in girls before marriage are not generally those that they would desire after marriage. Should a girl study carefully how to become a competent mother and wife, it is probable that this would act as a passive deterrent to her ever having the opportunity of becoming one.

Woman is then both an unskilled worker in industry and an unskilled worker at home. It is not her fault. She has the desire for craftsmanship and for good home-making, but society affords her little opportunity to satisfy these desires.

While industrial life has given woman greater independence, it has also given her uninspiring tasks and has deprived her of her former opportunity of learning about home-making.

Vocational education for women must then train women both for industry and for the home. If it does the former without the latter, it is preparing the average woman for at most only 10 years of her future life; if it does the latter alone, it is shirking the needs of those who will continue in industry, and is allowing the temporary workers to stay at ill-paid and unskilled jobs.

II. Gainfully employed women; their work and vocational needs.

The following pages contain an analysis of the nature of the work performed by women in industry and of the possibility of improving their situation through training. In 1910 the women employed were divided among the various occupational groups in the following proportions: Agriculture, 22.4%; professional service, 8.3%; domestic and personal service, 32.5%; manufacturing, 21.9%; and trade and transportation, 14.9%. While the number of women in all groups had increased absolutely since 1880, the relative importance of the various groups had considerably altered. Thus domestic service had decreased during these thirty years from comprising 44.6% of all gainfully employed women to 32.5%, while trade and transportation had increased from 6.2% to 14.9% and professional service from 6.7% to 8.3%. Agriculture remained approximately the same, although the 1910 statistics are probably not completely comparable with those of the preceding years, while manufacturing, although almost trebling absolutely, declined relatively from 23.8% to 21.9%.

These different fields of woman's work will now be analyzed in respect to their relative importance, the kind of work performed, and the possibilities for training. It is much to be regretted that we do not have later statistics than those of the 1910 census for the number of women employed in various occupations.

A. *Agriculture:*	*Number of Women Employed* [1]	*Percentage of Female to total workers employed*
	1,807,050	14.4%

Nearly 60% of the women employed in agriculture are colored, while 87% of the total are employed in the southern states.[2] Those that are not colored are chiefly of the " poor white " class and work on the small tenant farms. There is, however, a small percentage of native-born women of the best type helping with farm work. Some knowledge of scientific agriculture is needed by a considerable proportion, although the vast majority are, of course, farm laborers rather than managers.

B. *Professional Service:*	*Number of Women Employed* [4]	*Percentage of total number of women employed*
	779,825	9.6%

Eighty percent of this group are trained nurses, music-teachers, and, most important of all, school teachers. Taken as a whole they are the most favorably situated of all women workers. Problems there are to be sure, but the question of education is not primary.

[1] This is probably somewhat in excess of the actual number, see *13th Census*, vol. iv, pp. 27-28.

[2] Alabama, Arkansas, Florida, Georgia, Kentucky, Louisiana, Mississippi, North Carolina, South Carolina, Tennessee, Texas, Virginia.

[3] For description of working conditions, see A. M. MacLean, *Wage-Earning Women*, pp. 99-129.

[4] This number is somewhat larger than that listed in the table previously given. This is because it includes several occupations not included in the census up to 1900. When the previous table was given only these occupations were included under Professional Service for 1910 which had previously been included.

C. Domestic and Personal Service:	No. of Women	% of total No. of Women Employed	% of total No. in Group (Both Males and Females)
	2,463,413	30.5%	67.7%

Though, the relative importance of domestic service has steadily decreased, it is still pre-eminently woman's main industry. Formerly "working out" meant acting as a servant and it was the common employment of our native girls. Today over 56% of domestic "help" are either foreign-born or are negroes. These classes have crowded out the native girls, who have gone into other and more desirable kinds of work. In theory, domestic service is a reconciliation of the conflicting demands of the home and of industry. In working for wages, girls are at the same time learning how to manage a household. Present work and future occupation are thus joined together. Under good conditions, the efficient servant will ultimately be the efficient housewife. It must be frankly admitted, however, that little training is given today to the servant of the average household. The average housewife of today (unlike her grandmother) is seldom capable of efficiently instructing a maid in cooking or in housekeeping. As a result the maid-servant is compelled largely to blunder through things by herself.

Since education within the home has largely failed, some public system of household training seems then to be necessary. Some form of continuation school, such as will be described later, whereby all the house-servants in a locality could be given training in the principles of housekeeping, would be valuable. General instruction in personal hygiene, food values, and plain sewing, would fill gaps that now exist.

In discussing domestic service, mention should be made of the substitutes for the home. The growing importance of hotels, restaurants, and boarding houses, and not the invention of fireless cookers, vacuum cleaners, and the like, constitutes the real domestic industrial revolution.

The following figures show something of the growth in these occupations since 1880.[1]

Occupation	1880	1890	1900	1910
Boarding-house keepers	19,058	44,349	71,281	165,482
Hotel keepers	32,453	34,076	54,797	64,504
Restaurant keepers	13,074	19,283	33,844	60,832
Total	65,085	107,708	159,922	290,788

Thus we see that these occupations increased nearly four-fold while the population increased but 85 per cent. It will be noted that the above table did not include the employees of these establishments. Had they been segregated by the census a still greater increase would have been shown. The development of these occupations is a unique development in large-scale production. Their increase is due not only to increased travel on the part of Americans, but also because the difficulties attendant upon housekeeping have forced many middle- and upper-class families to abandon their homes and live in hotels and apartments.[2]

The large scale of these enterprises naturally causes a sub-division of labor that the one- or two-servant household cannot have. This is especially true, of course, of hotels. Chamber-maids, waitresses, and cooks pursue their particular occupation and seldom follow any other. As a result

[1] *12th Census, Special Report on Occupations*, pp. 36-37; *13th Census*, vol. iv, p. 94.

[2] See an article by I. M. Rubinow, "The Problem of Domestic Service," *Journal of Political Economy*, vol. xiv, pp. 502-519.

they do not have the all-round training for housekeeping that the maid-of-all-work has.

There are approximately 40,000 chamber-maids and 85,000 watresses, outside of those in hotels, boarding-houses and restaurants. Both of these classes need instruction. Cleanliness, promptness, speed, a retentive memory and accuracy are all necessities. Training to develop these qualities could be systematized, and the efficiency of these workers heightened.[1]

Another domestic industry that is developing into the factory stage is laundry work. In 1910 this employed over 663,000, of whom over one-sixth were employed in laundries and were not home workers. Though men formed but 2.5% of the home operatives, they comprised 32.1% of the laundry-hands. In this instance men are really assuming what was exclusively woman's employment.

Home laundry work is heavy and requires care more than skill. It is the last resort of broken-down women. In the factory the amount of machinery varies with the size of the laundry. Physical strength and endurance rather than skill or dexterity is required. It is this severe physical strain that has led to the introduction of men into the trade. Women work almost exclusively as markers, shakers, flat-work ironers and folders, starchers, dampeners, body-linen ironers, finishers, inspectors, assorters and

[1] In three large N. Y. City hotels, classes are held for chambermaids in which English alone is taught since the girls are all foreigners. *Cf.* *Pamphlet No. 263 of National Labor Commission,* "Experiments in Industrial Education in N. Y. City," pp. 12-13. The working conditions of chambermaids and waitresses are such, however, that great reforms are needed before they become fit opportunities for women's work. For the hardships of a waitress, see *The Survey,* vol. xxxvii, p. 174 (Nov. 18, 1916). A long working day, high strain at certain intervals, heavy trays, scanty opportunity to sit down, hastily-snatched food, together with the blind-alley nature of the job combine to render it objectionable.

[2] *13th Census*, vol. iv, p. 94.

wrappers. All these jobs are routine and mechanical in nature[1] and require little skill.

D. *Manufacturing and Mechanical:*

No. of Women Employed	% of Total Women Employed	% Women of total in group
1,820,980	22.4	17.2

For convenience and coherence this class will be subdivided into various groups.

1. Clothing Industries.[2]

Total No. employed	No. of women	% Women of Total
1,551,765	949,362	61.2

Thus over one-half of the women in manufacturing are engaged in the clothing industries.

(a) *Dressmakers and Seamstresses.*   *Total No. of women employed*
449,908

This, with rare exceptions, is completely a woman trade. It differs from the factory manufacture of women's clothing in that it chiefly covers the costume-field, while the factory

[1] For description of laundry processes see vol. xii of the *Report on the Condition of Women and Child Wage-Earners*, pp. 18-25; a fuller treatment is found in *Bull. 122, U. S. Bureau of Labor Statistics*, "Employment of Women in Power Laundries in Milwaukee," pp. 38-73. Here the injurious nature of some of the work, especially that of the foot tread press, is clearly brought out. See also Elizabeth B. Butler, *Women and the Trades*, pp. 178-203, where the laundry work in Pittsburg is described and analyzed.

[2] This classification of "clothing industries" is much broader than the one given in the census. It includes milliners, dressmakers, seamstresses, cloak, suit, skirt, and over-all operatives; shirt, collar and cuff employees, workers in shoe factories, and shoe-makers not in factories. It includes practically all the industries that are producing necessary and customary articles of clothing. As such, it gives a truer picture than the rigid Census definition of clothing industries, which excluded shoe-making, milliners, and dress-makers.

covers the ready-made field. Many of these dress-making shops are still in the handicraft stage in which apprentice-ship flourished. They buy their own materials and make up the goods, and sell directly to the consumer. Dress-making is essentially one of the last stands of the independent handicraft.

Dressmakers may be classified into three groups: (1) Those who work out by the day, (2) those employed in small establishments, (3) those employed in large shops.

(1) Practically all seamstresses and many dress-makers are not handicraftsmen but day laborers, who " sew out " and move from home to home. In the latter case the goods are generally furnished by the consumer and the seamstress simply makes them up at a specified rate.[1] These seam-stresses are working at tasks that are vitally necessary for the average wife. Consequently professional training in this task is also a particular preparation for home-making. Its relation to the home is not as close as that of domestic service, but it is nevertheless an indispensable branch of housekeeping.

The independent seamstress who works by the day knows the general kinds of sewing, and a few are highly skilled in elaborate dress-making.

(2) By a small shop is meant one which employs ten or less. The young worker in these shops needs fairly general skill and is supervised quite carefully by the head of the shop.

(3) The work in the larger shops is much more sud-divided. The large shop is more like a factory, with its separation of employer and worker, its large capital and the sub-division of the work. The larger the shop, the

[1] In this it differs from the domestic or the " putting-out " system in which a middleman furnishes raw material and sells the finished pro-duct. Here there is direct relationship between consumer and producer.

more specialized the tasks, and the less all-round the skill required. In Cleveland 21 different sub-divisions were found,
at which separate workers were engaged.[1] A Massachusetts
shop with 100 employees had equal specialization.[2]

In these shops the tendency is for each employee to do
only one special task. There are exceptions of course when
in order to fill a rush order, a worker may be transferred to
another branch. Men seem to fill the most skilled positions
such as cutting. Current investigation seems to indicate
that the small shops, though still predominating, are being
gradually driven out by the larger, and that in consequence
specialization is on the increase.[3]

Taken in the large, the requirements of the dress-making
trade are those of good, general training and intelligence
plus an ability to sew neatly either by hand or by machine.
There is moreover opportunity for designers who require
some artistic training, an appreciation of color harmony, and
a knowledge of fabrics, and textiles.[4]

(b) *Milliners*   *No. of women employed*
                             128,438 [5]

This trade likewise is monopolized by women. Like

[1] *Cleveland Foundation Education Survey*, Edna Bryner, "Dress-
making and Millinery," p. 31.

[2] United States Bureau of Labor Statistics, *Bull. No. 193*, May Allinson,
"Dressmaking as a Trade for Women in Massachusetts," pp. 44-45.

[3] See Allinson, *op. cit.*, p. 52, "The small and medium sized shops are
disappearing before the competition of the domestic or dayworkers on
the one side and the large shop on the other." See also Edna Bryner,
op. cit., p. 30.

[4] For the qualities that the dress-making trade requires of its workers,
see the *Vocational Survey of Minneapolis*, pp. 411-424.

[5] It is quite possible that the number of dress-makers and milliners
listed in the census may be above the actual number. It is quite well-
known among statisticians that professional prostitutes generally list
their occupation as either that of dress-making or millinery.

dress-making, it is still chiefly in the handicraft stage of production, where the independent owner makes up the goods with the aid of assistants, and sells them directly to the consumer. The tendency towards the factory stage is, however, visible in the presence of the factory-made hat which has become more important in recent years.

Retail stores may either make their own hats or merely sell the ready-made factory hats. In the latter case the employees are primarily saleswomen not craftswomen. A few milliners may be needed to make necessary alterations, but beyond this nothng. All-round workmanship is needed in a small shop which makes its own hats, because the work is little specialized. The milliner cannot standardize her hats, because she must keep a large variety of different hats in stock. As a result individual craftsmanship counts for much. A fine feeling for color, a capacity for dexterous combinations of materials, and a nice artistic sense are all needed.[1]

Millinery departments in stores have a much greater subdivision of labor than does the ordinary retail shop. Wholesale houses have a still greater sub-division. The larger the plant, the greater the sub-division and the less skill required of the employees.

Miss Perry, in her study found that workers performing mechanical tasks outnumbered the trimmers who do artistic work by the rate of 6 to 1 in Boston, and 7 to 1 in Philadelphia.[2] Three-quarters of the employees in Cleveland were mere copyists and only 7% were designers.[3]

Millinery is a seasonal trade. Like all seasonal trades, it has its periods of feverish over-activity and its correspond-

[1] The reverse side of the shield is the unsanitary, and poorly lighted nature of many of the workshops.

[2] Lorinda F. Perry, *Millinery as a Trade for Women*, p. 26.

[3] Bryner, *op. cit.*, pp. 60-61.

ing seasons of lethargy. Wages are low and prospects of advancement slight. Because of this and other reasons, only a limited number of girls should be encouraged to enter this trade.

(c) *Men's Hats*

Total No. employed	Total No. Women Employed	% Women
40,794	11,514	28.29

Unfortunately the number of workers in the straw hat industry cannot be ascertained.[1] Straw hat making is highly seasonal and the work in the late spring is feverish in its intensity. Not much skill is required. High power machines are used and the employee should know how to manage them. The Manhattan Trade School has tried to train the girls already engaged in the industry to be better workers, but the possibility of rising to more skilled positions is almost nil. The effectiveness of the workers at their present tasks might be heightened by trade education, but the maximum of efficiency would soon be reached. It is distinctly an industry which does not require skill, but merely endurance and nervous energy of its workers, and it is one which exhausts the energies of those who engage in it.

The woolen and felt hat industry for which statistics are given, is by no means as seasonal. More skill is required than in straw-hat making, but the skilled positions are rarely filled by women. They are employed in the lower grade jobs.

(d) *Collars, Cuffs and Shirts*

Total No. Employed	No. of Women Employed	% Women of Total
70,123	50,767	72.4

[1] Under the head of milliners the *Census* does not distinguish between the straw industry and that of straw hats. Many straw-hat workers moreover were undoubtedly included.

Women's work in these industries is decidedly low-skilled. In the manufacture of shirts all the skilled positions, such as that of cutter, are filled by men.[1] Women in consequence are found in the routine machine operations. Few or none of these require any special skill.[2]

The collar and cuff industry, which has its center in Troy, N. Y. employs women predominantly. The processes are almost completely automatic, work is highly sub-divided, with little or no necessity for technical skill. An investigation was made a few years ago of this trade in which it was found that no trade education was needed by the women engaged, since their work required little skill or dexterity. Endurance and a good physique were the chief requirements.

(e) *Clothing Factories*

Total No. Employed	No. of Women	% Women of Total
529,470	210,879	39.8%

This in turn has many sub-divisions.

(1) Men's Clothing.

In 1910, there were over 257,000 workers in this industry, 55% of whom were women over 16 years of age.[3] Since then, of course, the industry has grown very rapidly. It is characterized by a great division of labor and the grouping of the women in the lower grade of positions.

In the manufacture of coats the sub-division of labor varies in direct ratio to the size of the shop. In one coat

[1] Vol. xviii of the *Report on the Condition of Women and Child Wage-Earners*, p. 288.

[2] *Ibid.*, pp. 288-289. The work women do is monotonous to the extreme and is performed under conditions that are exceedingly fatiguing. Little or no skill is required.

[3] *13th Census*, vol. viii, p. 254.

shop[1] in New York, 49 different occupations were found which were performed by different operators, while in some shops as high as 62 different jobs were found. The most skilled occupations are those of cutting, fitting and basting, and these are almost completely manned by men.[2] Women work at the lower-grade tasks,[3] and an analysis of the tasks they perform shows that speed is the requisite rather than skill.

The manufacture of pants is less skilled than that of coats, and consequently women are found in it to a greater extent.[4] In those tasks in which skill is still required, however, men are predominant.

Vest-making is lighter work. Most vests are probably made by one worker with a few assistants. Some shops however, have carried the division of labor to an extreme point. Where sub-division of work does prevail, men again dominate cutting and other skilled trades while women are engaged at the more simple tasks.

Taking the industry in the large it is safe to conclude that women occupy the lower ranks of operations and work at jobs that require little skill or training.[5] Girls might be

[1] Vol. ii of *Report on Conditions of Women and Child Wage-Earners*, p. 462.

[2] *Ibid.*, pp. 443, 447.

[3] *Ibid.*, pp. 445-462. Whenever in the description of the 49 processes, it is mentioned that no skill is required, one is almost sure to find that the occupation employs women almost exclusively, *i. e.*, padding collars, lapel padding, felling tape, and pulling bastings are instances of this.

[4] *Ibid.*, p. 464.

[5] For a description of women's position in the clothing trade, see Mabel H. Willet, *The Employment of Women in the Clothing Trade*, 1902, esp. pp. 67-72. This study is somewhat obsolete but the point that women do the unskilled work, and men the more skilled is still valid. The investigation into the condition of women and child wage earners disclosed the fact that most women workers stopped at finishing, button sewing, and button hole making. See vol. ii, of the *Report*, pp. 476-78.

trained for some of the more highly skilled occupations such as pocket making and the sewing in of sleeves in which there are few women, at present.

(2) Women's Clothing.

This branch of the clothing industry employed over 162,000 people in 1910, of whom over 63 per cent were women above 16 years.[1] The proportion of women is thus higher than in the men's clothing industry.

In the dress and waist industry, women comprise 84 per cent of the working force.[2] This trade has many sub-divisions, there being as many as 24 different occupations.[3] Women abound in the simple non-operating tasks such as cleaning, finishing and assorting, and in the operative branches which do not demand much skill. The most highly skilled occupation, cutting, is exclusively monopolized by men, and one-third of all the men in the industry are found in this operation.[4]

It should not be inferred that all of woman's work in this industry is completely unskilled. Designing and draping are distinctly high-grade positions. Moreover over 25% of the women in New York shops make the entire garment and so need an all-round sewing knowledge that is not required in the larger shops where the division of labor has been carried to the extreme. On the whole, however, the knowledge that is needed by the female workers is not specialized craftsmanship, but general knowledge.

The cloak and suit industry more nearly approaches the men's garment trades than it does the dress and waist industry. Here the tailoring of heavy textiles predominates.

[1] *13th Census*, vol. viii, p. 254.
[2] *Bulletin No. 145, U. S. Bureau of Labor Statistics*, p. 158.
[3] *Ibid.*, p. 157.
[4] *Ibid.*, p. 169.

The heavier work causes men to be more numerous : thus they fill the pressing department.   Once more women are found to be in the lower-grade jobs and men in the upper.

(3) Shoe-making (factory).

Total No. Employed	No. of Women Employed	% Women of Total [1]
68,549	217,667	31.5

Here the effects of the division of labor are most clearly apparent.   Shoe factories are the heightened reflection of the tendencies operating in all industries.   The making of a shoe is so sub-divided that there are over two hundred different operations, each cared for by different workmen. Women predominate in the routine sewing operations, and in the packing, folding, and cementing departments.   These require little training.   Deftness rather than skill is needed.[2] Men on the other hand are found in the more skilled levels of work.   Over 95% of the cutters are men, as are likewise the lasters, while the finishers are chiefly men as well.

The shoe-makers or cobblers who are outside the factory are small handicraftsmen.   There are few women in this class and for our purposes they may be neglected.[3]

2. Textile Industries.

Total No. Employed	No. of Women Employed	% Women of Total [4]
898,992	410,174	45.6

[1] *13th Census*, vol. iv, pp. 350-353.

[2] The unskilled nature of women's jobs may be seen from a study of 214 women in Massachusetts factories; 86 or 48.2% required less than a week to learn their position, 86 or 48.2% required from 1 week to 4 weeks, while only 42 or 19.6% required over a month, see *Bull. No. 180, U. S. Bureau of Labor Statistics*, " The Boot and Shoe Industry in Mass. as a Vocation for Women," p. 50.

[3] The statement made in Chapter V that repair work was the chief branch of modern industry, which demanded skill is here corroborated. The modern cobbler does chiefly repair work.   Since he must know how to construct the whole shoe, he is much more skilled than the factory-hand.

[4] *13th Census*, vol. iv, pp. 380-393.

There are four main textile industries, (a) cotton, (b) woolen (c) knitting, and (d) silk manufactures. Other divisions such as lace, embroidery, and rope and sail manufacturies will be omitted because of their comparative unimportance.

(a) 148,000 women were employed in 1910 in the cotton industry where they formed 40% of the total force. 60% of the men were employed at occupations in which no women at all are employed.[1] The women are employed at the simpler and less skilled operations. Thus ring spinning is work that requires neither special mechanical knowledge or great physical strength,[2] and is performed almost wholly by women and by children. The spooling of the yarn and the "drawing-in" (a threading process) are also managed by women.

Men, on the other hand, monopolize mule-spinning because it is more difficult than ring-spinning. They do all the mixing, carding, and slashing, while all the loomfixers are likewise men.[3]

(b) 55,000, or 42%, of the 138,000 employees in woolen mills were women.[4] Here again they occupy the lower grade jobs. They comprise practically all of the furlers, rovers, drawers-in, sewers and menders, spoolers, and twisters. Loom fixers are again entirely men, while men predominate as carders, combers, slashers, sorters, and scourers. The same demarcation that is characteristic of the cotton industry is applicable here. Wherever there are skilled positions they are filled by men, while women are found wherever work is completely unskilled and routine.

[1] *Report on Conditions of Women and Child Wage-Earners*, vol. i, "Cotton and Textile Industries," p. 47.

[2] *Ibid.*, p. 403.

[3] For description of processes, see *ibid.*, pp. 399-408.

[4] *13th Census*, vol. vi, pp. 390-392.

(c) Fifty-five percent of the silk operatives in this country
were women in 1910.[1] This industry has developed very
rapidly, due to a cheap labor supply and the protective
tariff. Hand looms have been displaced by machine looms
more completely than abroad. Silk manufacturers have
located their plants where a cheap labor supply abounded.
Thus Paterson, N. J., where immigrants could be secured,
was chosen as the first center of the industry. Later the
seat of the industry was moved to the coal-mining centers
of Pennsylvania, where the wives and children of the
miners could be secured for low wages because of the necessity of eking out the low yearly earnings of the heads of
the households.

(d) In the knitting mills as well, there is little competition between the sexes. While women are engaged at the
light and unskilled posts, men do the heavy work and in so
far as skill is required, fill those positions as well. The
full-fashioned knitting machines are the most complex of
all the machines, and several years training is required to
know how to operate them. These machines are "invariably operated by men."[2]

3. Food Trades.

Total Number in Trade	No. of Women	% Women of Total
413,559	63,214	15.2[3]

Though this is woman's proverbial occupation, she forms
but 15% of the number of employees. This is a considerably smaller percentage than that which the total number of
working women form of the total working population. In
woman's traditional employment, therefore, as the industry
has moved away from the home, men have gone into it.

[1] *13th Census*, vol. vi, p. 388.
[2] *Ibid.*, p. 197.
[3] *Ibid.*, pp. 328-336.

In this instance, women have not followed, but have rather abandoned their work.

(a) *Bakeries*

Total No. Employed	No. of Women	% Women of Total
144,782	17,967	12.4% [1]

Women are confined chiefly to the clerical occupations and to packing. The intense heat and the heavy work of baking itself, has effectually debarred woman from entering the more important occupations. Such work as she does is mainly mechanical and automatic.

(b) *Candy Factories*

Total No. Employed	No. of Women	% Women of Total
42,684	20,648	48.0% [2]

Little good can be said of this as a trade for women. Wages are particularly low. In 1913-14, the majority of women in this trade in New York State received less than $6 a week.[3] Seasonal fluctuations with their over-employment and their unemployment are characteristic.[4]

Here, as elsewhere, men monopolize the skilled occupations. Pan work and operating the heavier machines which require some skill are distinctly men's occupations.[5] The " candy-maker " or table worker is likewise generally a man. Miss Phillips, in her study of the industry, enumerates seventeen jobs in which women predominate, that can be learned in a few minutes to a few hours."[6]   13 other jobs,

---

[1] *13th Census*, vol. vi, p. 328.

[2] *Ibid.*, p. 430.

[3] *4th Report, N. Y. State Factory Investigating Comm*, vol. ii, p. 326.

[4] *Ibid.*, pp. 321-323.

[5] *Ibid.*, p. 308.

[6] Anna A. Phillips, "An Investigation of the Candy Industry to determine the possibilities of Vocational Training," *4th Report, New*

10 of which are done chiefly by women, require little more than "a few hours' to a few days' " training.[1]

Chocolate and bon-bon dippers are the most highly skilled trades to which women may aspire, but for which as another study says "very few of the packers and wrappers ever qualify." [2]   Though two months or more of training are necessary to produce a good dipper, yet the requirements for entrance are exceedingly low.   "The requirements for a hand dipper," says Miss Phillips, "are that she appear neat and healthy and has hands that are not hot and do not perspire." [3]

(c) *Canneries*

Total No. Employed	No. Women Employed	% Women of Total
15,553	4,926	31.7% [4]

The investigations of the Consumers League have shown that this industry is one that as now conducted is extremely injurious to women.   Long hours of routine work at high speed are characteristic, their industrial life is so temporary that they would not have the opportunity to acquire skill, were any required.

York State Factory Investigating Comm., vol. iv, p. 1355; see also a study of the industry in vol. xviii, of *Report on Conditions of Women and Child Wage-earners*, pp. 119-137.   The federal investigation declared that there was "no competition between the sexes, males making the candy and females taking charge of the dipping, wrapping, and packing." The majority of the operations performed by women were described as "unskilled, consisting of simple operations or movements repeated indefinitely." *Ibid.*, p. 137.

[1] Phillips, *op. cit.*, p. 1357.

[2] *Alliance Employment Bureau*, "Inquiries into Trades for Factory Workers," p. 22.

[3] Anna A. Phillips, *op. cit.*, p. 1358.

[4] *13th Census*, vol. iv, p. 332.   These figures do not measure the number engaged in canning at the "peak" of the season.

4. Miscellaneous.

We will consider under this heading a number of industries that are not logically related. By grouping them together. however, we secure a more coherent treatment.

(a) *Cigar and Tobacco Factories* [1]

Total No. Employed	*No. of Women*	*% Women of Total*
195,379	79,486	40.7%

The cigar industry in this country was originally almost exclusively a woman's trade. The wives of Connecticut farmers made up the tobacco into crude cigars which were either sold directly to the consumer or exchanged at the country store for commodities. By 1850, however, factory methods were beginning, and the coming of Spanish, Cuban, and German cigar-makers into the factories displaced the women from their handicraft position. The immigration of trained Bohemian women about 1870 brought more women into the trade. Unlike the farmers' wives, they did not own the raw tobacco nor the homes wherein they worked, nor could they market the finished cigar. They were dependent upon a capitalistic entrepreneur for the purchasing of the raw material and the selling of the product. Consequently they worked under the domestic or " putting out " system rather than the handicraft system. The development of machinery made the work more unskilled and thus made it possible to employ more women. Women were also introduced into the trade by the employers in an attempt to break the power of the unions.[2]

It is difficult to separate cigarette from cigar making but in 1910 women formed 40% of the employees in the tobacco

[1] *13th Census*, vol. iv, p. 396.

[2] For the historical material about women in the cigar industry I have drawn largely upon Miss Edith Abbott's article on " Employment of Women in Industries: Cigar making, its History and Present Tendencies," *Journal Political Econ.*, vol. xv, pp. 1-25.

industry as a whole. The Federal Investigation into the Condition of Women and Child Wage-earners found that in 58 typical cigar factories visited, women comprised 67% of the total force.[1]

Woman's work in the factories is diverse in character. In some factories they are absolutely unskilled while in others they are the " pickers " and " makers," which are the two most skilled occupations in the trade. Taken as a whole, however, the federal report concluded that " Women predominated in the unskilled work, and that they are losing ground in the skilled occupations." [2] Women are more and more going into occupations like stripping and light machine operating, which require little skill.

Cigarette making is less of a domestic industry than cigar-making and is more in the factory stage. A cigarette plant employs on the average more men than a cigar factory,[3] and this permits the introduction of machinery to a greater extent than is possible in the smaller cigar factories.[4] This susceptibility to machine methods is moreover increased by the fact that cigarettes are a more uniform and standardized product than cigars and require fewer processes. Because of this fact, specialization is naturally greater in cigarette than in cigar-making.

[1] *Report on Condition of Women and Child Wage-earners*, vol. xvii, p. 89.

[2] *Ibid.*, p. 91.

[3] *Ibid.*, p. 77. " In 1905, the average number of wage-earners per cigarette factory was 28.8 while for cigar factories the average was only 8.3."

[4] The question as to whether large-scale production causes the introduction of machinery or whether the introduction of machinery causes large scale production is a logical tangle which is impossible to determine. It is not a question of cause and effect but of inter-action. A plant must be organized upon a fairly large basis to afford the heavy overhead expense of machine introduction; this introduction in turn increases the output and paves the way for expansion upon a still larger scale. Here as elsewhere in industrial life, growth is cumulative.

The Federal Report says of cigarette making, "Practically none of the female wage-earners can be called skilled. In many of these occupations, a brief training is required, but there is no operation in which the necessary knowledge cannot be easily gained in a few weeks."[1] The differentiation between the work of women and of men is brought out by the division of machine operations. Making oval cigarettes requires strength and mechanical knowledge on the part of the operator; hence these operators are nearly all men. Round cigarettes are made on a simple and light machine, therefore women predominate in that branch.

(b) *Clock and Watch Manufacture* [2]

Total No. Employed	No. of Women	% Women of Total
26,036	8,717	33.5%

In this industry, women work at a multiplicity of operations. Some of the work such as soldering and japanning is unskilled drudgery, some operations such as making mainsprings, finishing the parts, and adjusting the balance wheel require the highest delicacy of touch and accuracy of judgment. In case-making, an important and skilled branch of the clock industry, men predominate to the almost complete exclusion of women.[3]

(c) *Jewelry* [4]

Total No. Employed	No. of Women	% Women of Total
36,993	9,765	26.4%

[1] *Report on Condition of Women and Child-earners, op. cit.*, vol. xviii, p. 78.

[2] *13th Census*, vol. iv, p. 366. Women are relatively more numerous in watch-making than in clock-making.

[3] For an analysis of watch and clock-making, see *Report on Condition of Women and Child Wage-earners, op. cit.*, vol. xviii, pp. 111-119.

[4] *13th Census*, vol. iv, pp. 368-370.

Women monopolize the following occupations; chain-making, curbing, enameling, carding, and finishing; all routine and relatively unskilled occupations. The Federal Report says "comparatively little of the work done by them (by women and children) could be called skilled." [1]

(d) Paper Box Factories [2]

Total No. Employed	No. of Women	% Women of Total
22,976	14,324	62.3%

This is predominantly a woman's trade. The work has become highly specialized, and the use of machinery has spread rapidly. The occupations in which women are employed are in the main distinct from those in which men are engaged. [3] Neither technical training nor skill is required, but manual dexterity. Professor Leonard, after an exhaustive study of the industry, concluded that no provisions for vocational education were necessary because of the low-skilled nature of the work. [4]

(e) Paper and Pulp Mills [5]

Total No. Employed	No. of Women	% Women of Total
90,799	13,965	15.4%

Women are chiefly employed as platers, counters, cutters,

[1] *Report on Condition of Women and Child Wage-earners*, vol. xviii, p. 219.

[2] *13th Census*, vol. iv, p. 374.

[3] *Report on Condition of Women and Child Wage-earners*, vol. xviii, p. 258.

[4] See R. J. Leonard, "An Investigation of the Paper Box Industry to Determine the Possibility of Vocational Training," *4th Report, N. Y. State Factory Investigating Commission*, pp. 1243-1346, esp. pp. 1345-46, where his conclusions are given. For a somewhat more favorable view of the industry. *Cf.* Alliance Employment Bureau, *Inquiries into Trades for Factory Workers*, pp. 13-18. Case making for jewelry and silverware, a hand trade, is found by the Alliance Bureau however, to be one in which women do the low-grade work, see *ibid.*, pp. 23-29.

[5] *13th Census*, vol. iv, pp. 376-378.

and trimmers, sorters and rag-pickers. All of these jobs
are either completely unskilled or require but little skill from
the worker. The upper grades of the industry such as pulp
colorers, grinders, and beater-men have not as yet been
penetrated by the women.

(f) *Blank book, envelope and tag factories* [1]

Total No. Employed	No. of Women	% Women of Total
19,321	8,891	46.2%

Here also woman finds the chief source of her employment in the lower grades of work. Women fill positions
such as binders, folders, inspectors, unskilled machine-
hands, packers, pasters, and sorters; all quasi-automatic
positions. Men predominate in color-making, cutting, printing, and as pressmen; these are higher grade jobs.

(g) *Printing and Publishing* [2]

Total No. Employed	No. of Women	% Women of Total
355,674	76,676	21.5%

There are two branches to this industry: newspaper and
periodical printing, and book and job printing. Though
separate figures for the two fields are not given, women are
relatively more important in the latter than in the former.
In 1905, they formed 18.5% of those engaged in newspaper printing, and 23.4% of those in the book and job
end of the industry.[3]

Women are almost wholly confined to hand composing.
Here they set up the "straight" matter, but do not do dis-
play work. The introduction of machinery has taken over
much of the hand composing, but the machines are seldom
run by women. This is due to the fact that they do not

[1] *13th Census*, vol. iv, p. 376.
[2] *Ibid.*, p. 378.
[3] See *Report on Condition of Women and Child Wage-earners*, vol. x, p. 188.

run machines as swiftly or as skillfuly as men.[1] Thus women in the printing trades do not compete appreciably with men, save in the field of "straight" printing. Men have the better class of positions to themselves.[2]

Book binding in the 13th Census is listed in the printing and publishing trades. Miss Van Kleeck's study clearly shows the subordinate positions which women occupy in this trade. Women work chiefly as folders, pasters, sewers, and examiners.[1] These jobs are in the main so simple and repetitive that practical binding experts believe that industrial training is not needed for them.[4]

The more important tasks, such as trimming, rounding, backing and finishing, are performed by men. The line of demarcation between "men's work" and "women's work" is sharp and is one that is seldom crossed.

Summary For Manufacturing

This inductive study of trade after trade has shown, with perhaps monotonous reiteration, that women in practically every trade are congregated in the lowest unskilled jobs and that they thus do not really compete with men. Some cross-section studies that consider the field as a whole, not one specific trade, show this clearly. Miss Butler in her Pittsburg investigation secured the following statistics, covering woman's relation to skilled work.[5]

[1] Only 700 of approximately 13,000 machine operators in 1908 were women. See G. E. Barnett, *The Printers*, p. 318.

[2] For further information upon women in the printing trades see Belva M. Herron, *Labor Organization Among Women*, pp. 15-24. G. E. Barnett, *The Printers*, pp. 316-320. I have obtained much valuable information from an unpublished manuscript by Dr. F. A. Russell on *The Printing Trade of Illinois*.

[3] Mary Van Kleeck, *Women in the Book-binding Trade*, pp. 28-9.

[4] *Ibid.*, pp. 210-215.

[5] Elizabeth B. Butler, *Women and the Trades*, p. 369. These figures do not include the 6,500 saleswomen in mercantile establishments.

Kind of Work	No. of Women	Percentage
Skilled work	139	.8
Handicraft	305	1.9
Hand work requiring dexterity	3641	23.2
Machine operating	4885	31.1
Machine tending	2188	13.9
Wrapping and labeling	2118	13.3
Hand work requiring no dexterity	2475	15.8
Total	15651	100.0

Thus only 2.7% of these women at work could be called skilled; 23.2% (those in hand work which required dexterity) might be spoken of as semi-skilled. Many of these, however, " learn what they have to do in a week." 74.1% or over one-quarter mastered their job in three days or less.

The following table of 516 women workers shows that little training is needed for the positions women occupy in the textile trades.[1]

Days learning present occupation	Number of Workers	Percentage (Cumulative)
1	79	15.3
2 or less	105	20.4
3 or less	136	26.3
6 or less	317	61.4
12 or less	445	86.2
30 or less	496	96.1

These figures are exceedingly illuminating. 15.3% of the women workers learned their task in one day. 26.3%

[1] This table is adapted from figures given in Anna C. Hedges, *Wageworth of School Training*, p. 369. Miss Hedges' study is one of the most admirable pieces of work that has been done in America and is thoroughly trustworthy.

cr over one-quarter mastered their jobs in three days or less. 61.4% or over three-fifths, took only a week or less, 86.2% or seven-eighths, required two weeks or less, and 96.1% were able to learn inside of a month. Only 3.9% required more than a month.

It is, therefore clear, that women in manufacturing work almost uniformly at low-grade positions which in the main require neither innate skill nor training. Their labor chiefly consists in the monotonous repetition of simple movements.

E. Trade and Transportation.[1]

Total No. Employed	*No. of Women Employed*	*% Women of Total*
7,526,084	935,759	12.4%

Only 168,000 of the 3,200,000 employed in 1910 in the transportation industries were women, or approximately six percent. Indeed, in only one industry did they form an appreciable factor. 88,000 of this number are telephone operators.

(a) *Telephone operators* [2]

Total No. Employed	*No. of Women Employed*	*% Women of Total*
97,893	88,262	90.1%

Thus women monopolize the only industry in transportation in which they are appreciably employed.[3] Telephone operation in communities of any size is high-strung, taxing work. Quick muscular coordination, high power of concentration and illimitable patience are prime requisites for a successful operator. Indeed, the strain is so intense

---

[1] *13th Census*, vol. iv, pp. 92-93.

[2] *Ibid.*, p. 93.

[3] During the war, there was an increase in the number of women employed on the various railroads. At one time, approximately 110,000 were employed. By January, 1920, this had been reduced to 90,000. These were engaged chiefly in ticket selling and clerical work.

that the industrial life is very short. In Pittsburg the average length of time that a telephone girl stayed in the trade was only from fifteen to eighteen months.[1] This industry may well be called either skilled or semi-skilled. Telephone managers in various cities estimate that from one year to two years' experience is needed to produce an efficient operator.[2] Companies are beginning to recognize this fact and are establishing schools where the girls may be trained before they start work, but the low salaries paid militate seriously against their holding the operators for long.

(b) Saleswomen.

It is impossible to secure statistics concerning the number of women employed in the different kinds of stores. The Census differentiates between the owner of a drugstore and the owner of a men's clothing establishment, but does not differentiate between the employees. They are lumped together under such general headings as book-keepers, cashiers, clerks, salesmen, *etc.* Thus the division between the employees is by function rather than by trade.

Bookkeepers and cashiers will be discussed later in connection with office-work as an opening for women. We shall consider here only salesmanship and clerking as opportunities for work.

Clerks and salesmen should form two logically distinct groups. The former covers the administrative and accounting divisions of retail and wholesale trade, the latter the actual selling end. In the taking of the census, however, the enumerators failed to distinguish carefully between these two groups. Many salesmen were undoubtedly counted

[1] Elizabeth B. Butler, *Women and the Trades*, p. 291.

[2] Nelle B. Curry, *Investigation of the Wages and Conditions of Telephone Operatives*, pp. 2-23.

as clerks and vice-versa. Statistics for both groups are consequently given below.[1]

	Total No. Employed	No. of Women	% of Women of Total
1. Salesmen	875,180	250,438	26.6%
2. Clerks	387,183	111,594	28.8%

Can salesmanship be considered a skilled trade? Controversy has raged about that point. The trouble with the supporters of both views is that each has tried to make universal applications of its side of the case. The truth lies in the golden mean. Some types of salesmanship are skilled, while some are unskilled, and no sweeping statement can be made.

Saleswomen in five-and-ten-cent stores certainly are not skilled and do not need training. In fact they are sentinels rather than salesmen. They stand behind a counter, watch the customer make his decision; receive the money, wrap up the parcel and that is all. They are really guards to prevent theft, and also to bring goods from the shelves for the customers' choice, but they do not sell. The customer literally sells to himself.[2] Girls often work in these stores to acquire some experience so that they may enter other mercantile establishments.

Saleswork in many other stores is similar. A drug clerk, who does not put up prescriptions, needs only to know the stock and bring the customer what the latter demands. He does not need either skill or training. All stores which deal in standardized articles require little selling skill of their employees.

Thus certain branches of department-store work are essentially unskilled. The notion department and the lower positions in the house furnishing and crockery departments

[1] See *13th Census*, vol. iv, p. 22.
[2] See Iris P. O'Leary, *Department Store Occupations*, pp. 26-32.

require the worker only " to watch merchandise and hand out goods." [1]

Department-store work may be divided into three classes, (a) selling, (b) delivery, and (c) office force. The last two occupations may also be designed as " non-selling occupations, " and they comprise about fifty percent of the total employees.[2]

The selling department has a number of sub-divisions. Messenger or errand work is given to young beginners. This requires only the most rudimentary intelligence. Checking or packing is the next position. This demands (1) knowledge of the store system of making out sales-checks in order to correct errors, (2) the elements of arithmetic, (3) some skill in wrapping. The next position in importance is that of stock-girl. This worker should know (1) the various kinds of stock, (2) their place and the quantity kept, (3) the store system of marking, (4) the basic elements of arithmetic, and (5) invoicing.

Sales work is the next step. This requires both technical knowledge and a pleasing personality. The sales girl should know her stock thoroughly; together with the principles of color and design and the various grades of whatever textiles she may be dealing with. Moreover, she should master the store system of marking, of making out sales-slips (often a most complicated procedure), and the rules concerning " charging." She needs a thorough knowledge of arithmetic coupled with ability to reckon rapidly. Local geography, together with the ability to write a legible hand, and ability to spell names and addresses correctly are all prime requisites.

[1] I. P. O'Leary, "An Investigation of Department Store Work to Determine the Possibility of Vocational Training," *4th Report, N. Y. State Factory Investigating Committee*, vol. iv, p. 1370.

[2] *Ibid.*, p. 1379..

Taken all in all, the work of a salesgirl is by no means unskilled. The service which she renders is part of what the customer buys. A pleasant, tactful girl who is able to select goods skillfully is really selling the customer more utilities than an automaton who merely passes goods over the counter.

Sales work in other kinds of stores varies. General stores are similar to department stores, though not on so large a scale. Neighborhood stores with their personal clients, *etc.*, are important factors in many towns and cities.

The personal qualities of the salesgirl are after all more important than her technical knowledge. She must have the latter, but that in itself is incomplete. Mrs. Prince is correct when she says that education [1] of saleswomen must be "first for life and then for salesmanship." [2]

The stores are coming more and more to realize this. But while they tell their employees that they are skilled workers, they do not generally give adequate wages to the workers. While a minute examination of department store wages would lie outside the scope of this work, the statistics indicate an extremely low scale. [3] Moreover, there

[1] Much valuable literature has been written about the possibilities for skill and training in department store work. See Elizabeth B. Butler, "Saleswomen in Mercantile Stores," esp. chap. xi, *Report on Condition of Women and Child Wage-earners*, vol. v, pp. 39-44. D. F. Edwards, "The Department Stores," *Bull. No. 13, Nat. Soc. Promotion Industrial Education*, pp. 6-12. Iris P. O'Leary, *Department Store Occupations* (Cleveland Educational Survey). *The Minneapolis Survey*, pub. by Nat. Soc. Promotion Indus. Educ., pp. 464-515. *The Richmond Survey* (pub. as Bull. 162, U. S. Bureau of Labor Statistics), pp. 42-47 and pp. 227-254. Iris P. O'Leary, "An Investigation of Department Store Work to Determine the Possibility of Vocational Education," *4th Report, N. Y. State Factory Investigation Comm.*, vol. iv, pp. 1364-1405. Lucinda W. Prince, *What the Schools Can do to Train Girls for Department Store Work*, Bull. No. 13, Nat. Soc. Promotion Industrial Education, pp. 12-16.

[2] *Ibid.*, p. 15.

[3] For statistics on this point, see vol. v, *Report on Condition of Women*

has been hitherto an almost universal lack of a promotion system, and little or no reward for the careful or conscientious worker. The National Civic Federation, by no means unfriendly to the employers, declares that " The greatest injustice is slow promotion." [1]

The almost universal tendency of the large metropolitan stores is, indeed, either to discharge girls when they become competent to earn a higher wage, or so to discourage them that they resign. The stores prefer to use large numbers of unskilled girls at low wages rather than to employ more thoroughly trained employees at a higher salary. Their practice regarding the encouragement of skill is therefore, the reverse of their preaching.[2]

The movement to train saleswomen is one of the most interesting in the whole field of vocational education. Mrs. Lucinda Prince is the real originator of this movement, and by an ingenious combination of part-time instruction with actual selling practice in the stores has achieved remarkable results. Of late Mrs. Prince has turned her attention to training teachers of salesmanship, and her

and Child Wage-earners, pp. 39-45. Of the female employees in New York, Chicago, and Philadelphia Department Stores in 1909, 8.4% received less than $4.00 per week; 17.1% less than $5.00; 26.4% less than $6.00; 43.3% less than $7.00; 57.5% less than $8.00; 68.6% less than $9.00; 76.1% less than $10.00. Only 4% received more than $15.00 a week and only 2% more than $20. These figures, when taken into consideration with the fact that $9.00 was estimated at this time as the minimum sum necessary for the maintenance of a self-supporting woman, indicate the inadequacy of the wage. For New York figures, see those collected by the Nat. Civic Federation, *The National Civic Federation Review*, July, 1913, pp. 22-25. Even these figures collected by a body friendly to the employers, show that 20.6% received less than $6 per week; 36.5% less than $7; 51.3% less than $8, and 63.7% less than $9.00.

[1] *National Civic Federation Review, op. cit.*, p. 24.

[2] See an article by Elizabeth Dutcher, " Department Store *vs.* Trade Unions," *Department Store Magazine*, August, 1914, which emphasizes this point.

pupils are rapidly introducing her methods in practically all the large cities of the country.[1]

Many stores have also started schools to train the girls within their own store. The Department Store Association in New York City has started several schools for department store workers, while John Wanamaker has long had a system of training for his employees. Besides these private attempts, there are also in New York City, continuation classes for young department-store workers.[2]

(c) *Clerical Occupations* [3]

Total No. Employed	*No. of Women Employed*	*% Women of Total*
1,737,053	593,224	34.1%

This group has already been included in the statistics given for particular occupations. To give a separate treatment is then to count them twice. Their problem is, however, so different that it merits special treatment.

(1) Book keepers, cashiers and accountants.

Total No. Employed	*No. of Women Employed*	*% Women of Total*
486,700	122,665	25.2% [4]

The division of labor has extended to book-keeping. As in the factory, it varies with the size of the business. "Book-keepers in the strict sense" says Miss Cunningham, "who keep a complete set of books are seldom found now in the large offices. In their place are many clerks who each do a small part of book-keeping and are called ledger-clerks, cashiers and others according to the nature of the business

[1] See an article by Cassie L. Paine, "Origin and Growth of Movement to Train Teachers of Salesmanship." *Manual Training*, December, 1915, pp. 260-66.

[2] "Experiments in Industrial Education in New York City," *Bull. No. 263, National Child Labor Committee*, p. 12.

[3] *13th Census*, p. 94.

[4] *Ibid.*, p. 94.

of the employer. The results of the work of these many clerks are collected and combined by one book-keeper."[1] A modern book-keeping department often employs over 20 workers with but one bona-fide book-keeper.[2]

Here as in the factory, women work at the routine tasks. Where the sub-division of labor prevails, they are employed to do only one kind of book-keeping. Their field of work is essentially narrow. The "book-keeper" proper is rarely a woman but almost invariably a man.[3]

In smaller offices, however, the women have of course more all-round book-keeping work to do.

(2) Clerks (except in stores)[4]

Total No. Employed	No. of Women	% Women of Total
730,498	122,665	17.0%

This head includes a most diverse class: Governmental clerks, bank clerks, and envelope addressers are all counted in this category. Here women also occupy the inferior positions. Men monopolize the most responsible positions such as bank clerks, shipping clerks, and the higher positions in the offices of railroad and manufacturing firms.[5]

Miss Cunningham sums up as follows: "While the women clerks employed under Civil Service, may hold responsible and well paid positions, those found in business offices are usually doing work requiring little or no technical training and less general education than in other kinds of office work. They may be addressing envelopes, counting

---

[1] Women's Educational Industrial Union, *The Public Schools and Women in Office Service*, pp. 75-76.

[2] Bertha M. Stevens, *Boys and Girls in Commercial Work* (Cleveland Educational Survey), p. 37.

[3] *Women's Educational and Industrial Union, op. cit.*, p. 76.

[4] *13th Census*, vol. iv, p. 94.

[5] See Bertha M. Stevens, *op. cit.*, pp. 48-53, 81, 94-95.

or checking sales or transfer slips, recording all sorts of business transactions or engaged in that indeterminate work called general office work." [1]

(3) Stenographers and Typewriters. [2]

Total No. Employed	No. of Women	% Women of Total
316,693	263,315	80.3%

This is woman's proverbial stronghold. Stenography and typewriting has been the "way out" for multitudes of middle class women who have wanted to be financially independent. This branch of work is indeed skilled, and in fact requires far more ability than the average occupant possesses.

Accuracy, speed and a thorough knowledge of spelling, punctuation, and grammar, are absolutely necessary. Personal qualities are almost equally important.

The opening which lies ahead of the typist or stenographer is the private secretaryship. Indeed stenographic work shades into secretarial by infinitisimal degrees. This latter position requires broad general education together with initiative and responsiblity.

Though women predominate in this field, many firms prefer men. This preference is due to the fact that men are more permanent workers and consquently the more responsible officers can be recruited from their ranks. Consequently men tend to graduate from this class much more rapidly than do women.

III. *Women as Home-makers.*

Hitherto, we have considered only women in industry; we now turn to the other field of woman's effort,—homemaking.

[1] *Women's Educational and Industrial Union, op. cit.,* pp. 74-75.

[2] *13th Census,* vol. iv, p. 9. Stenographers and typewriters are differentiated from clerks and copyists because of their ability to write shorthand and to operate a typewriter.

The functions that the modern housewife performs are far different from those which she formerly exercised. When industry was in the domestic stage, the wife as well as the husband, was a producer of the family's income, and the husband, as well as the wife, directed the consumption of the family. The movement of industry from the home to the factory has separated and specialized these dual functions. The husband secures the family income; the wife spends it.[1]

There are many who deny that the management of a home is properly speaking a vocation. Their argument seems to be as follows: A vocation is one in which production is being carried on; the modern house-wife is a consumer; she is not following a vocation, consequently education for home management is not vocational, but rather general.[2]

This is true only if there is a sharp gulf between production and consumption. This gulf does not exist in life. It is true that we produce to consume. It is almost equally true that we consume in order to produce. Consumption is not only the end of production, but it is the means for further production. The consumer who can secure the utmost benefits from a limited income is a true producer. The wife who directs consumption into clean, wholesome, and efficient channels is a producer of values, and an aid to economic productivity.

We are thus justified in treating home-making as a vocation. It is indeed a vocation that has been neglected

[1] Mrs. Julian W. Heath estimates that 90% of the income of a middle-class family is expended by the wife.

[2] See C. A. Prosser, *What can the members of the General Federation of Women's Clubs do to aid the movement for Vocational Education*, p. 1. " General education prepares us to be intelligent consumers of the material and spiritual goods of life—vocational education prepares us to be intelligent producers of the goods of life."

too long. We Americans have tried to achieve prosperity by increasing our incomes. We are learning that we must also decrease or regulate our expenditures.[1] Since home making is a profession that the vast majority of women must practice, it follows that all girls should be trained for it, whereas only a minority need be trained for wage-earning proper.

What then, are the functions for which the housewife must be trained?[2] (1) She must be an efficient purchaser. Food and clothes, fuel and furniture, furnishings and fabrics must all be purchased by her. Thus she must know textiles and be able to appreciate the economic, aesthetic, and sanitary qualities of the various grades. She must know food values and market conditions; not only must she purchase foods in the proper amounts and proportions, but she must guide her expenditures by the family income. (2) She must direct the material management of the house itself. A knowledge of nutritive values of food and an ability to cook well and economically is necessary. If the housewife is to employ domestic labor, she should be acquainted with the elements of the labor problem and to be able to standardize and arrange the work to be done.

(3) She must be an accountant. The home as well as the business should be able to balance its expenditures, against its income. A family cannot expect to attain efficiency in its consumption unless it has this monetary record of its expenditures. (4) She must know the principles of health: Home sanitation, the maintenance of a physical inventory, and the elements of nursing and infant welfare

[1] *Cf.* Wesley C. Mitchell, "The Backward Art of Spending Money," *American Economic Review*, vol. ii, pp. 269-281.

[2] I have derived many hints from an admirable article by Mrs. H. M. Hitchcox, "The Business of Home-Making," *Proceedings Ninth Annual Convention of the Nat. Soc. Promotion Industrial Education*, pp. 187-195.

are all necessary. Moreover, she should be so equipped that she may train her children completely until the age of six and after that constantly supplement the work of the school.

(5) In order to be a good mother and house-wife, her work must not be restricted to the confines of the home itself. She should know the proper opportunities for family recreation, and if they are not present, be able and willing to cooperate to secure them. It is an integral part of her qualifications that she be interested in and able to pass upon school training and administration.

(6) Woman must not be completely subordinated to the home itself. " Kirche, Küche, und Kinder " should not fill her whole horizon. Most men have emphasized the importance of training in home-making because of the fear that otherwise they would not be comfortable. We should recognize that woman is a free functioning personality, and that the training given to make her more efficient should not obliterate the emphasis upon her right to think and act for herself.

IV Summary

Women in industry perform low-grade, routine operations. They are seldom employed in the same occupation with men. The wages of men and women are indeed fixed in different markets.[1]

(1) Women in agriculture are not skilled farmers and need little or no training.

(2) Little skill on the whole is required, in domestic and personal service as it is now conducted. There are however, opportunities to develop and train this class of workers which have not been seized.

---

[1] See a note by Emilie L. Wells, *Am. Ec. Rev.*, vol. ii, p. 439. Also Sidney and Beatrice Webb, *Problems of Modern Industry*, pp. 63-64.

(3) In manufacturing, women are at the bottom of the industrial ladder. They work chiefly at automatic tasks and taken as a whole, do not need much vocational training for their specific tasks.

(4) The situation is brighter in mercantile occupations. More training is undoubtedly needed by the workers, although it is questionable whether this can extend very far.

These conclusions, based upon a study of specific occupations, do not prove that women should be denied vocational training. They merely indicate that if women are to stay in their present position in industry, industrial training is, on the whole, unnecessary. If women, however, desire to attain higher places in industry, vocational training would constitute an avenue whereby they might escape from their present positions.

The great barrier to women entering these higher grades of labor is, of course, marriage. Matrimony necessarily makes women temporary workers. It renders them unwilling to undergo prolonged training for a brief industrial career, and makes employers, on the other hand, reluctant to give them a chance at the higher positions lest they suddenly leave the industry and necessitate the breaking in of a new worker. As long as the modern type of family exists, it is probable that the mass of women will continue to work at the lower grades of labor, although they need not be confined to as low-grade work as they now are.

Women do need education during their industrial life, but this education should be primarily for life and only secondarily for industry. Health, civics, and industrial history are needed to make the girl an efficient and interested citizen. Instruction in dress and purchasing is also essential. Finally, it should not be forgotten that ultimately most of the girls will become wives and mothers. Individual manufacturers cannot be expected to educate their female employees for this career, but the state must do so. If it is a social duty to prepare men for their vocation, it is equally a duty to prepare women for theirs.   Training for home-making and for life, as well as for industry, should then be an integral part in any system of vocational education for women.

CHAPTER VII

MANUAL TRAINING

THE first movement to put vocational content in our school system was that to introduce manual training. Our system of manual training came to us from Russia, which in turn derived it from Finland. In the late fifties, Cygnaeus, a Finnish educator, devised a system of hand work for the schools, which was an extension of the educational theories of Pestalozzi and Froebel. The kindergarten method of Froebel was based upon the belief that children are educated through the senses rather than by purely intellectual processes, and that hand-work thereby has distinct educational value. Froebel believed that the child secures self-expression and mastery by the use of objects and he organized a series of " gifts " and occupations "which interest and develop the child."

Cygnaeus supplemented the Froebelian materials by giving the older children as well certain kinds of handwork such as joinery, turning, basket making, *etc*. These occupations were designed to train the hand in developing a sense of form, and of aesthetics. The system of Cygnaeus had two fundamental characteristics: (1) it was for primary schools; (2) the occupation taught should not be regarded as preparation for a trade but always as a means towards formal and general education. In 1866, Finland made the system obligatory in all primary and normal schools.

Russia copied and amended this system but did not put it into effect in the primary schools as in Finland, but in the Technical Institutes which admitted only boys of 18 and over. The system was sub-divided and the tools, and the material used in the construction of the article were each studied. There was no intention of giving training for specific industries. The work was designed solely to train the eye and hand, and to develop accuracy.

The Russian educational exhibit at the Centennial Exposition, Philadelphia, in 1876, contained a full account of the methods practised in the Imperial Institute and illustrated the system with sets of models and other materials. This exhibit attracted a great deal of attention and brought the movement into our educational life. The movement was at first called " sloid " (its name in Sweden) but Professor Woodward of St. Louis gave it the name of " manual training " which was generally adopted.

President John D. Runkle of the Massachusetts Institute of Technology was an enthusiastic propagandist of this new movement, and due to his efforts tool instruction was established at M. I. T. in 1877. Due to the work of Professor Woodward, a Manual Training School was started in St. Louis in 1880 and from then on the movement gained ground rapidly.

The adherents of the old cultural education and the supporters of manual training engaged in spirited discussion over the merits of the system. The former claimed that manual training was not educative and that it should not be introduced into the curriculum. The latter argued that education should be for life and that manual education was as truly cultural and preparatory as was literary education itself.

Slowly but surely manual training began to gain ground. The National Education Association became more and more friendly to the idea. Various schools began to introduce it into their curricula and industrial drawing in particular became a common subject in the high school curriculum. New manual training schools sprang up in St. Louis Chicago, Toledo, and Louisville. New Jersey in 1885 encouraged the spread of manual training by offering to duplicate the appropriation of any annual sum from $500 up to $5000 by any locality. In the late eighties, Massachusetts made it obligatory upon every city of 25,000 or over to provide manual training in the high school system.[1]

As manual training developed it grew to have quite different principles from those which the founder Cygnaeus had worked out: (1) as in Russia, it was used chiefly in the high schools and not in the primary, but also (2) it came to have a distinct commercial purpose. It was used in part as a means of training workmen for their industrial life, if not for their specific trade.

Manual training was taught in the high schools in three ways: (a) It was taught as a part of the general curriculum, which all high school students must study. The reluctance of teachers to admit manual training to the high school curriculum and their indifference and hostility towards it after admission made this system difficult of administration. The teachers selected to conduct the manual training courses were not only often out of sympathy with the subject but were in many instances incapable of teaching it. (b) It was taught as a separate course of study in the general high school, parallel to the college preparatory, the English and the business courses. Here greater cohesiveness was given to manual training, and since the department was differentiated from the others, greater specialization could

---

[1] For the early history of manual training in this country, see H. Ross Smith, "Development of Manual Education in the U. S.," *8th Annual Report of Commissioner of Labor*, 1892, pp. 14-79; *Report Commissioner of Education*, 1893-4, vol. i, pp. 877-949; *Report Commissioner of Education*, 1903, vol. i, pp. 1019-1041.

result.   (c) It was taught in an independent high school devoted to manual training alone.   Cultural studies were present in the curriculum but they were subordinated. These independent schools were established because: (1) the traditions of existing high schools were antagonistic to manual training.   (2) Since manual training required a longer school day than ordinary high school work, the manual student would be compelled to stay at school longer than his fellow students in other departments.   This inevitably caused dissatisfaction and made pupils reluctant to enter the manual training department.   In a school within which hours were uniform this difficulty could not arise. (3) A concentration of interest would result from isolating the manual training work.   (4) There would be a concentration of administration and responsibility.   Undoubtedly the main reason was in order to get the schools out of the hands of the educators who disliked practical studies and to get them into the hands of those who were sympathetic to the movement.

This movement of manual training from a study within the high schools to separate schools of its own was not strictly chronological.   Some manual training high schools were started independently at an early date,[1] but the general movement tended to pass through these three stages.   The number of independent manual training high schools increased from 15 in 1894 with 3,300 students to 40 in 1897 with 13,900 students.[2]   This development illustrates the biological principle that function precedes structure.

Manual training thus came to be used to train workmen as well as to give general education.   For a long time, the supporters of manual training protested that this was not

[1] Notably the St. Louis manual training school which was founded in 1879.

[2] *Report Com. of Educ.*, 1906, vol. ii, pp. 1043.

true. Professor Woodward declared in 1890 that " In a manual training school the aim is not the narrow one of learning a trade. Neither is dexterity sought in special operations which may be only small parts of even a trade. The object of every feature is education in a broad and high sense. Its influence is subjective. In the case of tools, intelligent use, rather than dexterity, is aimed at. Some one has suggested that manual culture was a better name than manual training in as much as the manual features take on so clearly the form of culture." [1]

Despite these protestations, however, manual training came to be regarded as a means of industrial training. It was used not to train boys for a specific trade but to give an all-round mechanical education which would greatly increase their industrial efficiency. In 1903, Professor Woodward himself stated " by multiplying manual training schools we solve the problem of training all the mechanics our country needs." [2] This last statement shows how the idea of mechanical education had permeated the system of manual training and had changed the earlier conception of manual training as a cultural subject only.

This development of manual training away from its original purpose was caused by three forces:

1. In the Scandinavian countries woodwork had been the chief form of manual training. When introduced into this country, it was applied to metals as well. Wood lends itself to tool manipulation since the pupil through the use of the tools acquires dexterity and co-ordination of eye and muscle. Steel, however, does not lend itself so

---

[1] Calvin M. Woodward, *Manual Training in Education*, pp. 61-68.

[2] C. M. Woodward, " Manual Industrial and Technical Education in the United States," chap. xix in the *Report of the Commissioner of Education for 1903*, vol. i, p. 1039.

readily to this purpose. Here the machine and not the tool becomes more practicable. With this comes the subordination of the individual. No longer is he the craftsman but he is now merely the unleasher of objective power. Cultural education diminishes while the mastery over machine processes increases. Consequently, vocational education steals in unawares.

2. The creation of the independent manual training high school freed the movement from the cultural spirit. Once independent, the theory that manual training should be merely cultural became weaker and it was but natural that vocational education should make a stronger appeal. When fighting for its life, manual-training adherents could not declare too pronounced views lest the whole movement be swept away.

3. The industrial condition of the time was more fundamental than either of these two factors. Apprenticeship had long since been on the wane. Skilled workmen were needed for the upper grades of machine labor. There was a real dearth of competent foremen and machinists. What was more natural than that the employing class should try to capture the manual training movement and make it an organ which would satisfy their needs for skilled labor? The separation of manual training from the literary education of the day made it possible to take hold of these schools and help dictate their policy. Indeed the business and commercial interests often played the part of educational midwife and assisted at the birth of many of these independent schools and were strong believers in their separation from other high schools. The manual training schools of St. Louis, Chicago, and Cleveland, indeed owed their creation almost entirely to the interest of the business classes.[1]

[1] *Commissioner of Education*, 1893-4, vol. i, pp. 884-885, 889-890 and 893.

Manual training was not, however, confined to the high schools alone. It spread into the elementary grades as well. In 1908 there were 502 cities which gave manual training in the public schools.[1] This form of manual training was really the result of two influences, (a) the spreading downward of manual training from the high schools, (b) the spreading upward from the kindergarten. The vocational features of manual training disappeared in this process and in the elementary grades it was purely cultural.

The total number of students given some form of manual training has steadily increased. This development is best shown by several tables.

We shall first consider the number of separate manual training schools and their total enrollment.

NUMBER OF PUBLIC TRAINING SCHOOLS OF HIGH SCHOOL GRADE [2]

Year	Number	Enrollment
1894	15	3,362
1895	15	4,892
1897	40	13,890
1913	51	50,975

Thus while the number of schools has increased about three-fold the number of students has increased fifteen-fold.

These figures do not measure the total number receiving manual training. In 1913, there were 200 additional manual and industrial training schools with a total attendance of 82,839.[3] Of this number, 52,870 were students of secondary rank receiving instruction in the manual arts. The remainder who received manual training were elementary pupils.

[1] *Report Commissioner of Education*, 1900-09, vol. ii, pp. 1046-49.

[2] *Report Com. of Educ.*, 1906, vol. ii, p. 1050; *Report Com. of Educ.*, 1913, vol. ii, p. 517.

[3] *Report Com. of Educ.*, 1913, vol. ii, p. 552.

Nor is this all. Manual training courses have continued to be given to an increasing degree, in the regular public high schools. In 1913, 1,167 public high schools had 50,543 students in manual training courses.[1]

In 1913, therefore, the following number were receiving some form of manual training in secondary institutions:

Institution	Number	Percentage of Total
1. Public Manual Training High Schools	50,975	33.0
2. Manual and Industrial Training Schools	52,870	34.2
3. Public High Schools	50,453	32.8
Total	154,298	100.0

The relative numerical importance of these schools is therefore equal. The 51 high schools devoted to manual training had as many students in manual training as the 1,167 high schools giving some manual training courses.

The distribution by sex of these students follows·

Institution	Boys	Girls	Total
1. Public Manual Training High Schools	32,134	18,841	50,975
2. Manual and Industrial Training Schools	35,264	17,606	52,870
3. Public High Schools	43,821	6,632	50,443
Total	111,219	43,079	154,298
Percentage	72.1	27.9	100.0

Nearly three-quarters of the students of manual training are therefore boys.

Manual training is especially strong in the North Atlantic States. The following table shows this most clearly:

	Number of Schools in North Atlantic States	% of Total Number	Number of Pupils in North Atlantic States	% of Total Number
1. Public Manual Training High Schools	18	35.3	24,215	47.5
2. Manual and Industrial Training Schools	92	46.0	53,805	68.4

[1] *Report Com. of Educ.*, 1913, vol. ii, pp. 498-516.

Nearly one-half the students in the specialized manual training high schools and over two-thirds of the students in
manual and industrial schools are residents of the North
Atlantic States. They are indeed residents of a specialized
section of the North Atlantic States. Since the upper tier
of the New England States had no special schools for
manual training, all the students in this group came
from Massachusetts, Rhode Island, New York, New
Jersey and Pennsylvania.

Manual training has not proved a solution of the problem
of industrial education nor can it. We have seen that the
vocational purpose was an afterthought, grafted upon an
educational system originally designed as purely cultural.
Manual training courses in public high schools have been
too often farcical as regards adequate preparation for industry. Only a few hours a week are devoted to them; the
equipment is scanty; the teachers are ill-trained. Work is
generally confined to carpentry, cabinet making, and woodwork in general. Little or no attention is paid to other
branches of industry. Moreover, the work is done on a
handicraft rather than upon a machine basis. A great deal
of care is lavished upon the production of one article and
the fact that the machine industry demands quantitative
rather than qualitative production is neglected.

Nor have the specialized manual-training high schools
been more successful. Here facilities are better but still
inadequate. In 1912 the expenditure per student in these
schools for tools was only approximately $2.00 for the year
and a similar amount for materials. Certainly not much
trade knowledge could be acquired with such equipment. As
Dr. David Snedden says, "the spirit of approach has been
that of the amateur or dilettante rather than of the person
interested in obtaining vocational fitness." [1]

[1] David Snedden, *The Problem of Vocational Education*, p. 43.

Manual training has been ineffective, moreover, because it has not reached the class who most need industrial education. Since it has been practically confined to the high schools, the children of the poorer class have been debarred from whatever benefits it may possess. It is in the main only the soft-handed class that can afford to keep their children in school for the entire high school course. The high school pupils who do study manual training are, consequently, being prepared for occupations they will never enter.

The following statistics covering the life occupations of graduates of five large manual-training high schools in Philadelphia, St. Louis, Boston and Cambridge show how useless training has been as a means of providing skilled workers for the trades.[1]

Occupations	Number	Occupations	Number
Students	287	Artists and Engravers	32
Clerks	282	Railroad men	22
Draftsmen	215	Bookkeepers	20
Superintendents, m a n a g e r s, foremen	198	Dentists	13
		Surveyors	13
Merchants and M a n u f a c - turers	160	Inspectors	12
		Newspaper Men	12
Civil Engineers	115	Designers	12
Salesmen	95	Insurance Agents	8
Electrical Work	91	Contractors	5
Teachers	79	Plumbers	5
Lawyers	63	Druggists	4
Physicians	58	Opticians	4
Architects	53	Carpenters	4
Machinists	52	Clergymen	3
Electrical Engineers	48	Pattern-makers	3
Mechanical Engineers	36	Unclassified a n d w i t h o u t occupation	400
Chemists	33		
		Total	2437

[1] *Report Mass. Commission on Industrial and Technical Education,* 1906, p. 196.

Thus, only 168 or 6.9% of the total number of graduates went into mechanical work. The electrical and mechanical engineers, the machinists, railroad men, plumbers and carpenters were alone in going into occupations for which their manual training was designed to prepare. In spite of all the courses given in wood-working, only four, or two-tenths of one percent, became carpenters.

As a system of vocational education manual training has therefore been a failure. It has lately been found that it may have great value as a part of a system of prevocational education whereby the pupil may become better acquainted with his aptitudes and better able to make a rational choice of occupation. Under this plan, manual training ceases to be chiefly a high school study but becomes an integral part of the curriculum in the grades.[1]

[1] See Leavitt and Brown, *Pre-vocational Education in the Public Schools*, pp. 20-24.

CHAPTER VIII

TRADE AND INDUSTRIAL SCHOOLS

TRADE schools may be divided into two classes: (1) Public and eleemosynary trade schools. (2) Commercially conducted trade schools.

Trade schools aim to prepare for specialized trades. Unlike manual training schools, they are definitely vocational in purpose; cultural training is negligible and attention is concentrated upon the specific trade for which the pupil is being prepared. They are designed as a substitute for apprenticeship,[1] are generally open only to boys and girls over 16 years of age, and are based upon the theory that industrial training is better given in the school than in the shop.

The trade-school movement for manual training and has passed through two stages: (a) Private trade schools, (b) Public trade schools.

The New York Trade School, founded by Col. Richard T. Auchmuty in 1881, was the first of its kind in America. Courses were given in brick-laying, plastering, plumbing, carpentry, house, sign and fresco painting, stone-cutting, blacksmithing, tailoring, and printing. The bricklaying and tailoring trades were especially well taught.[2]

The Williamson Free School of Mechanical Trades in

[1] See *17th Annual Report of the Comm. of Labor*, 1902, p. 10. "Training in trade schools is intended to supply the place of the old-time apprenticeship which has nearly disappeared under the conditions of present day industry."

[2] For a description of these courses see *8th Annual Report, U. S. Comm. of Labor*, 1892, pp. 80-83.

Delaware County, Pennsylvania, was founded in 1888 and opened in 1891. The founder declared that the abandonment of the apprenticeship system and the failure of the public school system to devise a substitute necessitated the institution of a school that would train poor and deserving boys for the mechanical trades. The benefits of the school including board, instruction and clothing for the entire course were made absolutely free for all students. This necessitates a thorough winnowing of the candidates for admission, in order to obtain the most worthy. The pupils are formally apprenticed to the Board of Trustees for the period they are in the school.

The following trades were taught in 1910: bricklaying, carpentry, stationary engineering, machinists, pattern-making. The graduates of this school during the years 1905-1909 totaled 268, of whom 91% were actually engaged in the mechanical trades.

The Baron de Hirsch Trade School was founded in 1891 from the endowment of the Baron de Hirsch Fund. Candidates for admission must be Jews and must be at least 16 years of age. Among the trades taught are those of the machinists trade, plumbing, electrical work, carpentry, and house, fresco and sign painting. The school work here is not designed as a complete substitute for apprenticeship but is rather intended as a partial preparation for the trades.

Other private schools founded before 1900 were, (a) The California School of Mechanical Arts in 1895. This gives training in the pattern-making, forging, and machinists trades. (b) The Wilmerding School of Industrial Arts. This was founded "to teach boys trades, fitting them to make a living with their hands, with little study and plenty of work." This school is closely affiliated with the California School. Work is given in carpentry, brick-laying, plumbing, tinning, the electrical trades and cabinet making.

(c) The trade school department of Pratt Institute, Brooklyn, N. Y. This gives trade instruction in several branches, notably carpentry, plumbing, pattern-making, and machine practice and tool-making. (d) The Miller School of Albemarle, Virginia. This gives trade instruction in the later years of a general educational course.

Private schools started after 1900 include the Manual Training and Industrial School of New London, Conn., in 1903;[1] the Winona Technical Institute of Indianapolis, Indiana, in 1904; the Milwaukee School of Trades in 1906; and the David Ranken School of Mechanical Trades in St. Louis, Mo., in 1909.

All of these schools have been established by private endowment and are outside the public school system. Emphasis was completely placed on the vocational aspect and general education was in the main neglected.

In 1906 the era of publicly administered trade schools began.[2] In this year the Philadelphia Board of Education established a public day trade school to be supported entirely from the public funds. In 1907 the Milwaukee School of Trades was taken into the public school system of Milwaukee. The Columbus, Ohio, Trades School was started in 1909 and trade instruction was given in printing and wood-working. In 1909, Buffalo, New York, instituted a public trade school, followed by Yonkers in 1910. Connecticut in 1909 established at Bridgeport and New Britain two state-supported all-day trade schools. The Portland, Oregon, School of Trades was established in this period under the direction of the school board.

[1] This school was aided financially by the city but not controlled by it.

[2] The Newark Technical School was opened as early as 1885 under state administration and gave some trade courses. It was however so isolated and had so many other purposes in addition that it cannot be said to have initiated the movement.

In recent years Massachusetts has established a number of public trade schools. In 1914, there were in that state nine trade schools for boys and three for girls.[1] In that year, 772 girls were being trained for the trades of dress-making, millinery, power-machine operating, cutting and fitting, and cookery and sewing. In the same year, 1667 boys were being prepared for machine woodwork, cabinet making, carpentry, machine-shop work, printing, sheetmetal work, automobile manufacture, electrical work, pattern-making, and power plant engineering.[2]

This development of public trade schools creates certain essential differences. In the first place, more subjects of general educational value are introduced into the curriculum than was the case with private trade schols. English, civics, industrial history, geography, industrial hygiene, *etc.*, are generally found in public trade schools while they were largely non-existent in private. Another difference is that the public trade schools do not uniformly place the minimum age of entrance at 16 as do the private schools.[3]

Just as in a previous period, manual training had been expected to solve the problem of industrial education, so in the decade 1900-1910, trade schools were thought to constitute the solution. The Annual Report of the Commissioner of Labor in 1902 praised the independent trade school and treated the problem as well on the way to solution.[4] The

[1] *Bulletin No. 5*, Mass. Board of Education 1914, "Massachusetts Independent Vocational Schools," p. 7.

[2] *Ibid.*, pp. 17-39.

[3] For a description of these various schools see the *25th Annual Report of the Commissioner of Labor*, 1910, pp. 41-141. Also C. R. Richards, "Some Notes on the History of Industrial Education in the U. S." In the *Proceedings of the National Educational Assoc. for 1910*, pp. 678-79.

[4] *17th Annual Report Commission of Labor*, 1902, pp. 10-12.

Massachusetts Commission on Vocational Education, appointed by Governor Douglas in 1906, in its report envisaged the trade school as the core of any adequate system of industrial education. Arthur D. Dean in his book on *The Worker and the State,* a brilliant argument for industrial education, published in 1910, advocated trade schools as the fundamental basis of industrial education. Mr. Dean declared that " the next step in education is clearly in the direction of building up a great system of public trade schools." [1]

This belief in the efficacy of trade-school education was increased by the reports of certain educational " experts " about the hundreds of successful trade schools in Germany. Continental experience was appealed to in support of the system of training craftsmen in all-day trade schools. Unfortunately, however, these " experts" had misunderstood the real nature of the German trade schools and had taken them to be identical with those of the United States.

When Dr. George Kirchensteiner, the celebrated Munich educator came to this country in 1910-1911, the fallacy of this comparison was shown. Dr. Kirchensteiner said, " If I seek to compare German Trade Schools I find that our higher trade schools most resemble your technical colleges. Only we must not forget that there is no transition contemplated from our higher trade schools to our technical universities and that one or two years practical work must be presented or taken in special preparatory courses before admittance to the school.

" *Our numerous lower trade schools have no counterpart in the United States...The trade schools of the United States are generally intended to take the place of apprenticeship. The German trade schools on the other hand are*

[1] Arthur D. Dean, *The Worker and the State,* p. 159.

*intended, with few exceptions, to make up for the deficien-
cies of apprenticeship.*" [1]

Only those who had had at least four years practical
work were admitted to these German schools. Consequently only thoroughly trained workmen were received in
them.[2]   The difference between this system and the American trades schools is thus clearly evident. Our trades
schools were designed to give trade instruction in the schools
and prepare men for the industries directly.   German trade
schools were designed merely to supplement the actual training previously given by the industry itself.   Therefore,
while our trade schools were a substitute for apprenticeship,
German schools were a supplement to it.

A further quotation from Dr. Kirchensteiner brings this
point out more clearly : " Schools that replace apprenticeship
are rare in Germany.   In Austria and Switzerland schools
of this kind have existed for the last twenty years, but during these twenty years they have remained at a standstill.
Nor can I discover any strong inclination in these three
countries to spend public money on such schools." [3]   Other
studies of the German system of industrial education only
confirm Dr. Kirchensteiner's statements.[4]

When one examines the situation, the relatively small
number of trade schools that have come into being since
1881 is especially striking.   Several philanthropic men have
endowed such trade schools and the public has started several
more, but the total number is relatively insignificant.   In

---

[1] Dr. George Kirchensteiner, *Three Lectures on Vocational Training*,
pp. 47-48. The italics are mine.

[2] *Ibid.*, p. 32.

[3] *Ibid.*, p. 47.

[4] See Holmes Beckwith, " German Industrial Education and its Lessons
for the United States," *Bull. No. 19 U. S. Bureau of Education*, 1913,
pp. 49-131 ; George E. Myers, " Problems of Vocational Education in
Germany," *Bull. No. 33, U. S. Bureau of Education*, 1915, pp. 7-35.

1911, after thirty years of agitation and example, there were not more than fifteen such schools and today there are probably few over twenty, while the number of graduates turned out is almost negligible in comparison with our industrial population.

California for example has two splendid trade schools yet these are woefully inadequate in supplying her with journeymen. The California Bureau of Labor Statistics declared in 1904 that " The number of journeymen in California engaged in the occupations covered by the curriculum of the Lick and Wilmerding schools is approximately 30,290. The average number of students graduating yearly from these schools is about 30 or approximately one to every thousand journeymen." [1] In 1912, Mr. H. E. Miles stated that the total regular students in all the trades schools in the country were fewer than 2,000 and that the number graduated by these schools was approximately 700 a year.[2]

The number today is undoubtedly somewhat greater. The Massachusetts trades schools alone have 2,400 pupils. Since the twelve Massachusetts schools comprise approximately one-half of the total number of trade schools, and since most of the other schools have about the same attendance as the Massachusetts schools it is safe to conclude that there are today not far from 5,000 students in the public and private trade schools of the country.

Such a number is plainly inadequate for a system that was designed to take the place of apprenticeship. Moreover, the number of trade schools is not increasing and shows no signs of growth. Although they have had nearly thirty years time, they have failed to perform their mission. The reasons why they have failed in the past are furthermore reasons why they must fail in the future.

[1] *Report of the California Bureau of Labor Statistics,* 1904, p. 29.
[2] H. E. Miles, *Proceedings National Educ. Assoc.,* 1913, p. 963.

(1) The first great reason for their failure is the heavy expense. The cost to the individuals who attend these schools is heavy. An all-day trade school necessarily keeps the boy and girl from work and they must consequently sacrifice the wage they otherwise could earn. Since the school commonly admits only those over 16 years of age, this potential wage is of considerable amount. If we compute the average weekly wage as $8.00, the yearly earnings would be $416, minus time lost through unemployment. It is a real sacrifice for most working-class families to forego these earnings and we cannot expect many boys to give up this money in order to continue in school.

The cost, however, is heavy not only for the pupils and for their families but also for society itself. A trade school necessitates a somewhat expensive building, elaborate technical equipment and costly materials upon which the student must practice. In order to give efficient training, it must make itself into something like a shop, and this cannot be done cheaply. The actual cost per pupil is a difficult matter to ascertain and the statistics are not available to give an exact statement, but some incidental figures illustrate the point. The yearly expense per student in the Williamson School of Mechanical Trades, for instance, is over $300.00, while in the David Ranken school the yearly cost is $228.00 per capita.[1] According to the supervisor of industrial education in Milwaukee, Wisconsin, the cost per student in the Public Trade School of that city is approximately $250.00 a year.[2] Mr. Miles' statement that the yearly cost of instruction per pupil ranges between $200.00

[1] *Report of Canadian Royal Comm. on Indus. Training and Technical Education*, pt. iii, vol. ii, p. 1414.

[2] D. F. Perry in the *Eleventh Year Book of the National Society for the Study of Education*, 1912, p. 83.

and $300.00 seems, therefore, to be a fair and conservative estimate.[1]

Many of the trade schools have tried to reduce the expense by economizing on the use of materials and tools. This economy necessarily has lowered the quality of training given since a good school cannot have poor equipment. If trade training in the schools is desired, the community must pay the cost.

(2) The trade schools, moreover, have failed of their purpose not only because of the expense to those trained and to the state, but also because the school cannot, in the very nature of things, adequately prepare a boy to enter industry as a skilled worker. The trade school cannot be a substitute for apprenticeship, because the school cannot take the place of the shop. The shop is essentially dynamic; goods are being made and sold and the test of efficiency is applied to action. The school is essentially static, there is an inevitable air of business unreality about the work carried on. Try as teachers or students may, the feeling that they are playing at work rather than working is almost unescapable.

To avoid this, many trade schools have adopted the policy of disposing of their product commercially. It is believed by many that production for sale will cause greater efficiency and an approach to actual shop conditions. It is urged, moreover, that the sale of the product will lessen the net expense of the school.

Among the schools that have consistently followed out this policy are the Manhattan Trade School for girls in New York,[2] the Milwaukee Trades School,[3] and the

[1] H. E. Miles, *Proceedings of First Annual Convention of the National Association of Corporation Schools*, p. 275.

[2] See Violet Coen, "Shop Methods and the Utilization of Product," *Proceedings of the Ninth Annual Convention of the National Soc. Promot. Indust. Educ.*, pp. 215-219.

[3] Charles F. Perry in the *Eleventh Year Book of the Nat. Soc. for the Study of Education*, p. 85.

Bridgeport Trades School. Schools that do not market their product include the Williamson School of Mechanical Trades, the David Ranken School, the New York Trade School, and the Baron de Hirsch Trade School.

Some of the objections to the selling of the product are speedily disposed of. One objection is that since no wages are paid, the school product can and will undersell products competitively produced, and that workers and enterprizers will consequently be forced out of business. The sale of school-made goods does present, though in a much lesser degree, the same danger as the sale of prison-made goods. It can however easily be met. Selling only at market price as is done in Milwaukee is one solution, while still better is that of city or state use of the products so manufactured. Either of these methods prevents the market from being swamped with the products of " cheap labor."

(3) There are other objections, however, which are more weighty. Commercial products manufactured in the school are of two kinds: (1) articles made up in logical sequence during the course in trade experience and afterwards sold; (2) orders received from customers, which are filled regardless as to whether or not they fit into the course of study prescribed. The difference between these two plans largely consists in that the former makes the commercial disposal of the product merely an incident and does not allow it to interfere with the prescribed course of study, while the latter lays greater stress upon the marketing of the product and makes the course of study dependent upon the orders received. The first plan presents few dangers, the latter many.

Under the latter plan, the school virtually imitates the shop. Production for sale tends to become the predominant purpose. The director becomes anxious to make profits and to turn out marketable products which meet the favor of the trade. In so doing the original purpose of trade schools tends to be neglected. The production of goods rather than the production of skilled artisans is emphasized. The changing of boys about from one kind of work to another is inimical to production for profit and the result is that they are often confined to one or a few lines of work. This is financially profitable for the school but not educationally profitable for the boy. A boy must be taught all varieties of work before he can master a trade. Such teaching is, however, as we have seen, costly, and the temptation to confine him to one job is great, but wherever he is so confined, he is being treated as a worker not as a student.

" Rush orders " present somewhat similar dangers. The continuity of work is broken and the student's attention is concentrated upon the production of an article which is not pedagogically connected with the work he has previously been doing. Furthermore, the speed with which the work must be done is apt to be injurious to the skill of the student.

The dangers of this kind of commercial production are great. They may be avoided by alert and determined directors,[1] but they are always a menace. It is difficult if not impossible for a trade school to seek both profit and trade training.[2] If it holds to the first, it must neglect the second. The primary purpose of a trade school is not to turn out commercial material but to teach trades.

Nor does the sale of the product materially diminish the expense. The Milwaukee trade school sells its product

[1] See E. E. McNary, " If Commercial Articles are Produced How Should the Educational Value of the Training be Safe-guarded," *Proceedings Eighth Annual Convention of the Nat. Soc. for Promot. of Industrial Education*, pp. 149-152.

[2] See Lewis Gustafson, " Longer Course Schools for Training Superior Workmen," *Proceedings of the Eighth Annual Convention Nat. Soc. Promot. Industrial Education*, pp. 190-192.

yet its annual expense per student is approximately $250.00.[1]
Thus in trying to avoid the unreality of the school training
by selling the product, new dangers are created.

(4) There are other factors however which inevitably
make the school an inadequate place to teach a trade.   Even
though the product be commercially sold, the elimination of
waste is rarely carried to the degree that it is in the shop
itself.   Moreover usually only simple trades can be taught
as the appliances necessary to teach a complicated trade are
so costly as to make them prohibitive. Most schools for
boys confine themselves mainly to the building, and the
machinists trades; and for girls to the dressmaking and
millinery trades.   The trades schools have therefore not
touched the problems of other trades outside of these few.
The expense of equipment is such that it inevitably confines
their activities to certain narrow limits.

(5) Another obstacle exists even in those trades wherein
training is given, namely that of keeping the school equipment up to date.   Modern competitive industry scraps its
machines quickly.   It discards them if better ones are invented.   A school finds it impossible to keep pace.   In
consequence it is common for the trade school to be teaching
trades to boys with obsolete equipment.   Such students will
not be able to practice their trades efficiently when they enter
industrial life as it is.

One justification for trades schools often urged is that they
can prepare for specific local trades.   There is, of course,
a great deal of geographical specialization in the United
States.   Thus, the shoe industry is concentrated in the cities
of Haverhill, Lynn and Brockton, Massachusetts; shoe
machinery construction in Beverly, Massachusetts; glove
making in Gloversville and Johnstown, New York; the silk
industry in Paterson, New Jersey, and the coal towns of

[1] C. F. Perry, *op. cit.*, p. 80.

Pennsylvania; automobiles in Detroit and Flint, Michigan, and in Indianapolis, Indiana; furniture in Grand Rapids, Michigan; collars and shirts in Troy, New York; cheap jewelry in Attleboro, Massachusetts; locomotives in Philadelphia, Pennsylvania, and Schenectedy, New York; ready-made clothing in New York City, Chicago, and Rochester; and talking machines in Camden, New Jersey.

What is more natural, it is claimed, than that each of these towns should start a trade school to prepare for their local industry. This belief, however, rests in part on the assumption that the young men will continue to stay in the same city where they were educated. There is, however, no such permanence in American industrial life, since American workers change their residence quite frequently. The Russell Sage Foundation found that only 16% of over 22,000 men investigated in 78 different cities, and that only one-quarter of the American born, were then living in the same city in which they were born. A trade school preparing boys for local trades would not then be primarily preparing them for their life-career. The boys and girls should not be trained in an industry which few of them will later enter. If any trade training is given it should be in industries which are nationwide not local.[1]

Because of these inherent defects, not only are trades schools not increasing in number but those that do exist are finding their greatest development in other than their original purpose. The David Ranken School in St. Louis is giving special attention to apprentices who are learning the trades in the shop. Apprentices in the plastering and sheet-metal trades are given supplementary instruction in the David Ranken School.[2] This trade school has there-

---

[1] L. P. Ayres, *Some Conditions affecting Problems of Industrial Education in Seventy-eight American School Systems*, p. 7.

[2] Lewis Gustafson, "The Recognition of Industrial Education in Apprentices by Organized Labor," *Proceedings of the Eighth Annual Conv. Nat. Soc. Prom. Industrial Education*, pp. 134-43.

fore changed from the original purpose of replacing apprenticeship to supplementing it.[1]

2. *Commercially Conducted Trade Schools.*

Public and elementary trade schools form but a small percentage of the total number of trade schools. Trade schools that are conducted for profit form the vast majority. This type of trade school followed in the wake of the private business schools. It differs from the latter in that it teaches occupations other than the purely commercial ones of stenography, typewriting and bookkeeping.

No one can estimate how many such schools there are. They are not subject to inspection and in consequence official statistics are almost wholly lacking. They are found in the out-of-the-way corners of cities, and are often unknown by the community about them. Many of them evanescent, some are going out of business and others entering.

Some investigations, however, show how numerous they are. In 1915 there were in Chicago alone, 46 commercially conducted trades schools. Nine of these were automobile schools; six taught dressmaking and design; four millinery; three motion-picture operating; two barbering; and two comptometer operating.[2] In Minneapolis, Minnesota, there were in 1916, 14 such private schools with an annual attendance of approximately 2000.[3] The trades taught included telegraphy, tractor operating, window-dressing, barbering, automobile driving, pharmacy, "beauty culture," dress-making, and sewing. The total income of twelve of these schools

[1] Lewis Gustafson, " Experts cannot be trained in school alone. Experts must come from a combination of school and trade experience," *ibid.*, p. 192.

[2] Caroline Bengsten, " Private Trade Schools in Chicago," *Manual Training and Vocational Education*, vol. xvii, pp. 497-510, March, 1916.

[3] " Report of the Minneapolis Survey for Vocational Education," *Bull. 21, Nat. Soc. Promot. Indust. Educ.*, see chart p. 122.

was over $84,000 per year. The tuition fee ranged from $20 to $100 but averaged about $50.[1]

Such figures indicate what a vast number of these trade schools already exist in the country as a whole. 2000 would probably be a conservative estimate of their number.

Though some of these schools are highly efficient, many are exceedingly poor. On the whole they are wasteful and inadequate and do not teach the trade properly. Much of their expense is competitive. In order to attract students and to enroll them, advertising and "baits" are necessary. Advertisements in the daily papers, circulars, commissions for securing students, discounts for cash payments of tuition and promises to secure positions for graduates are common practices.[2] A large part of the tuiton fee is thus devoted to these competitive expenditures instead of being devoted to trade training itself. Practically all these expenses would disappear in a well articulated public system where competition for students was not necessary for existence.

The equipment of the trade school is such moreover that in most cases it cannot give adequate instruction. Thus, the equipment of one school in Minneapolis teaching tractor operating was absolutely worthless, while two dress-making schools had only about $100 worth of equipment apiece. Many of the Chicago schools had no facilities for teaching the trades they pretended to teach. Even the best schools cannot afford the costly apparatus necessary to instruct students. Even in the best of schools, the instruction given is intensely specialized. Trade training and nothing else is given while civics, economics and English are eliminated.

Such a system suffers from all the evils of profiteering. The aim of the proprietors is primarily that of immediate

[1] The capital equipment of these schools was estimated at about $50,000 and the number of instructors totaled 75.

[2] Caroline Bengsten, *op. cit.*

profits, not that of thorough training. If the student has more money, he is generally urged to take an additional course to perfect himself in the details of the trade. If his money is exhausted, he is hurried out. The inevitable tendency is to shorten the course so that a fresh batch of students may be secured. Thus, schools for barbers " teach " the trade in six weeks, automobile schools in two months but the graduates of such schools are only " quarter-baked " workmen.

Vicious as most of these private schools are they have arisen because of a real need. The breakdown of apprenticeship threw the burden of training the upper class of workers upon other agencies. The public school system, swayed as it was by tradition, responded so slowly that it did not meet the need of the age. Individuals were quick to see the opportunity and to bend it to their advantage. They started schools as business undertakings to supply these workmen. They were far from ideal but they bridged the gap. They did it expensively and wastefully, they gave insufficient preparation but they did give some trade training, even though slight. They cannot, however, be a permanent solution.

There is however another grave defect in addition to those already mentioned. The tuition fee of $50 or over is sufficient to bar out the largest section of our working population. Therefore, if private trade schools were to be relied on, we would be perpetuating a caste organization of industrial society and would prevent children of the lower strata from rising in the industrial scale.

3. Technical High Schools.

These schools differ from trade schools proper in the following ways: (1) They educate their pupils for different ranks in industry. Whereas trade schools were designed to turn out ordinary skilled workmen, technical high schools aim to train for positions above this lower level. Their industrial purpose is therefore to provide the non-commissioned officers of industry and not, like the trade schools, to be a mere substitute for apprenticeship. Because of this difference the curriculum of the technical high schools is not as narrow as that of the trade schools. Subjects of more general interest, such as history, economics, and English are treated and mathematics forms an important part of the curriculum.

(2) Technical high schools admit students at a different age than do trade schools. Almost uniformly trade schools fix the age of entrance at 16. Since technical high schools are an integral part of a city's public school system, they must take the graduates from the grammar grades without regard to age.

It is sometimes said that the purpose of the technical high school should be to prepare students for colleges of engineering. This duty however can be performed equally well by the ordinary high school. Others declare it should give general education with some practical work, but this function in turn is performed at present by the manual training high schools. Neither of these purposes would justify the existence of separate technical high schools. As Mr. Bogan says training for some form of industrial leadership should be the dominating purpose of the technical high school.[1]

Several cities have adopted these specialized high schools as a part of the public school system. Notable among such schools are the Lane Technical School and the Harrison Technical School of Chicago, the Stuyvesant High School of New York City, the East and West Technical High

---

[1] William J. Bogan, "What is the True Place and Purpose of the Technical High School in the American Public School System?" *Proceedings Sixth Convention, National Society Promot. Industrial Education*, p. 188.

Schools of Cleveland, Ohio, and the Cass Technical High School of Detroit, Michigan. These schools do not confine themselves to one particular trade but instead teach several.[1]

Since trade preparation, not college preparation, is their chief purpose, two and three year courses are offered as well as the customary four year course.

These schools have undoubtedly retained many children in school who otherwise would have left. The population of Cleveland, Ohio during the decade of 1900-1910, increased by above 18,000 people annually. Nevertheless during the years 1906-8 the High School enrollment did not increase, being 4,873 in 1906 and 4879 in 1908. Three vocational high schools were instituted from 1908 to 1912. One of these was a commercial high school, while the other two were technical high schools. The enrollment in the Cleveland High Schools in 1912 was 7,800 or a gain of nearly 3,000 pupils in four years. This increase had indeed almost entirely taken place in the vocational schools. The technical schools gained 17% in the year 1911-1912 while the academic high schools gained only 6%.[2]

The technical high school cannot, however, give advanced work adequately because it cannot successfully imitate shop conditions. The difficulty of getting the students to treat production seriously, the attendant waste of materials, the lack of speed and the minimization of quantitative production all hamper the work.

Such schools moreover encounter the same economic difficulties that the trades schools experience. The education

[1] See an article by James F. Barker, "The Separate Technical High School," *Eleventh Year Book of the National Society for the Study of Education*, pp. 49-67.

[2] James F. Barker, "The Place and Purpose of the Technical High School," *Proceedings of Sixth Convention National Society Promotion Industrial Education*, pp. 195-6.

is too costly and the poorer pupils cannot afford the time required.   Mr. H. E. Miles estimates that the cost per student year in the Stuyvesant High School of New York City and the Cass Trade High of Detroit Michigan to be $100.[1]   This type of school, furthermore, does not touch the children who because of poverty must leave school at 14.   It must recruit its members almost entirely from the upper grades of labor and not from the lower grades.   Like the trade schools it does not afford a ladder by which men may climb from the unskilled to the skilled labor group

4. Trade Preparatory Schools.

These schools are for the 14-16 year old boy and girl. Unlike the trade school they admit younger pupils and are not designed as substitutes for apprenticeship.   They do not aim to turn out highly skilled workmen but rather to give a general preparatory training which will afford a basis for later specialization.

There are hundreds of specialized trades in the United States which if taught in the schools would necessitate minute specialization of the school and the creation of an elaborate and complicated system.   Many groups of trades are however similar in materials used, tools employed and in the nature of the final product.   Education in the principles common to a group of these trades can be given to the 14-16 year old child and afterwards he can choose a particular trade and specialize in it.   Such groups of trades having basic similarities are: [2]

---

[1] H. E. Miles, *Proceedings First Annual Convention National Association Corporation Schools*, p. 274.   This includes an allowance for interest upon the cost of the school plant.

[2] I am largely indebted to the admirable classification of the sub-committee of the National Education Association on intermediate industrial schools. See *Proceedings of the 1910 Convention, National Education Association*, pp. 715-719.

(1) Woodworking callings: this includes carpenters, cabinet making, coopers, and saw-mill workers. Many of the subdivisions are exceedingly specialized but they have many common tools and they work upon the same material.

(2) Iron and Steel trades: this includes blacksmiths, iron and steel workers (in mills) machinists, plumbers and gas fitters.

(3) Book-binding and pasting trades: among there are, bookbinders, box makers, and paper makers.

(4) Printers Trades: Though there are many specialized trades yet there are principles common to all.

(5) Leather trades: including, boot and shoe makers, harness and saddlery makers, tanners and trunk makers.

(6) Textile mills, cotton, hosiery, silk and woolen mills. The problem here is more difficult since many of the processes are dissimilar.

(7) Clothing trades: including dressmaking, millinery, seamstress work, tailoring, shirt and collar making, *etc.* All these trades involve sewing. If machine work is used, many of the machines and processes are almost identical.

(8) Stone work industries: This includes masons, roofers, and slaters, marble and stone cutters, *etc.*

(9) Interior work, building trades: Among these, painters, paper hangers, and plasterers. There are many common trade problems in the occupations of this group.

(10) Food industries: This includes butchers, bakers, candy makers.

(11) Tobacco trades: including cigar, plug and cut tobacco, and cigarette making. All these deal with the same material and educational material common to all could be worked out.

(12) Miners and quarrymen.

These groups afford an idea of the field which is open to

the trade preparatory schools. Several such schools have been instituted. Among these are the Industrial School of Columbus, Georgia,[1] the Intermediate Industrial School of Albany, New York; the Rochester Factory Schools, and the New Bedford, Massachusetts, Industrial Schools. In these schools such subjects as industrial history, mathematics, drawing, geography, and other cultural material are given in addition to the general trade preparatory work.

Such schools are performing a very valuable function in giving this generalized training as a basis for later work. The principle is pedagogically sound. It does not try to give a training which it is incompetent to offer from the inherent ineffectiveness of the trade school proper.

Nevertheless under our present system it fails of effectiveness because it cannot teach the class for which it is intended. The families of many 15-16 year old children cannot afford to keep them in school without financial aid. Therefore, they cannot benefit by this training and are debarred because of their economic situation.

5. Industrial Schools.

This term is commonly used in two senses, (a) to designate a school giving instruction in several trades forming an industry, (b) to designate a school for those who are regarded as mentally, morally, socially or economically inferior. It differs from a trade school in that it gives instruction in several trades rather than in one. It is similar to manual training schools in that a manual training school which specialized in wood working might be called an industrial school because of its preparation for this specific industry. On the other hand industrial schools often give such general industrial training that they might well be listed as virtually manual training schools.

[1] See *Bulletin Number 25, 1913, United States Bureau of Education*, "Industrial Education in Columbus, Georgia," pp. 12-30.

These similarities, however, should not obscure the difference between industrial and manual training schools. An industrial school gives much more concrete training and its work is intensive rather than extensive.   It aims to turn out a man who is a master of a particular industry instead of one with merely general information about several.

The term "industrial school" connotes furthermore a school giving vocational education to the dependent, defective and criminal classes.   The Elmira Reformatory began trade instruction in 1886.   It was intended to teach every corrigible prisoner some trade before he was released.   By 1892, 32 distinct trades were being taught to over a thousand youths and men.[1]   Industrial training has been since introduced into many prisons; notably in the Michigan State Prison.

The rapid progress of vocational education in reform institutions is indicated by the fact that in 1913, only 22 out of 106 retained the word "reform" or reformatory in their title and that nearly all the remainder declared that they were "industrial schools."   In practically all of these institutions children are received because of legal commitment, not on account of criminal acts committed by them, but to rescue them from criminal surroundings and from homes where they were ill treated or suffered because of economic dependence.[2]   In 1913, 35,575, of the 50,812 inmates were being taught some trade or occupation.[3]

Industrial training is given also to the deaf and blind.   In 1913, 70% of the 5,000 blind in public institutions were receiving instruction in the industrial departments;[4]   while

[1] For an account of the Elmira system see *Eighth Annual Report of the Commissioner of Labor,* 1892, pp. 623-650.

[2] See *Report Commissioner of Education,* 1913, vol. ii, p. 623.

[3] *Ibid.,* pp. 624-628.

[4] *Ibid.,* pp. 646-648.

6,800 or 62% of the 11,000 pupils in State schools for the deaf, were being taught some industrial occupation.[1]

Many of the feeble-minded in public institutions are also being taught trades. Approximately 6,500 of the 25,000 inmates were taught some industrial occupation in 1913.[2]

Industrial schools are the predominant type of higher educational institution for the negroes and Indians. 88 of the 214 schools for negroes specifically state in their title that their primary purpose is industrial, and nearly all of these 88 call themselves "industrial schools." Of the 68,000 enrolled in secondary and higher schools for the negroes, 31,000 received industrial training. Some of the Negro schools, notably Hampton and Tuskeegee, have attained a very high level of efficiency. Many of the most influential Negroes are advocating that higher education for their race be chiefly confined to vocational training, rather than to cultural training.[3]

The education which the government has provided for the Indian is almost wholly vocational in character. Institutions such as the Haskell Institute of Lawrence, Kansas, and the Carlisle Indian School, are primarily nothing but advanced and thorough industrial schools. There are 73 industrial training schools for Indians. 13,000 or 88% of the 15,400 students in these schools received industrial instruction.[4]

The somewhat contemptuous attitude which educators and the public have adopted towards vocational education

[1] *Report Commissioner of Education*, 1913, vol. iii, pp. 655-657.

[2] *Ibid.*, pp. 671-672.

[3] The late Booker T. Washington and his successor Col. Moten have been the chief supporters of this idea. W. E. B. DuBois, the negro educator and the editor of *The Crisis*, opposes this view and lays greater stress upon so-called "cultural education." The vocational theory however seems to be winning more adherents.

[4] *Report Commissioner of Education*, 1913, vol. ii, p. 526.

is evidenced by the preceding statements. Vocational education was thought to be necessary for criminals, wayward youths, and defectives. It was also adopted as the basic element in the instruction of the two races that are regarded as socially inferior; the Negro and the Indian. For all these elements in our population, vocational education was encouraged.

For the normal child of the white race, vocational education was however discouraged. No better illustration of the leisure class ideals which have permeated our educational system could be given. Our educators have implicitly reasoned as follows: " Manual work is debasing and slavish. Intellectual pursuits are ennobling. Therefore, only the notably inferior classes should be educated for manual work, while the rest should be given purely intellectual training."

The practical difficulty with any such theory as this is that most of those who are not given vocational education must later do manual work, for which their purely " intellectual " training has not prepared them. This is the predicament which has followed upon the taking over of the leisure class ideal of education as the basis of our democratic school system. Formerly education had very frankly been for the leisure class who were few in number. When free education was established for all citizens, the content of the old education was adopted by the new system. Whereas formerly education had prepared those who studied for their future occupation, i. e., to enjoy life without working; now the vast majority did not have the economic means to be able to put their education to that use.[1]

[1] For a brilliant treatment of this subject see John and Evelyn Dewey, *Schools of Tomorrow*, pp. 229-250.

CHAPTER IX

TRAINING OF EMPLOYEES BY THE PLANT

HITHERTO we have been considering efforts being made outside of industry to prepare men for their work. This chapter will deal with the organized efforts made by business establishments themselves to train their employees for the work they are doing or are expected to do.

Every workman has of course, always needed some training in the work he has to do and has received some instruction. This instruction has, however, been generally given by a harassed and overworked foreman who seldom knew how to explain a process. At its best such training was incomplete and sketchy, while at its worst it consisted largely of ill-tempered rebukes. In either case it was costly, because of the decreased production, the breakage and damage, and the abnormal labor turnover that resulted.

In recent years, business units have begun to adapt themselves to the situation and many concerns have functionalized the training of employees in a separate department charged with this work. The training of the workmen instead of being one of the many tasks of the shop foreman, becomes the concern of a plant official or department. Such a step, like the creation of a functionalized employment department, is but the carrying out of the principle of functional foremanship as advocated by Mr. Frederick W. Taylor.

In those plants where such departments exist, it is of course true that the foremen still retain considerable authority and responsibility in the training of the employees. Complete functionalization has therefore not been effected even in those plants where the training department has the firmest foothold and probably will never be completely accomplished. The trend is, however, distinctly towards centralizing training so far as possible under one definite agency. The training given by these business units is of two varieties: (1) instruction in a separate class or school which is for the time being somewhat apart from the actual production process, (2) instruction at the job itself. The first of these gives more the theoretical background for shop work while the second gives concrete production training in an actual shop setting. Much confusion has arisen because many writers have confined their attention to the school work given by a concern and have treated it as the sole branch of educational activity and have ignored the training at the job itself. The term " corporation school " has in itself contributed to not a little of this confusion.

As a matter of fact, many plants use only one of these methods while some use both. In general, it is undoubtedly true that large concerns created special schools for their apprentices and workmen before they established functionalized departments to instruct the workmen in the shop work itself. This was true both because it is always easier to create a new agency apart from the regular organization of the concern than it is to effect a reorganization in the plant itself, and because business men, although ostensibly somewhat scornful of the schools, were yet unable to think in other than school terms. As we shall see, however, the trend has been of late, distinctly towards an emphasis on training at the job itself.

The growth of the general movement is evidenced by the

fact that so far as is known, Hoe and Co., the famous manufacturers of printing presses, were the first large concern to institute a formal school for training their apprentices and workmen in 1872. In 1888, the Westinghouse Machine Co. of East Pittsburg, Pa., started another such school but for over a decade, few other corporations followed their example. In 1901 the Baldwin Locomotive Works inaugurated a somewhat similar system.[1] In the same year the General Electric Co. started its first school for apprentices in its Schenectady plant, and in the following year extended it to its Lynn plant. In 1903 the International Harvester Co. tried to provide organized training for its apprentices.

After 1905, the movement grew rapidly and widely. Many railroads adopted the plan, the first of which was the Central Railway of New Jersey in that year. In the next year the New York Central and the Union Pacific adopted the scheme, while the Atchison, Topeka, and Santa Fé followed in 1907. By the action of these three roads the system was taken from the Atlantic to the Pacific within a year. The plan was quickly adopted by other roads notably the Delaware and Hudson in 1907, the Chicago and Great Western, and the Erie, in 1908, the Lehigh Valley in 1910, the Baltimore and Ohio in 1911, the Illinois Central in 1912, the Southern Pacific in 1913. In 1915 in addition to the roads previously mentioned, the following also had apprenticeship schools: (1) The Boston and Maine, (2) the Canadian Pacific, (3) the Central of Georgia, (4) The Lackawanna, (5) the Grand Trunk, (6) Oregon Short Line. (7) the Southern, (8) the St. Louis & Southwestern, and

---

[1] See an article by S. M. Vauclain, " The System of Apprenticeship of the Baldwin Locomotive Works" in J. R. Commons, *Trade Unionism and Labor Problems*, pp. 304-315.

(9) the St. Louis and San Francisco.[1] In that year there were in all 108 such railway schools.[2]

Corporation schools developed rapidly in manufacturing as well as in transportation. A few of the corporations who instituted such a policy, between 1905 and 1913 and the dates of their action are given in the following table:

Year	Corporation	Place
1905	Cleveland Twist Drill Co.	Cleveland, Ohio
1906	Burroughs Adding Machine Co.	Detroit, Mich.
	Consolidated Gas Co.	New York, N. Y.
	Western Electric Co.	Chicago, Ill.
	Westinghouse Air Brake Co.	Wilmerding, Pa.
1907	Lupton Sons Co.	Philadelphia, Pa.
	Cadillac Motor Co.	Detroit, Mich.
1908	Brown and Sharpe	Providence, R. I.
	Cincinnati Planer Co.	Cincinnati, Ohio
	R. R. Donnelly and Sons	Chicago, Ill.
	Fore River Shipbuilding Co.	Quincy, Mass.
	Solvay Co.	Syracuse, N. Y.
	Yale and Towne Mfg. Co.	Stamford, Conn.
1909	Westinghouse Electric & Mfg. Co.	E. Pittsburg, Pa.
	Leland and Co.	Worcester, Mass.
1910	Franklin Mfg. Co.	Syracuse, N. Y.
	General Electric Co.	Pittsfield, Mass.
1911	Warner, Swasey and Co.	Cleveland, Ohio
1912	Royal Typewriter Co.	Hartford, Conn.
	Foote and Davies Co.	Atlanta, Ga.
1913	Packard Motor Co.	Detroit, Mich.
	Fort Wayne Electric Works	Fort Wayne, Ind.
	Curtis Publishing Co.	Philadelphia, Pa.

The year 1913 was marked by the organization of the National Association of Corporation Schools. This asso-

[1] The development of the railway systems of corporation schools is well illustrated in the charts included in the *Proceedings Second Annual Convention*, pp. 410-411; *Proceedings of Third Annual Convention*, pp. 168-169.

[2] *Proceedings Third Annual Convention Nat. Assoc. Corp. Schools*, pp. 168-169. There were in addition 32 railway schools of the Grand Trunk and the Canadian Pacific located in Canada.

ciation was organized to act as a clearing house for the interchange of ideas, to collect and make available data about successful and unsuccessful schemes of educating employees, and to promote an interest in the training of their employees on the part of corporations. The corporation school thus ceased to be the concern of any one individual plant alone, and became the subject of general concern. The strength of the movement was thus enormously increased.

The growth of this organization is well illustrated by the following table.

MEMBERSHIP IN NATIONAL ASSOCIATION OF CORPORATION SCHOOLS [1]

Date	Number of business concerns members
Sept., 1913	37
June, 1914	52
June, 1915	65
June, 1916	102
March, 1917	105
March, 1920	146

These figures are not a complete index of the actual number of corporation schools started in this period. A few of the companies belonging to the association did not actually have such schools or training departments, while the additions to the association are in part due merely to the coalescence of already existing schools. The growth of the association does, however, indicate the heightened interest in the general idea of corporate training for employees.

The National Association of Corporation Schools in fact soon broadened its whole program so that it included the entire educational aspect of industry. To its primary purpose of constituting a forum, the association added the following three functions:

[1] Compiled from the monthly bulletins of the National Association Corporation Schools.

1. To develop the efficiency of the individual employee.
2. To increase efficiency in industry as a whole.
3. To influence courses of established institutions more favorably towards industry.

The association has tried to lay down standards for safety and health precautions; to investigate schools for office-workers, adult workers, and for apprentices proper, and to recommend successful features for adoption; to study policies of advertising and retail salesmanship; and to institute approved methods of vocational guidance.   In the school work that is given the subjects taught naturally vary with the plant.   For the machinists trade, mechanical drawing, shop mathematics and blueprint reading are the most important studies.   The training is based upon the problems which arise in the daily work.   The school studies are in the main used simply to clarify the practical problems. Text-books, loose-leaf lesson sheets and oral instruction, are all used in these schools.   In general, the supervisors of apprentices believe that loose-leaf lesson sheets obtain better results than texts, as the sheets allow greater elasticity and make the studies apply much more concretely to the practical problems of the particular shop.[1]

The average amount of time which the apprentices are required to spend in the schools is approximately four hours a week, generally in two sessions of two hours each.[2]   The instructors in these schools are normally taken from the force of the corporation itself instead of being hired from without.   This connects the school with the problems of the workshop, and is less expensive because it does not

[1] 30 plants out of 33 declared that lesson sheets were more satisfactory than textbooks. See *Proceedings Third Convention Nat. Assoc. Corp. Schools*, p. 165.

Proceedings Third Annual Convention Nat. Assoc. Corp. Schools, pp. 141-145.

necessitate the employment of a man upon full-time pay to do only part-time work. It does, of course, have the disadvantage that the teacher may be hurried by his other duties that he does not have time properly to prepare his school work.[1]

In 1914 the following number of apprentices attended the corporation schools of 51 different companies.[2]

Type of Industry	No. of Schools	Number of Apprentices
Railways	17	4,451
Manufacturing concerns	34	3,638
Total	51	8,089

Since the sources of information were limited there were necessarily many plants whose apprentices were not included in the preceding table. Approximately 80 per cent of these apprentices were being trained for the machinists trade for repair work. Thus in the railway schools practically all the men were being trained for repair-shop work. This confirms the statement made in an earlier chapter that manual skill is being largely concentrated in the repairing of machines. Other trades taught are carpentering, plumbing, molding, boiler-making, painting, and decorating, electrical work, blacksmithing, mechanical drawing, pattern-making, and testing.

These apprentice-schools are almost all located in the eastern states. Of forty-one shop schools for apprentices in manufacturing industries which were investigated in 1915, only one was located west of the Mississippi River and only three south of the Ohio River. Fourteen were in the states

---

[1] For the pedagogical qualities of corporation school work, see A. J. Beatty, *Corporation Schools* (Bloomington, Ill.) especially chaps. iv to viii, inclusive.

[2] These statistics are compiled from a chart made by the sub-committee on trade apprenticeship. See *Proceedings of Second Convention Nat. Assoc. Corp. Schools*, pp. 404-405.

of Wisconsin, Illinois, Indiana, and Ohio, and the remaining twenty-three in Pennsylvania, New Jersey, New York, Connecticut, Rhode Island and Massachusetts.[1]   The railway shop schools on the other hand were much more widely scattered.   Forty-eight of the 108 shops in this country, or nearly one-half, were west of the Mississippi, and 11, or 10%, were south of the Ohio.[2]   Most of the corporations that prescribed school training for their employees provide this school themselves and have the work given inside the plant.   Some, however, either rely upon the public evening schools or upon the correspondence schools to meet the need but meet part or all of the expenses for their employees.

In addition to these specialized schools for the more-highly skilled workmen many concerns have established schools of a more general nature for their unskilled and semi-skilled workmen.   These classes are designed to arouse in the employee interest in and a general knowledge of the business. Consequently, lectures are generally given on such topics as (a) the history and importance of the industry, (b) the technological processes of the industry, (c) policies of particular organization itself including its origin, growth, selling policy, labor policy, methods of promotion *etc.*   Within the last few years many plants employing large numbers of immigrant-workers have instituted Americanization classes which have devoted themselves largely to teaching English.   Lectures are also given in many plants on safety measures and in some, on health care.

It has been unfortunate, however, that the attention of educators and of the public has been fixed upon the school training given by modern business concerns rather than

[1] See *Proceedings Third Convention, Nat. Assoc. Corp. Schools*, pp. 168-169.

[2] *Ibid.*, pp. 168-169.

upon the shop training, for the former has always been less important than the latter.   The real education which a business concern gives to its workmen is always mainly centered about the actual days work itself and " school work" is at best extrinsic to the real core of the production process.   Men learn to become good workmen at their job only, by mastering that job and this cannot be accomplished by theoretical instruction, whether inside or outside the factory walls.   The development of the functionalized training department, however, has introduced order into the education of workmen on the job where all was previously chaos.   A definite plan of training is set up and an agency created to administer it.

The nature of this shop training must naturally vary with the type of worker to be trained.   Where advanced apprentices are being trained for executive and high-grade engineering positions the men are changed from one branch of the work to another, once they have mastered a field. They are carefully supervised and a wealth of individual instruction is given them.   The most notable concern giving this type of training is the General Electric Company which annually employs approximately 300 college graduates as apprentices.   These men are given training in the testing department for one year; after that, as Dr. Steinmetz says, " we provide situations for those who desire to remain with the company and for those whom we consider first class men, further training in an extension course." [1]

Where men are being trained for the highly skilled mechanical positions, as in the railroad apprentice schools and many of the large corporations, the shop work of the learners is generally supervised by a specialized agent.   This

[1] C. P. Steinmetz, " Engineering Schools of Electrical Manufacturing Companies," *Proceedings First Annual Convention, National Association of Corporation Schools.*

man primarily oversees the training given to the apprentices rather than training the apprentice himself. Promotion is thus individualized and the lock-step method is broken; once adept boys have mastered an operation, they can be changed to another job without waiting for their less capable fellows. Should the apprentice need more instruction than can be given by the foremen, the functional supervisor can of course give supplementary training. To do adequate work such a supervisor should not be burdened with the care of overseeing too many apprentices. The general consensus of opinion seems to be that thirty or fifty apprentices per supervisor is the maximum number than can be directed efficiently.[1] In practice, however, many plants have a much higher ratio than this although one manufacturing concern has as low a ratio as six apprentices per instructor.[2]

The war-time labor shortage caused many employers to install training systems. In these systems, the learners were almost universally trained upon the job itself. Perhaps the most noteworthy development was that of the " vestibule school." This has been admirably defined by Dr. H. C. Link as[3]

a preliminary training school in which to observe and coach new employees. The vestibule school is to the industrial organization what the vestibule is to the home. In the home it is a place where the entrant stops, wipes his shoes on the mat, adjusts his garments, and performs those duties which prepare him to enter the house proper. In the factory or office it is a place which detains the incoming employee until he has become adjusted to a new environment and has been prepared to handle the essential elements of his prospective work. Having passed through this preliminary stage, he is the more ready to enter upon the work of the main shop or office.

[1] *Proceedings Second Annual Convention, National Association Corporation Schools*, p. 437.

[2] *Ibid.*, p. 439.

[3] Link, *Employment Psychology*, p. 273.

.The novices are given training under instruction, on actual production jobs somewhat apart from the main plant process itself. This training department may be completely separated from the rest of the plant, or, if it is unwise to equip such a complete cross-section unit of the plant, it may occupy segregated floor space in each of the regular departments. The segregation permits close supervision and instruction, while the production work gives absolute concreteness of aim. Scores of plants instituted such schools during the war, among which may be mentioned the Lincoln Motors Co. of Detroit, the Recording and Computing Machines Co. of Dayton, and the Curtis Aeroplane and Motor Co.[1]

The novices are generally trained in only one operation and naturally their period of training is short. Women in the Recording and Computing Machines Co. were trained for a unit job from three to ten days.[2] The worker is also given a certain amount of supervision once he leaves the school and starts work in the plant proper. Employees changed to new positions are also frequently sent back to the " vestibule school " for training on their new job.

The development of the vestibule school corroborates the statement made in Chapter V. that most industrial operations do not require long training and at the same time indicates what the probable development of industrial education inside the plant will be.

[1] For a description of these training departments see C. V. Carpenter, " How we Trained 5000 women," *Industrial Management*, May, 1918, pp. 353-57. H. E. Miles, " Vestibule Schools for the Unskilled," *Industrial Management*, July 1918, pp. 10-12. J. W. Russell, " Installing a Training Department," *Industrial Management*, March, 1919, pp. 177-183. H. N. Clarke, " Breaking in the New Worker," *Industrial Management*, June, 1919, p. 497. See also H. E. Miles, " Vestibule Schools," *The Survey*, March 6, 1920, pp. 700-706.

[2] Carpenter, *op. cit.*, p. 355.

It should not be thought that plant training has been confined to the manufacturing end. Many concerns have installed systems of training for their clerical force and salesmen as well.[1] Here again are found the "Vestibule schools" with their emphasis upon the "actual" job and the auxiliary training work given in school classes.

It is very easy to see that the new system of training employees inside the plant applies many of the features of the old apprenticeship system to modern conditions. Supervised training is given the employee on actual productive work. There are however, certain very vital differences: (1) Unlike the old apprenticeship the new system rarely aims to teach the worker the whole trade. Save in only a few instances the novice is trained at only a limited number of operations. The vestibule school with its instruction at a single operation illustrates the trend towards specialized training. (2) There is in general no fixed period of time which the learner must serve. Some of the corporation schools do have minimum periods for the apprentices to the highly skilled trades, but in the main the work is conducted on a go-as-you-please basis with no fixed period of training. (3) The indenture is rarely used and whatever instruction is given is almost wholly outside any possible legal supervision. (4) Whereas apprenticeship formerly applied almost exclusively to minors, the present system trains workers of

---

[1] Among the companies that have systematic plans of training their office workers are the National Cloak and Suit Co., the Larkin Co., the Curtis Publishing Co., the Burroughs Adding Machine Co., and the Dennison Manufacturing Co. General financial institutions such as the Equitable Life Insurance Co., the National Surety Co., and the National City Bank of New York City have similar plans. Among the firms that have a thorough system of education for their salesmen are the New York Edison Co., the National Cash Register Co., the Burroughs Adding Machine Co., the Dennison Manufacturing Co., the Packard Motor Co., the American Optical Co., the Cadillac Co., and the United States Cigar Store Co.

all ages. (5) The present system confines its training to instruction inside the plant. Unlike the old apprenticeship, it does not and cannot hope to superintend the learner outside the work place. Nor can it adequately develop the cultural and spiritual aspects of the worker as was the purpose of the institution of apprenticeship.

In conclusion, what may be said to be the merits and demerits of corporation schools and training departments?

They have real advantages, since a corporation knows its problems as no school can know them and its training work has great concreteness. Theory and practice are joined together in every week's activity. A corporation, therefore, can train its employees for their specific tasks more efficiently than can any other organization. The movement is then a real attempt to restore the good features of apprenticeship and to make modern industry a place of learning as well as of doing.

They have, however, certain very decided inadequacies:

(1) The school or training department is scarcely practicable for a small business, since a concern must be of considerable size before it can afford to establish a separate educational department with a special supervisor of training. The corporation school and the specialized training department, must then be accounted one of the advantages of large scale production and as one of the by-products of the capacity of a large concern for specialization and differentiation. A plant must apparently have at least several hundred employees before it becomes profitable to introduce the corporation school. Indeed nine-tenths of the concerns making up the National Association of Corporation schools number their employees in the thousands.

(2) 51 out of 57 apprentice schools would not admit apprentices under 16.[1] Only four schools would admit child-

---

[1] *Proceedings of Second Annual Convention Nat. Assoc. Corp. Schools,* pp. 408-409.

ren of 14 or under. The fourteen-year-old child is too immature and undependable to be profitably given skilled training by private plants and other agencies are needed to care for those two years in a child's life.

(3) The policy of the corporation school is necessarily shaped by the employer alone. It is, therefore, almost inevitable that social questions such as the merits and demerits of trade unionism should receive biased treatment.

(4) The primary purpose of a corporation school or training department is necessarily profit. As Charles P. Steinmetz, perhaps the ablest and broadest-minded man in the corporation school movement, says: " The limitation of the corporation activities in the educational and similar fields is that given by the limitation of the corporation purpose to earn dividends for its stockholders. No human activity in this or other fields can be justified before a stockholders meeting, which does not show a favorable financial balance, however much the corporation directors may desire philanthropic work." [1]

This cash-value test of education is of course dangerous, since what may be immensely profitable to society, may not be profitable to the individual corporation. In the corporation schools the training is thoroughly practical. There is no cultural education at all. Although the vestibule schools do furnish admirable preparation for specific trades, nevertheless, they do not provide broad vocational or civic training. Workmen need to posses a broader equipment than the knowledge of only one process if they are to protect themselves against unemployment. As citizens moreover, their needs are greater than can be satisfied by the business exigencies of the individual plant.

[1] C. P. Steinmetz, " Presidental Address," *Third Annual Convention National Association Corporation School*, p. 52.

(5) The question may fairly be asked: Does this plant training pay for itself after all? There can be but little doubt that the " vestibule " training does. The expense of training is more than compensated by the increased production at work, the freeing of the foremen from instruction, the reduction of breakage and damage whether to the machine, the material or the fellow workmen, together with the reduction of the labor turnover which results.

(6) Finally, it is by no means clear however, that the more elaborate apprentice courses and corporation schools are a paying proposition. In the first place, most of the arguments advanced to prove the economic success of these schools are decidely inadequate. Mr. F. C. Henderschott of the New York Edison Co. declared that in the year after the introduction of a school for salesmen and other workers the business of his company increased 20.5% as compared with the average yearly increase of 12%.[1] The conclusion was that the school work had been chiefly responsible for this increase. Mr. Henderschott is here guilty of the *post hoc ergo propter hoc* fallacy. A number of other factors might have caused the increase equally as well.

The truth of the matter is that the corporation faces the same obstacle in training its apprentices and skilled workers that the small manufacturers were confronted with in the 19th century, namely that the apprentice may leave upon or before the termination of his term and go to some other company. This is a real deterrent to the individual employer providing training. He is liable to go to the expense of training the boy only to the end that some one else shall obtain the benefits of his skill. The employer must face the question: considering the transient nature of the working force does

[1] F. C. Henderschott, *Proceedings First Annual Conv. Nat. Assoc. Corp. Schools*, p. 404.

it pay *him* (not does it pay the industry) to train his young workers?

The following table shows the number of apprentices taken on trial by various concerns up to 1914, the number graduated, and the number in the employ of the company in that year.[1]

Name of Company	Number of Apprentices on Trial	Number Graduated	Graduates Employed with Company
Am. Locom. Co.	807	126	98
Bos. & Me. R. R.	83	27	20
Cen. R. R. of N. Y.	260	36	16
Del. & Hudson R. R.	290	113	86
Erie R. R.	1007	161	104
Gr. Trunk R. R.	1660	225	99
Penn. R. R.	406	219	181
South Pac. R. R.	304	4	4
Cadillac Mot. Car. Co.	580	80	35
Cincin. Planer Co.	50	10	3
Clev. Twist Drill Co.	28	7	1
Foote & Davis Co.	35	0	0
Ft. Wayne Elec. Wks.	11	0	0
Gen. Elec. Co., Lynn, Mass.	1710	156	60
" (Pattern-making)	177	20	11
" (Moulding)	171	22	8
" (Stenography)	19	3	2
" (Mech. Drawing)	254	57	24
" (Testing)	98	1	1
" (Business)	17	4	2
· " (Electrical)	274	93	46
Leland & Co.	30	8	6
Packard Mot. Car. Co.	86	0	0
Western Elec. Co.	111	25	15
Westinghouse Elec. Mfg.	779	133	63
Yale & Towne	212	55	37
Total	9,459	1,585	922

[1] This table has been compiled from raw data gathered by the sub-committee on manufacturing and mining, *Proceedings Second Annual Convention National Association Schools*, 1914, pp. 408-409.

Thus only 16.7% of the apprentices who were taken on trial graduated from the course of training and only 58.1% of those who graduated or 9.1% of those taken on trial were at that time in the employ of the company.

Can an undertaking be called profitable when, of every 100 men trained, only 16 complete the course, and only 10 work permanently for the concern that trained them? These corporations have in other words trained 90 men who are working elsewhere for every 10 men so trained who are working for them.

This statement however, needs to be qualified. Many dropped out soon after training began, others were eliminated along the way and the expense undergone by the companies in training such a boy was much less than it would have been had he gone all the way through, and then left to work elsewhere.

It is a curious paradox, however, that it does pay some concerns to lose their apprentices to other plants. The apprentices that leave the employ of the General Electric Company, go as a rule into executive positions with companies using electrical apparatus. Since they have been trained in General Electric methods and accustomed to General Electric machinery and since, moreover, the General Electric has tried to develop an *esprit de corps* among its apprentices, there is every incentive for them to buy General Electric goods. There can be little doubt that sales of the General Electric Company have increased in part just because of this loyalty on the part of its old " boys " who are now with other firms. This is however, an unusual case. Most apprentices do not leave a company to become loyal purchasers from that company, but rather to become employees of a competitor. After all allowances have been made, it is at least possible and in many cases probable that the cost of training the boys is on the whole, greater than the return received.

It seems probable, however that the plant training given in the future will be more in the nature of shop instruction in specialized processes rather than in the more elaborate system of a long-time apprenticeship training. However some skilled workmen are needed and if some plan similar to the Wisconsin apprenticeship system were introduced for the more skilled trades, undoubtedly a greater stabilization would result, and the employer would be given greater assurance of a return upon his investment of training.

CHAPTER X

EVENING AND CORRESPONDENCE SCHOOLS

THIS and the following chapter consider schools that are midway between those of the last two chapters. Chapter VIII. discussed schools that had as their basic assumption that the school could train for industry. The corporation schools described in Chapter IX. are based upon the belief that training in an industry can come only from actual experience in the industry itself and that the school work is merely supplementary. Continuation and coöperative schools stress the importance of shop work more than does the trade or industrial school, but they also lay greater stress upon the school-work that is to accomplish the practical details.

The continuation school differs from the day trade school in that the student is studying while he is already engaged in industry. It differs from the corporation school in that the student is generally instructed outside of the place where he is employed and his education is under the direction of agencies other than his employer.

Continuation schools have two broad purposes: (1) Industrial and (2) social. The industrial purposes of the continuation schools are to prepare the worker (a) for the job he chances to be holding at the time, (b) for a higher position within the same industry, (c) for other industries. The social purposes are (a) to teach the English language (in the case of foreigners), (b) to give general instruction in citizenship, (c) to increase the capacity for enjoyment of cultural things.

Continuation schools may be divided into two main classes, (1) those that are conducted outside of working hours, which are considered in this chapter, and (2) those that are conducted during working hours, which are considered in the following chapter.

Evening schools were an early phenomenon in this country. The early masters were compelled to give some literary education to their apprentices and evening schools were established to provide for this so that the masters might pool the education of their apprentices. Samuel Crane of Dorchester, Mass., kept an evening school from 1790-97 for the apprentices in paper mills and for other studiously inclined boys. There were many evening schools in the middle colonies which had as their chief purpose the furnishing of education to these indentured apprentices.[1] Of course students other than apprentices were admitted to these schools, but the necessity of complying with the educational requirements of the apprentice law gave a certain amount of patronage to these schools and was at least one of the causes for their formation.

Such evening schools continued and increased during the nineteenth century, and the necessity of providing for the education of the apprentices was still one of the causes for their institution. In 1828, the Ohio Mechanics Institute started a school in Cincinnati to which apprentices and sons of members were eligible upon payment of 50 cents a year.[2] In 1840, the Baltimore, Md., board of education organized six evening schools for apprentices and others.[3] Thus evening schools had their origin, in part at least, as a continuation of the apprentice system.

[1] A. W. Brawley, *Schools and School Boys of Old Boston*, p. 24. Quoted by A. J. Jones, *Continuation Schools in United States*, pp. 84-85.

[2] Chas. Cist, *Cincinnati in 1841*, p. 132.

[3] *Report Baltimore Board of Education*, 1860, p. 335.

Evening schools may be classified from the standpoint of control under two heads: (1) Those under private management, (2) those under public management.

1. Evening Schools Under Private Management

The private schools may be primarily conducted either for eleemosynary purposes or for profit. Prominent among the privately managed schools that are conducted primarily for public purposes are those of the Young Men's and Young Women's Christian Associations.

The following table shows the increase of students in round numbers in the Y. M. C. A. Schools.[1]

Year	No. of students enrolled
1893	12,000
1900	26,000
1905	33,000
1915	83,000

The increase during these twenty-three years was, therefore, approximately six-fold. The expenditure per student also increased during this time from $4.33 in 1893 to $13.90 in 1915, or an increase of over 200%.[2]

In 1895, three-quarters of the men who took this school work were clerks, but in 1905, only 43% were clerks, while 51% were artisans.[3] The average age of these students in 1909 was 23 years, and about 18% were under 18 years of age.[4] The subjects studied are classified under six heads: (a) Commercial, including business law, arithmetic, book-keeping, stenography and typewriting. (b) Political, including government, economics, social history, etc. (c) Industrial, including carpentry, drawing, wood-carving,

[1] *Annual Report, Educational Department of the Y. M. C. A.*, 1905, pp. 39-50; *Year Book, Y. M. C. A.*, 1915-1916, pp. 24-50, *op. cit.*

[2] *Annual Report Educational Dept. 1915-16 Year Book, op. cit.*, p. 24.

[3] *Annual Report Educational Dept., op. cit.*, p. 29.

[4] *25th Annual Report Commissioner of Labor*, p. 363.

etc. (d) Scientific, including higher mathematics, physics, chemistry and electricity.   (e) Language, including English, French and Spanish,   (f) Special, such as law, art and automobiling.   (g) Employed boys.   This is work specifically adopted to the needs of those already employed. With the decline in the relative importance of the clerical class, commercial subjects have also decreased in importance.

The work is supervised by the educational department of the International Association.   Though its power is only advisory, it acts as a clearing house for information and advice.   This committee prepares uniform examinations upon the subjects taught and sends them to the local associations.   The certificates are granted to those who pass these examinations and in 1901 the certificates had been accepted as credit by 110 colleges and universities.   Not many of the local associations use these examinations, however, for only 2.7% of the 82,000 students in 1915 were given the international certificate.[1]   Though the Y. M. C. A. is doing good work it can never be expected adequately to solve the problem.   First, it reaches and can teach only a comparatively small percentage of those that need training.   Only those sections that have an association can benefit by its work.   The growth of the educational work is, therefore, dependent upon the growth of the movement, as a whole, and many places that need evening education can not receive it.   Not only is there this geographical restriction of the field of service, but large sections of the population within any given territory either will not, or cannot, attend such schools.   Though the Y. M. C. A. is attached to no religious body, yet its influence and leadership is overwhelmingly Protestant in nature rather than Catholic.   This, to be sure, is caused in part by the re-

[1] *1915-16 Year-books, Y. M. C. A.*, p. 24.

fusal of most Catholics to coöperate with it. The Catholic population, however, looks somewhat askance at it and is loath to utilize it in any way. If Catholics dislike the Y. M. C. A. because it is Protestant, " free-thinkers " dislike it because it is religious. Its somewhat evangelical characteristics cause it to be looked down upon by so-called " rationalists " and to be viewed with a vague distrust by other non-religious or anti-religious people.

Nor are its obstacles geographical or religious alone. There are economic barriers as well. The tuition fees average over $11.00 per student. To this must be added, (1) dues in the Y. M. C. A. itself, membership in which is generally a pre-requisite for attending classes, and (2) the cost of text-books. It is safe to estimate that an average expenditure of $20.00 would be necessary to take the school-work offered. Knowing what we do about wages and the cost of living in the United States, we can readily see that this amount debars a large class.

Finally, despite the efforts to standardize and improve the quality of work offered, it cannot be said that the training given is always of a high order. It is often more in the nature of an advertisement for the local Y. M. C. A. than a serious and earnest attempt to improve conditions. Very often the equipment is inadequate and the teachers incompetent.

The Y. W. C. A. also gives instruction in a parallel manner to that of the Y. M. C. A. Its members are fewer and its influence less than that of the men's association, but it confronts the same obstacles.

Another type is that of the privately endowed schools that give evening work. Some of these give all day trade instruction as well. These schools thus perform the double mission of a day trade and an evening school. To the extent that they do give evening instruction to those already employed, they may be listed under the head of eleemosynary evening schools.

Examples of schools that give evening instruction only are (1) the North Bennet Industrial School, (2) Franklin Union, (3) the Massachusetts Charitable Mechanics Association Evening Trades School, all of Boston, Mass., (4) the Ohio Mechanics Institute of Cincinnati, Ohio, (5) the St. George's Evening Trades School, (6) the Preparatory Trade School, (7) the Italian Evening Trade School of New York City and (8) the Virginia Mechanics Institute of Richmond, Va.

Examples of schools that give day instruction as well, are (1) Cooper Union, (2) the New York Trade School of New York City, (3) Pratt Institute of Brooklyn and (4) Franklin Institute of Philadelphia. Cooper Union was founded in 1854, for definite continuation school purposes. It was designed "to give instruction, to those already employed at trades, in such departments of knowledge as might fit them to become foremen, employers and good citizens." Here both the industrial and social purposes are clearly evident. The industrial training was evidently to be given in order that the worker might rise from his position to a higher rank, whether within the same industry or without. The idea of training the worker merely for the particular task at which he is then engaged, which is one of the most important purposes of the modern continuation school, is wholly absent.

Little or no argument is needed to demonstrate the inadequacy of philanthropic evening schools. Philanthropists are relatively few and their gifts are insufficient to meet the need. The problem is too big to be solved by the fortuitous donations of individuals.

In addition to these philanthropic evening schools, there are schools conducted primarily on business principles. In a previous chapter we have discussed day trade schools operated for profit. Private enterprise, however, does not confine its attention to the daytime. Its night-schools afford an opportunity for those who work by day to study by night. Little need be added to the description of these schools that has already been given. They are in the main inefficient and ill-equipped, and are so expensive that a large class is barred from making use of their advantages.

2. *Public Evening Schools*

Most important of all are the public evening schools. It is impossible to obtain statistics about the early extent and influence of the public evening schools. Here and there in the reports of city school systems and in the reports of the Commissioner of Education, we find references to their existence, but definite figures are difficult to secure. The first compilation by the Bureau of Education was in 1887-88, and the following table shows the growth of the system since then.

Year	*Total number of pupils in evening schools in cities over 8,000* [1]
1887–88	135,654
1896–97	183,168
1898–99	185,000
1900–01	203,000
1902–03	229,213
1904–05	292,319
1907–08	357,923
1909–10	374,364
1911–12	419,981
1913–14	614,068
1914–15	678,393

These statistics indicate an extraordinary growth since 1911-12 of 260,000 in round numbers or an increase of about 62%. Part of this increase is due, undoubtedly, to

[1] See *Reports Commissioner of Education*, 1887-88, pp. 223-27; 1897, vol. i, p. 9; 1898-99, vol. i, p. 60; 1901, vol. i, p. 9; 1903, vol. i, p. 9; 1905, vol. i, p. 8; 1908, vol. ii, p. 422.

the better reporting of school statistics which the Bureau has secured since 1912. In spite of this, however, there seems little reason to doubt that during the last five years, evening schools have greatly extended their influence.

The evening schools find their chief strength in the cities of over 100,000 population. 45% of all the pupils en-. rolled in 1914-15 belonged to cities of this class.[1]

411,000 or 60% of the students in the evening schools in 1914-15, were males and 267,000 or 40% were females.[2] That the evening schools do not do advanced work is evidenced by the fact that over two-thirds of the pupils were enrolled in the elementary grades, and slightly less' than one-third in the secondary schools.[3] The evening schools, moreover, will contain in one class, people of different ages and nationalities. Employed boys and girls of from 14-21 years study along with men of over 30 years of age. American-born children of American parents study in the same room or the same school with foreign-born men—for there are over 175,000 foreign-born immigrants who are studying in evening schools of the country.[4]

In consequence, the evening school curriculum permits only rudimentary work. The courses offered in the evening schools are, indeed, designed more to atone for deficiencies in the common school education which the pupil for one cause or other has experienced, than to act as a continuation of the common school studies. Its training is, therefore, so general in nature that it gives little assistance to the boy in industry who wants to be prepared either for the

[1] 313,253 of the total of 678,393. See *Report Commissioner of Education*, 1916, vol. ii, pp. 72-75.

[2] *Ibid.*

[3] *Report Commissioner of Education*, 1912, vol. ii, p. 30.

[4] See F. E. Farrington, " Public Facilities for Educating the Alien," *Bull. 18, 1911, U. S. Bureau of Education.*

job he is then holding or for a better one. The American evening school is really a duplication of the day school system, running only at different hours, and its content rarely shows that the educational authorities have realized that they have a different problem to face.

These evening schools are definitely a part of the school system of the various cities. Massachusetts and Connecticut make their creation mandatory to stamp out illiteracy. Nine states (California, Georgia, Kansas, Missouri, New Jersey, Ohio, Pennsylvania, Vermont and Wisconsin) have permissive legislation allowing the establishment of evening schools. These laws amount to but little because they merely formally approve the action of a city but do not encourage it. States which do not have permissive legislation often have as many evening schools as those that do. Of more direct aid are the grants which eleven states : California, Connecticut, Minnesota, Indiana, Maine, New Jersey, New York, Pennsylvania, Rhode Island, Washington and Wisconsin make for the support of evening schools.

Though public evening schools have undoubtedly performed valuable service, they do not, as at present constituted, offer a solution to the problem of industrial education for the following reasons :

(1) The curriculum is so elementary that it offers little opportunity for the boy at work to improve his position.

(2) The teaching force is always overworked and often incompetent. In 1914-15 each teacher (upon the average) instructed forty pupils.[1] This ratio is far too high. Approximately 60% of these teachers, moreover, also taught in the day school as well. Double work of this sort is so exhausting that no one can continue to do justice to both positions.

[1] *Report Commissioner of Education*, 1916, vol. ii, pp. 72-75.

Furthermore, the teachers who instruct in the night school are generally less efficient than the teachers in the day schools.   They are either new teachers gaining experience in night work or those whose scholastic rank is low and who are, in consequence, confined to night work.   The number of night-school teachers is also swelled by many who follow some other occupation by day and do night-teaching in order to earn a supplementary income.   To this latter class, teaching is but an auxiliary line of effort, a crutch to help them hobble along, not the main course of interest.   Few of them know anything about pedagogy and their technique is of the scantiest.   Because of all these factors, enthusiastic and efficient teaching is a rarity in the public evening schools.

(3) The students who are working by day are generally so tired that they cannot profit from the instruction given.

Modern industry is essentially exhausting.   Manufacturing, clerical and commercial occupations are geared at high speed, and an adolescent has little or no surplus energy to expend after a day's work.   To expect faithful attendance at, and close attention in an evening school which itself seems inefficient and tired is to expect an impossibility.

The following table shows in round numbers, the enormous loss in attendance which evening schools experience.[1]

Year	Total number enrolled in evening schools	Average daily attendance	Percentage daily attendance of total enrollment
1908–09	379,000	155,000	41.1%
1909–10	374,000	145,000	39.6%
1911–12	420,000	149,000	35.6%

These statistics are corroborated by those of New York City.   Ever since public evening schools were opened in 1847, irregular attendance has been a constant characteristic.

[1] See *Reports Commissioner of Education*, 1910, vol. ii, p. 689; 1912, vol. ii, p. 30.

In the first year, only 35% of those enrolled attended upon the average; forty years later, in 1887, the percentage was 33.8, while in 1910-11 it was 34.1.[1] It is safe to conclude, therefore, that evening schools instruct upon the average only slightly over one-third of those who enroll. Miss Van Kleeck found that in New York, 8% of those who enrolled never attended even one session.[2] These may be written off as complete deadwood. A comprehensive treatment of any scheduled subject cannot be given with this irregular attendance, and all logical continuity is destroyed.

Even to those who attend faithfully, the evening school is essentially unsatisfactory. The students are tired from the day's work and cannot concentrate upon their studies. The teaching is generally listless and there is an air of irrelevancy about the whole situation that leads the mind to go "wool-gathering." As Miss Van Kleeck says, "the facts seem to us to show conclusively that if a system of compulsory continuation schools for young wage-earners is to be developed, their sessions must be held by day and not by night."[3]

3. Correspondence Schools

Correspondence schools are really schools outside working hours conducted at long range. A few students may devote their entire time to the course of studies and for these, the correspondence schools are trade preparatory and not continuation schools. The vast majority, however, take correspondence courses as a supplement to their daily work. These courses are used to accomplish the three industrial purposes of continuation schools, *i. e.*, to pre-

[1] See Mary Van Kleeck, *Working Girls in Evening Schools*, pp. 143-148.

[2] Van Kleeck, *op. cit.*, p. 145.

[3] Van Kleeck, *op. cit.*, p. 165.

pare a worker for the job he is then engaged at; to prepare him for higher positions within the same industry; and to prepare him for other industries. The last two purposes are of course stressed more by the correspondence schools than the first.

The two varieties of correspondence schools, like the evening schools, are public and private. The public correspondence schools are usually attached to the universities of the country. In 1913, thirty-two colleges and universities gave correspondence courses with a total enrollment of approximately 20,000.[1] The Universities of Chicago and Wisconsin have been the pioneers in this field and have given instruction to tens of thousands by means of correspondence. The Massachusetts Board of Education has recently instituted a state extension system which is largely based upon the correspondence idea.

In all these public systems the courses given are mainly cultural and not directly vocational.[2] Subjects such as literature, language, history, education, *etc.*, seem indeed to be the most popular. It would be erroneous to conclude that no vocational courses are offered, since the Universities of Wisconsin and Pennsylvania and the Michigan State College of Agriculture offer courses in engineering, agriculture, industry, and business. But such work is distinctly subordinated to the cultural instruction.

The correspondence schools conducted for profit are far more important in point of numbers enrolled than are those conducted primarily for public service. Due to the multiplicity of such private schools and to their secrecy, it is impossible to secure statistics which will accurately indicate their influence and importance. An estimate of several

[1] Louis E. Reber, "University Extension in the United States," *Bulletin, 1914, U. S. Bureau of Education, No. 19*, p. 20.

[2] For analysis of courses given, see Reber, *op. cit.*, pp. 21-26.

hundred thousand pupils enrolled would be, however, most conservative. Some of these schools are downright frauds, giving little or no instruction in return for the fees paid. Most of the schools of caricaturing and drawing are of this stamp. Others have as their main purpose, the sale of a set of books and are really book-firms instead of correspondence schools. Still others specialize in correspondence work but give inadequate instruction, while there are some very reputable concerns which offer a fair degree of opportunity to the student.

The curriculum of this class of correspondence schools is completely practical. Few or no cultural subjects are included. The sole standard that a student of this class of school considers is " will this raise my pay-check? " There is consequently a multitude of courses offered in the fields of engineering, business, agriculture, *etc.*

Though a great deal of incidental good is done in furnishing instruction to ambitious young men, the private correspondence schools constitute in the main, a vicious and inefficient system of education for the following reasons: (1) Many of them are fraudulent. It is difficult for the post-office authorities to detect whether or not a concern is doing a legitimate business. By liberal advertising, it is possible for a company to reap a harvest before a fraud order can be issued. It is possible, moreover, for a concern to stay within the letter of the law and yet exploit its patrons. (2) The degree of efficiency, even among the technically honest firms, is not high. A staff of ill-paid clerks is generally employed at answering letters and replying to questions. Even though the work is standardized, these people cannot furnish complete and accurate information or high-grade instruction. (3) The charges for tuition are too high. The fees per course vary from $20. upwards; the average charge by the International Correspondence

Schools being $75. This constitutes a severe drain upon a poor man's resources, and their collection is only possible, because they are paid in installments rather than in a lump sum. Were the tuition fees actually invested in the educational side of the business, no complaint could of course be made, but such is not the case. (4) An enormous amount is wasted in competitive advertising and canvassing. Most of the expenses of a modern correspondence school are indeed in the sales and not in the educational department. One large school claiming an enrollment of 350,000 pupils had twenty branch offices each with its quota of salesmen and employed in all over 2,500 people. Only 370 of these were, however, connected with the educational work! Fifteen percent of the force was devoted to the actual instruction itself, while eighty-five was employed in the administration and sales side of the business. This indicates a shocking disproportion of energy and resources, and is one that would not exist under a publicly operated system with the wastes of competition eliminated.

(5) A further criticism of private correspondence schools is that only a small percentage ever finish the courses that they begin. Veiled in secrecy as the records are, only estimates are possible. The Minnesota Department of Labor Statistics found that less than one-third of those who began courses in Minneapolis, finished them.[1] The percentage, for the country, as a whole, of those who complete their course is probably even less. The Canadian Commission on Technical Education declared it to be as low as 5 or 10 percent.[2]

(6) Finally, correspondence school courses even at their

[1] "Vocational Survey of Minneapolis, Minn.," *Bulletin 199, United States Bureau of Labor Statistics*, p. 113.

[2] *Report Canadian Commission on Industrial Training and Technical Education*, pt. iv, p. 1688.

best, are a decidedly unsatisfactory means of education and should be used only as a last resort. The instruction lacks personal touch; there is an inevitable delay in replying to questions which is generally at least as long as a week, and sometimes a fortnight or a month. This robs the study of much of its interest and the student soon loses heart and generally drops out. These schools cannot be called a solution, in any real sense, of the problem of industrial education.

The huge numbers who have sought further technical education at their hands is, however, adequate proof of the fact that the present educational system of the country has failed to meet the needs of the times. Because of the lack of a better system, men have turned to privately managed schools both at long and short range to secure the training that they have needed.

CHAPTER XI

PART-TIME SCHOOLS

1. Introduction.

THERE are two varieties of part-time schools: (1) The co-operative school, (2) the part-time continuation school. These schools differ from evening schools in that they operate within and not without working hours, and that children at work are excused to attend them.

The typical co-operative school alternates school and shop training, giving school training to one set of students for a week, or some such period, and then sending this group to work in some industry and taking in another group who have been employed in industry the preceding week. After another period, the process is reversed. There is thus an alternation between school and shop, between theory and practice. The typical part-time continuation school on the other hand takes all the workers for a few hours every week. The continuation and co-operative schools are alike in that they give training within working hours but they differ in the following respects: (1) In the co-operative schools, there is a rotation of men from school to shop which does not exist in the continuation school. (2) The co-operative school generally takes students and finds a place for them in industry, while the continuation school takes boys and girls already engaged in industry and gives them school training. (3) Much more time is devoted to school work under the co-operative than under the con-

tinuation school. Whatever the length of the "shifts" in
the former system, the proportions devoted to school and
shop respectively are approximately half and half. In the
continuation schools on the other hand, the hours devoted to
school work are never more than eight a week or less than
16% of the normal working time of the child laborer. (4)
The work in the co-operative school is closely co-ordinated
with that of the shop and the work of the students in the industry itself is supervised by the school authorities. In the
continuation school, on the other hand, the school training
is merely super-imposed upon the shop work and the school
authorities do not interfere with the work done in the industry itself. (5) Typically, attendance at the co-operative
school is voluntary while attendance at the continuation
school is generally compulsory. The co-operative school is
established and maintained by the voluntary co-operation of
employers with the educational authorities. The part-time
continuation schools in the United States are in the main
compulsory upon both the employer and juvenile worker.
(6) The curriculum of the co-operative school is almost
wholly designed to increase the technical efficiency of the
individual worker while that of the continuation school
normally lays considerable stress upon the social aspects of
industry and life. This difference in the curriculum is
probably occasioned because attendance is voluntary in the
co-operative school while it is generally compulsory for the
continuation school. In the former case, the educational
authorities are forced to bid for the support of the employers and the employers naturally demand that the school
curriculum be made more practical and be confined to subjects of almost immediate trade value. As a report of the
Fitchburg, Massachusetts, Co-operative Plan says:

From the first, the employers who offered their assistance in-

sisted that the course be such as to make those going into it
better mechanics, capable of advancing to the highest possibilities in the trade. The prescribed studies of the ordinary
courses that were included in the coöperative industrial course
were, as a rule, changed in form and structure. Many of the
time-honored courses were carefully shelved, and such subjects
were selected as would fit the students to be intelligent mechanics and thoughtful artisans.[1]

The continuation school is not compelled to offer such
inducements to attract a clientele. Courses in industrial
history, industrial hygiene, civics, *etc.*, are therefore more
common in the continuation than in the co-operative schools.

2. Co-operative Schools.

(1) The Co-operative system of the University of Cincinnati.

Dean Herman Schneider is the originator of the co-operative system of education. While an instructor at Lehigh
University, he conceived the idea of co-ordinating the University work with the large industrial plants in Bethlehem,
Pennsylvania. Some of the Lehigh graduates were working for two years as apprentices in the local plant after
graduation. It occurred to Professor Schneider that the
apprentice course and the college work could be combined
in a six-year course with alternate weeks of work and study.
This method, he believed, would solve a number of problems. First, it would avoid a duplication of shop-equip-
ment. This would at once enable the student to work with
up-to-date equipment, a practical impossibility for a school
to supply, and it would relieve the University of the expense of maintaining elaborate mechanical laboratories.
Secondly, it would free the University curriculum of purely

[1] M. R. McCann, "The Fitchburg Plan of Co-operative Education."
U. S. Bureau of Education, Bull., 1913, No. 50, p. 13.

descriptive courses, knowledge of which could be better obtained in the industry itself.   Finally, since the students would be earning money while they studied, many worth while men would be enabled to attend college who otherwise would not be able to do so.   Though the plan was favored by practising engineers, it was rejected by the Lehigh authorities.

When Professor Schneider accepted a position at the University of Cincinnati in 1903, however, he convinced the University authorities of the soundness of the plan and in 1906, a beginning was made to put it into effect.

Twelve industrial plants and 28 students contracted to begin the work which was mapped out to cover a six-year period with alternate weeks at the University and in the shop, together with a three-months period of complete shop-work during the summer. The students were to be grouped in pairs, the men taking turns working at a machine and attending classes. This prevented any discontinuity in the work of the plant. The manufacturer on his part guaranteed to move the student-worker about from position to position. Thus, in the electrical engineering course, the manufacturer guaranteed to employ and train the boy for a year and a half in the foundry, for the next year and a half in the machine shop, for two years in the commutation, controller, winding, erecting, and testing departments and the remainning year in the drafting rooms.

The plan was threatened with disaster at the start since Dean Schneider required all of the candidates, in the summer before entrance, to work in some manufacturing plant. The hard work in hot weather discouraged all but six or eight and Dean Schneider was compelled to fill up the ranks from those who were insufficiently prepared.   Over 400 inquiries from prospective students were received during the first year and a large percentage of these made formal application.

for admission.[1]   By 1911, the experimental period was over
and the system could well be called a success.   By that
time a number of changes in the original plan had been
made: (a) The six years course of 9 months per year was
changed into a five years course running for 11 months per
year.   (b) The period of alternation between shop and
college was lengthened from one to two weeks.   (c) The
iron-clad contract with the employers was modified and the
employers were given power to change a worker whenever
desirable.   The shop-work was checked by the University
authorities to prevent a boy from being kept at one operation
too long.   (d) The business side of the undertaking was
taken from the instructional staff and given to a special
official.

The Cincinnati plan was designed for University men but
it has been copied by several cities who applied the principle
to co-operation between the high schools and industry.   The
system has thus spread downward in the educational scale.

(2) The Fitchburg, Massachusetts, Plan of Co-operative
Education.

The Fitchburg system is a direct outgrowth of the Cincinnati plan.   Dean Schneider on one occasion described his
system to a group of metal manufacturers, among whom
was Mr. Daniel Simonds of Fitchburg, Massachusetts.   Mr.
Simonds became very enthusiastic over the plan and succeeded in inducing the school authorities of his city to start
it in connection with the high-school work.

A director with both shop training and technical education, was employed and in the first year 18 pupils were registered in the course.   The main features of the plan are:
(a) The course covers three years.   One year of regular

[1] C. W. Park, " The Co-operative System of Education," *U. S. Bureau
of Education, Bull., 1916, No. 37,* p. 13.

high-school work being required before the pupil is eligible for entrance. (b) A preliminary summer must be spent in the shops to test the capabilities of the boy. (c) An alternation of weekly periods between school and shop with a consequent pairing off of students. (d) Signing of an agreement or "indenture" by parents and manufacturer. The parent contracts that the boy will complete the school course unless prevented by very unusual circumstances, while the latter contracts to teach the boy the trade mentioned in the agreement. (e) The boy is to be paid wages beginning at 10 cents per hour and finishing at 12½ cents or a total of about $550 for the three years course. (f) The creation of a director who was to supervise the school and shop work of the boys and co-ordinate the two.

Since its inception in 1908, the plan has flourished. From 1908 to 1913 a total of 134 boys had been enrolled and at that time, about 55 boys were taking the course.[1] The boys graduated have in general gone out into the trade for which they have been prepared and their comments upon the system are very enthusiastic.[2]

(3) The Beverly, Massachusetts, Plan.

This system, which was instituted in 1909, is unique in several features. A separate school, called the Beverly Industrial School, was created, which was limited to 50 pupils who were to alternate between shop work and school in groups of 25. The United Shoe Machinery Company agreed to fit up a separate department in their factory to accommodate the 25 boys. These boys were to be given all the necessary equipment and trained to be full-fledged

[1] M. R. McCann, "The Fitchburg Plan of Co-operative Industrial Education," U. S. Bureau of Education Bull., 1913, No. 50, p. 28.

[2] See fifteen commendatory statements by former pupils quoted in "Vocational Letter No. 7," U. S. Bureau of Education, May, 1915.

machinists. The company moreover contracted to furnish the material and purchase the product at established prices. One-half of the price is given to the pupil and the remainder goes toward the maintenance of the school shop, while any deficit is made up by the company itself.

The theoretical instruction is given in high school buildings by a separate staff and the system is administered by a board of industrial education, controlled by the city school board, but upon which the manufacturers have representation. No formal indenture is required, and boys over 14, who have completed the 6th grade, are eligible for entrance.[1]

(4) The Textile Industrial Institute of Spartansburg, S. C.

This is a half-time school supported by private contributions and subsidies from cotton mills. School instruction is given in the common branches and practical courses in homemaking subjects. It is designed to train superintendents and overseers for the cotton mills of the South.

(5) The Co-operative System of York, Pennsylvania.

This follows the alternative week plan. Manufacturers in the following trades co-operate with the high school authorities: machine construction, pattern-making, cabinet-making, plumbing, auto-repairing, molding and electrical work. Over $32,000 was earned by the boys in the first four years of the system. An interesting development in York has been the creation of an auxiliary shop, under the control of the school. It was found that it was necessary to build a separate school shop to insure the students securing all-round training. Thus the co-operative plan in York at least has encountered the same difficulty which spelled ruin for the old apprenticeship system.

[1] See the *First Annual Report of the Trustees of the Industrial School of Beverly, Massachusetts,* 1910, pp. 5-28.

(6) The Co-operative System in New York City.

The introduction of the co-operative system into New York City is the direct result of the labors of Dean Schneider. In 1914 he was employed as an educational expert by the city, and the Board of Education upon his recommendation installed the plan. As in Fitchburg, a preliminary year of high school work is required and unit periods of a week are used. The school work is co-ordinated with the shop experience, mathematics, for instance, being treated from the standpoint of shop problems. 9 high schools and 87 firms co-operated for the year 1916 in taking care of 486 pupils. The weekly earnings of the pupils averaged $5.78.[1]

(7) Other experiments.

Solvay, New York has adopted the co-operative plan in connection with its high school work. The Lewis Institute of Chicago also uses it for some of its students, while the Cincinnati Public School system has established a co-operative course for the training of messenger boys. Centralia township in Illinois has recently put the co-operative plan into practice, while Pittsburg, Pennsylvania, has tried the system in co-operation with various industries and during the last year has worked out an especially close relationship with the department stores of that city.[2] Little Rock, Arkansas, has recently adopted an interesting variant of the usual co-operative plan in its school for printers. Instead of the usual week and week about system, the Little Rock plan calls for five half days in school each week and six half days in the industry itself.[3]

[1] "Experiments in Industrial Education in New York City 1916," National Child Labor Committee Pamphlet, No. 263, p. 12.

[2] See Edward Rynearson, "The Pittsburg Co-operative Plan," School Review, September, 1919, pp. 533-44.

[3] Vocational Summary, September, 1919, p. 95.

3. Part-Time Continuation Schools.

In the United States, the part-time continuation school has been a development of the last ten years. How recent has been its growth in this country can be seen from the fact that when Arthur J. Jones in 1907 wrote his monograph on *The Continuation School in the United States,* he did not mention the type of school that we now regard as " the continuation school."

The development of the continuation school principle in the United States may be divided into two periods: (1) The agitational and experimental period prior to the passage of the Smith-Hughes law. (2) The period since the passage of the Smith-Hughes act, marked by its adoption by nearly a score of states.

The real movement for the establishment of part-time continuation schools began in 1910 when Ohio passed the first law definitely referring to continuation schools. More important still, was the tour of the country in the same year by Dr. George Kirchensteiner, the celebrated founder of the Munich system of continuation schools.[1] Dr. Kirchensteiner's influence was increased by the prestige then popularly attached to Germany's " efficiency " methods. Dr. Kirchensteiner very strongly emphasized the fact that the German system of industrial education was not based upon the all-day trade-school, as people had assumed, but instead upon the part-time continuation school. Drawing upon his own experience, Dr. Kirchensteiner pled for the adoption of the system in the United States.

As a result of Dr. Kirchensteiner's visit, the leaders of the movement for industrial education in this country came to understand the real nature of the continuation school and

[1] Dr. Kichensteiner's tour was under the auspices of the National Society for the Promotion of Industrial Education.

many of them became enthusiastic advocates of it.   From this time on, the continuation school movement gained ground with every year.   Prior to the passage of the Smith-Hughes Act in 1917, seven states (Ohio, Wisconsin, New York, New Jersey, Massachusetts, Indiana and Pennsylvania) had made some form of legislative provision for continuation schools and various systems were being put into effect.   The laws and developments in each of these states prior to 1917 will now be considered in turn.

(1) Ohio.   In 1910 the Ohio legislature passed an act specifying that: " Any board of education *may* require children, between the ages of fifteen and sixteen years who are employed, to attend continuation schools not to exceed eight hours per week between the hours of 8 A. M. and 5 P. M." [1]   The act further provided that all minors over fifteen and sixteen who had not completed the sixth grade in required subjects should be required to attend school for a corresponding period of time. [2]

Since the Ohio Law did not require local boards to establish continuation schools but merely permitted them to do so, and since no state aid was given to those localities which might take advantage of the act, little could be expected from the law.   Cincinnati was, in fact, the only Ohio city which installed continuation schools.   Even here, however, not all employed children between fifteen and sixteen were required to attend but rather only narrowly restricted classes.   In the year 1914-15, the number of pupils enrolled in these continuation schools was only 951. [3]   This figure included a considerable number of students under the

[1] " Digest of State Laws Relating to Public Education," *Bull. United States Bureau of Education, 1915, No. 47,* p. 550.

[2] *Ibid.,* p. 550.

[3] *86th Annual Report of the Cincinnati Public Schools* for year ending August 31, 1915, pp. 338-343.

co-operative plan who were not really attendants of part-time continuation schools. The per capita cost of instruction in these continuation schools was as follows:[1]

Year	Cost per Student
1909–10	$12.32
1910–11	20.50
1911–12	8.70
1912–13	9.13
1913–14	9.44
1914–15	7.26

(2) Wisconsin. In 1911, the Wisconsin Legislature passed a series of acts providing that the various local boards of education in localities of over 5,000 population must establish an industrial, commercial, continuation or evening school upon petition of twenty-five persons qualified to attend these schools. Whenever such a school was established for minors between fourteen and sixteen, every such child must attend it for not less than five hours a week for six months in a year and their employers must allow these minors a corresponding reduction in the hours of work. Other features of the act were: (a) the establishment of a liberal system of state aid to such schools; (b) the revision of the apprentice laws so that all apprentices must receive at least five hours of instruction per week; and (c) the creation of a state board of industrial education.[2]

By a law which went into effect July 1, 1916, the age of compulsory attendance was raised from 16 to 17 years and the number of hours required for school per week was increased from 5 to 8.[3] Furthermore, the length of the

[1] This includes the voluntary attendance at these continuation schools, ibid., p. 355.

[2] Report Commissioner of Education, 1911, vol. i, pp. 306-07, also Bull. No. 2, Wisconsin State Board of Industrial Education, p. 4.

[3] This requirement was not to be imposed for the 16 year old class until September 1, 1918. Till then only four hours a week were required.

school year was increased from six to eight months. In these ways, therefore, the amount of continuation school training required was more than trebled.

The enrollment in the day and evening continuation schools during the year ending June 30th, 1917, was approximately 38,000. Such schools are in operation in all of the 30 cities of the state. The total cost of these schools was about $700,000 for the year of which the state pays approximately one-half. The average cost per student was $18 a year.

(3) The New York Law of 1913.

In 1913, the Education Law was amended so that, it *permitted* local boards of education to establish continuation schools

in which instruction shall be given in the trades and in industrial, agricultural, and homemaking subjects and which shall be open to pupils over fourteen years of age who are regularly and lawfully employed during a part of the day in any useful employment or service, which subjects shall be supplementary to the practical work carried on in such employments.[2]

Should such continuation schools for employed children between fourteen and sixteen be established the local board of education was given the power to require the attendance of any person within this age period. In addition to this

[1] Respective amounts of time required for continuation schools by Wisconsin Acts of 1911 and 1916.

Act	Years	Weeks	Hours per Week		Total number of hours required
1911	2	× 26	× 5	=	260
1916	3	× 35 (app)	× 8	=	840

[2] *U. S. Bureau of Education, 1915, Bulletin 47*, "State Laws Relating to Public Education," pp. 698-99; *Bulletin University of State of New York, No. 542*, May 1, 1913, pp. 16-17.

every boy between fourteen and sixteen not graduated from elmentary schools must take not less than six hours of school work a week for sixteen weeks.

State aid was provided for any continuation school running thirty-six weeks and having one full-time teacher and a minimum of fifteen pupils. This subsidy was to be two-thirds the salary of such a teacher but not to exceed a total of $1000 per school; and in the year 1916-17 these were attended by only 163 children between the ages of 14 and 16![2] As we shall see, New York has since passed a compulsory continuation-school law.

(4) New Jersey. The New Jersey Vocational School Law of 1913 gave permission to the various school districts to establish part-time continuation schools. State aid to an amount equal to that raised by the district (exclusive of buildings but not to exceed $10,000 for any one district) was pledged.[3] Despite this subsidy, only one continuation school had been established by 1916 with a total of fifty-seven pupils.[4] New Jersey has since passed a compulsory continuation-school law.

(5) Massachusetts. Massachusetts was the pioneer state in real industrial education. The celebrated *Report of the Douglas Commission* in 1906 caused the state to provide state aid for vocational education. The dominant ideal at that time however was that of the all-day trade school but the inadequacies which this system displayed soon forced the adoption of other plans as well.

[1] *U. S. Bureau of Education, 1915, Bulletin 47, op. cit.*, pp. 698-99.

[2] *News Letter National Society Promotion Industrial Education*, May, 1917, p. 21.

[3] "Digest of State Laws Relating to Public Education," *Bull. U. S. Bureau of Education, 1915, No. 47*, p. 697.

[4] *News Letter*. National Society Promotion Industrial Education, May, 1917, p. 21.

In 1911, trade extension schools, with voluntary attendance, and open to persons between fourteen and twenty-five, were authorized.[1] An investigation of the general question of part-time education was also authorized and in 1913 the State Board of Education submitted its report recommending the establishment of continuation schools. The Board recommended that all unemployed children between fourteen and sixteen be compelled to attend school and that the local boards of education be empowered to require the attendance of children of these ages at a continuation school for at least four hours a week.[2] The legislature accordingly enacted that

the school committee of any city or town may, with the approval of the state board of education, require that every child who is over fourteen and under sixteen years of age, and who is regularly employed not less than six hours a day, shall attend at the rate of not less than four hours per week during the time that such school is in actual session.[3]

This was a permissive-mandatory law in which the legislature declined to make attendance compulsory but permitted local boards of education to do so if they deemed fit.

Boston was the only city to take advantage of this law. In 1915, the first continuation schools were opened in that city and the enrollment for the year 1915-16 was 3,300, employing 39 teachers.[4]

The continuation schools were intended to be of three varieties: (a) those to extend the general education of the

[1] *Acts of 1911*, chapter 471, section 1, paragraph 7, and section 3.

[2] " Needs and Possibilities of Part-Time Education," a *Report by the Massachusetts Board of Education*, 1913, pp. 21-23.

[3] House Bill No. 424, Massachusetts Acts 1913.

[4] *News Letter*, National Society Promotion Industrial Education 1917, p. 20.

pupil; (b) prevocational continuation schools, to give the employed child practical experience in several trades, furnish information about various industries and assist, through vocational guidance in selecting an occupation; (c) vocational continuation schools; these last were to give actual vocational instruction. This last class in turn was composed of two further varieties, (1) trade preparatory, (2) trade extension schools. The former was to give training in occupations unrelated to those followed by the pupils during the working day. Its aim was to teach skilled trades to those not already engaged in them or to allow pupils to change from present occupations to more congenial ones for which they are better adapted. The Trade Extension School, on the other hand was to train the pupil in subjects closely connected with the work at which he was employed and give him practical training in the advanced processes of his particular trade.[1]

· The curricula of these varied types quite naturally differed. All the schools were to give 25% of their time to general training for citizenship, to include courses in civics, personal and industrial hygiene, together with recreation, and cultural subjects. The general improvement school, however, devotes 50% of its time to such subjects as English, arithmetic, geography, and history. These are designed to remove the previous deficiencies of the pupil and add to his general resources. The remaining 25% is to be spent in the discovery and development of the pupil's vocational interests and powers. The pre-vocational school, on the other hand, devotes 50% of its time to shop-work and 25% to vocational guidance, while the vocational continuation schools devotes 75% of its time to actual shop-work and

[1] For a more detailed description of these types, see *Bulletin of the Massachusetts Board of Education*, 1915, number 6, whole number 43, pp. 9-10.

related subjects. In 1919, Massachusetts referred the question of compulsory part-time attendance to a referendum vote of all localities where there were more than 200 employed minors from 14 to 16. It is significant that every city voted to require such schools.

(6) Indiana. In 1913 Indiana established a system of state-aided vocational schools and among the types provided for by law was the continuation school. The act authorized the local boards to require all children between fourteen and sixteen years who were regularly employed to attend school not less than five hours a week between the hours of 8 A. M. and 5 P. M.[1] State aid to the extent of two-thirds of the cost of instruction was extended to those schools approved by the state board of education, and a special tax levy of one cent upon every hundred dollars of taxable property was made to provide funds for this purpose.[2]

The state board of education announced that state aid would be extended only to those schools which gave " instruction in the present wage-earning occupations of the pupils, instruction designed to make them more efficient and productive workmen in that occupation or trade." Schools which aimed to increase the general intelligence of the workers were not to receive assistance. The board declared that though, " it is important to provide a means whereby the workers who have gotten into blind-alley jobs, may be able to fit themselves for more skilled occupations, a school having this for its aim cannot be state aided under the law."[3] The part-time continuation schools that have

[1] House Bill No. 101, Indiana Legislature, approved February 23, 1913, section 11.

[2] Ibid., section 14.

[3] " Vocational Education in Indiana," Bull. No. 6, Vocational No. 4, Indiana Department of Public Instruction, p. 25.

been established are for apprentices and workers between 14 and 25 years who are engaged in skilled trades. Mr. Book says, " No general continuation work for young people engaged in juvenile or temporary occupations has as yet been organized because this type of education was not state-aided by our law." [1]

The narrowness of this system can be readily seen. It does not provide for boys and girls in blind-alley trades and thereby ignores the majority of juvenile labor. Confining its attention, as it does, solely to the occupation at which the young worker is engaged, it does not permit him to prepare himself for other and better occupations. It is extremely doubtful, moreover, whether it permits him to educate himself for more responsible positions in the same industry. The general social purposes are pared to a minimum, only the course of civics being required.

During the year 1915-16, Indiana had thirty-three part-time schools (including co-operative schools) with a total enrollment of 235. Day courses in homemaking for women, which may be called continuation schools, enrolled a total of 1970.

(7) Pennsylvania. In 1913, Pennsylvania provided for the establishment of a system of compulsory continuation schools in connection with a stringent child-labor law. The continuation school law reads, " It shall be unlawful for any person to employ any minor between fourteen and sixteen years of age, unless such minor shall during the period of such employment, attend, for a period, or periods, not less than eight hours each week, a school approved by the state superintendent of public instruction." [2]

Children employed on farms or in domestic service are

[1] W. F. Book, " Vocational Education in Indiana," *Educational Administration and Supervision*, vol. iii, p. 451 (October, 1917).

[2] Act of General Assembly, No. 177, Laws of Pennsylvania 1915, sec. 3.

not subject to this act, although all other children are. These continuation schools may be conducted in schoolhouses or in factories and stores. They must not be held on either Saturday or Sunday and must be between the hours of 8 A. M. and 5 P. M.

When a school district has fullfilled the regulations of the department of public instruction, such district receives $200 annually for every teacher having had three or more years of teaching experience, and $150 for every teacher having had one to three years of experience. The state also pays 50% of the cost of equipment in such a school. The proportions of the school time devoted to various branches are as follows: (a) 40% to academic subjects and general education. This includes English, composition, industrial geography, hygiene, (personal, industrial and social) and civics. (b) 20% to fixed vocational subjects applicable to all industries. This includes industrial mathematics with problems specifically adapted to industrial bookkeeping. Another required subject is shop-sketching and free-hand drawing. (c) 30% to variable vocational subjects. This includes the study of the machines and processes at which the pupil is employed during the day. The local board is given the power of constructing a curriculum of this portion of the time.[1]

For the year 1915-16, three hundred and fifty-one continuation schools employed 372 teachers and had a total enrollment of 35,628 pupils, which had increased to approximately 40,000 by June, 1919.

State legislation prior to the Smith-Hughes Act, therefore, was based upon conflicting attitudes on the following two questions: (1) Whether or not the state should require

[1] For a further description of the Pennsylvania system see W. E. Hackett, *Manual Training*, January, 1916, pp. 377-79.

attendance at the continuation schools. Wisconsin and Pennsylvania were the only states where the legislature made attendance compulsory for all. Massachusetts, New York, Ohio and Indiana had permissive mandatory laws by which the legislature empowered the local boards of education to require attendance. Experience was clearly showing, however, that the latter type of law was very ineffective in meeting the situation because of the reluctance of the local boards to impose any additional tax burden. Wisconsin and Pennsylvania, on the other hand, were demonstrating that state-wide compulsory continuation schools backed up by a system of state aid were the only effective means of educating the juvenile worker. (2) Whether or not the curriculum of the continuation schools should be narrowly vocational. As we have seen, the Indiana law permitted education only for the job at which the juvenile worker was employed and did not allow the trade preparation training or social subjects in the curriculum. Pennsylvania and Massachusetts, on the other hand, permitted a more diversified form of education and included civic and social subjects as well as the more strictly vocational.

The Smith-Hughes Act of 1917 greatly accelerated the movement for continuation schools. The act provided that at least one-third of the money apportioned to the respective state for teachers of home economics, trade and industrial subjects *must* be spent in part-time schools or classes and furthermore that the subjects taught must increase the civic or vocational intelligence of employed persons over fourteen years.[1]

As a result, seventeen additional states passed compulsory continuation school laws in 1918, so that there are now nineteen such states. The following table summarizes the chief provisions of these laws:

[1] Section 11 of the Act.

PROVISIONS OF PART-TIME COMPULSORY EDUCATION LAWS [1]

States	Minimum number of minors required to establish classes	Ages of required attendance	Hours per week required attendance	Length af School Year	Law in Effect
Arizona	15	14–16	5	150 hours	1919
California	12[5]	14–18	4	Same as public schools.	1920
Illinois	20	14–18	8	Same as public schools.	1921
Iowa	15	14–16	8	Same as public schools.	1919
Massachusetts	200	14–16	4	Same as public schools.	1920
Michigan	50	14–18	8	Same as public schools.	1920
Missouri	25	14–16	4	Same as public schools.	1919
Montana	15	14–18	4	Same as public schools	1919
Nebraska	15	14–16	8	144 hours	1919
Nevada	15	14–18	4	Same as public schools.	1919
New Jersey	20	14–16	6	36 weeks	1920
New Mexico	15	14–16	5	150 hours	1919
New York	20[3]	14–18	4–8	Same as public schools.	1919
Oklahoma	20	16–18	..	144 hours	1919
Oregon	15[3]	14–18	5	Same as public schools.	1919
Pennsylvania	50	14–16	8	Same as public schools.	1913
Utah	15	14–18	4	144 hours	1919
Washington	15[4]	14–18	4	Same as public schools.	1920
Wisconsin	..[3]	14–17	8	8 months	1911

It will be noticed from the above table that ten states require attendance until eighteen, one to seventeen and seven to sixteen years of age. The minimum age at which part-time education begins is almost universally fourteen save in Oklahoma where it is sixteen due to the fact that com-

[1] Taken from *Third Annual Report, Federal Board for Vocational Education*, December, 1919, p. 21, and paper delivered by L. H. Carris before *National Society for Vocational Education*, February 21, 1920. Mr. Carris' paper gives an admirable summary of this legislation.

[2] Establishment required only in cities of over 5,000 population.

[3] Attendance upon evening school may be substituted.

[4] Districts may organize schools upon written request of 25 residents.

[5] High school districts having 50 or more pupils must establish part-time classes.

pulsory full-time education is required there until sixteen. Nine of the states require two years of this part-time education, one requires three years, and nine require four years.

The number of hours of part-time education required per year also varies. The Smith-Hughes Act requires that at least 144 hours be given before the school may receive federal aid and all states provide at least this amount. On the basis of weekly attendance, seven states require four hours, two require five hours, one requires six hours, six require eight hours and one has a minimum requirement of four hours with a maximum of eight. Twelve states require as many weeks for the part-time schools as for the other public schools. One specifies that thirty-six weeks should be required; another, eight months and still others do not specify the number of weeks but fix a yearly minimum length. Taken all in all, the minimum of 144 hours a year is exceeded by at least seven states, most notably by Wisconsin, Illinois, Pennsylvania and New Jersey.

It will be noticed that the laws provide a minimum number of minors necessary to form a class ranging from 12 in California to 200 in Massachusetts. In all but four states, however, not more than 20 are required. Some limitation seems to be necessary from an administrative standpoint; but care should be taken lest the minimum be placed too high, thus preventing children in small towns and localities from receiving such training.

The state laws almost universally require the schools to be held during the minors' working hours and usually state that they must be held between the hours of 8 A. M. and 5 or 6 P. M. The hours spent in the part-time school are to be deducted from the maximum number of hours which the state law permits the minor to work. For instance, if children are allowed to work 48 hours per week and are required to attend a part-time school for 4 hours, the number of hours which a minor can legally work is thereby lowered to 44. Only one state, Oregon, permits the attendance at an evening school as a substitute for attendance at a part-time school.

Most of the acts have been passed so recently, many having not yet gone into effect, that it is difficult to pass judgment upon their effectiveness. The whole movement, however, is a most significant step in the abolition of the hitherto abrupt break between school and industry and in extending partial educational control over the child for an additional period of time. It is probably only a question of time before the other states will enact compulsory part-time laws as well and the example of Wisconsin and Pennsylvania rather than the permissive-mandatory laws will furnish the model for future legislation.

Both the part-time continuation school and the co-operative school posses certain obvious advantages over the all-day trade school and the corporation school. Unlike the former they can take both those under sixteen and those who are poor and give them an education which admirably combines theory and practice, and do all this at a lower cost per pupil. Unlike the latter, they can apply to small plants, their teaching will be less biased and their continuation will not be dependent upon their pecuniary profitableness to the individual employer. These statements should not be understood to mean that the trade school and the corporation school have no place. Far from it. They have a real place but it is a supplementary one. They cannot become the chief element in the system of industrial education.

While it may have been doubtful a few years ago as to whether the part-time continuation school or the co-operative school would become the dominant form of school, this issue has been settled by the part-time laws passed within the last two years. It is the continuation school that will be-

come the corner stone for the American system of industrial education as it has been for that of Germany and,
under the Fisher Act, has become for that of England.   The
chief reason for the adoption of the part-time school plan
in preference to the co-operative school was perhaps its
greater adaptability for the purpose of compulsory attendance.   It was seen that voluntary attendance for further
training would not be sufficient to cope with the problem.
Compulsion was necessary.   It would be impossible, however, to compel attendance at school for half of the time of
the employed boy.   Such a universal requirement would
disrupt every employer's business, cut the child's wages in
half and impose a crushing burden of expense upon the
state.   Part-time education of from four to eight hours a
week is less costly and disconcerting to all parties.

The part-time continuation school, however, has at least
two further advantages which are less frequently considered :
(1) There is much less danger than under the co-operative
plan of overcrowding any particular trade with workers.
Under the co-operative system, two sets of learners alter-
nately occupy the same place in industry.   Should the co-
operative plan be adopted completely in any one locality,
there would be danger that a double labor force would be
trained which could not be assimilated upon graduation. (2)
More than any other plan, the continuation school gives a
greater opportunity for the abler members of the lower
economic classes to rise in industry.

This may perhaps be illustrated as follows.   Let us represent the present industrial system as a multiple-storied
house, the first floor of which is composed of the unskilled
jobs, the second story of the semi-skilled positions, the third
of the skilled jobs the fourth of the high grade clerical work
and the upper floor of the engineering and managerial positions.   How do the present occupants of these various floors

attain their positions? Obviously anyone can walk in on the
ground floor and enter the ranks of the unskilled workers.
But how can one reach the upper floors? It depends upon the
system of industrial education. If the trade or the co-operative school is the predominant method, entrance to these
floors is only from outside of the house, not from the inside.
There would be some passage between the unskilled and semi-
skilled and the skilled, but it would on the whole, be slight,
especially between the latter two classes. Once a juvenile
entered the ground floor and joined the ranks of the unskilled laborers, he must largely abandon hope of climbing
to the upper floors. The only way to reach them would be
by climbing the staircase outside of the building (the trade
or co-operative school) which would open at the various
floors and then admit him. But should he try this, he
would be outside the building and to climb up the stairway
would take several years. Since he was outside, he would
not be in the industry and consequently, he would not be
earning. Since he could not support himself while he was
climbing the staircase, he would be forced to stay inside and
continue working on the ground floor at unskilled labor.

Who then would reach the upper floors? Those whose
parents could afford to support them while they were learning and climbing the stair case. These children could reach
the two upper floors and join the skilled laborers and brain
workers without ever having entered the lower floors at all.
Thus, each group of workers would be recruited from a
particular class and those in the lower floors could not rise
to the upper. Such a system of industrial education, to
carry our analogy one stage further, would be like a house
with no inside but only outside stairways. This was the
German system of education and inevitably produced there
what it will produce everywhere, namely, class stratification.
It does not give equality of economic opportunity.

The continuation school supplies those inside stairways that are lacking under a trade or co-operative school system of industrial education. It enables men to earn while learning and hence makes it possible for them to rise from the bottom and helps to break down class stratification. The continuation school seems thus to be the best single system of industrial education that there is. The trade school, the corporation school, and the co-operative school can all find places in which they may function efficiently, but they should be auxiliary and subordinate to the continuation school.

CHAPTER XII

Vocational Guidance

VOCATIONAL guidance aims to direct the child into those occupations in which he can find the greatest efficiency and happiness. Upon leaving school, children now generally take the first job that turns up without stopping to inquire whether it is a position that has future promise or is one for which they are adapted. Says the Federal Investigation into the Conditions of Women and Child Wage-Earners:

There is much to indicate . . . that the opportunities and advantages were alike unknown to them (the children). Nothing seemed to suggest to a child the desirability of learning a trade or entering an industry in which he would have a chance of rising so he took the first thing that came to hand.[1]

Since the child rarely knows the nature of the industry he enters and practically never knows his own capacities, an enormous amount of economic and social maladjustment follows. One index of this is the rate at which juvenile workers change their positions, which has already been indicated in Chapter IV. The vast multitude of men and women working at distasteful jobs for which they are not adapted forms one of the great modern wastes of human energy as well as one of the chief sources of unhappiness and baulked human impulses.

The vocational guidance movement seeks to lessen this maladjustment. Such a movement could never have arisen

[1] *Report on Conditions of Women and Child Labor*, Senate Doc. 645, 61st Congress, 2nd Session, vol. vii, p. 186.

in the days of handicraft: it is a product of the complexity of modern industry. In the small village preceding the Industrial Revolution a boy had only to make his choice between a few trades, each of which was a whole. He walked by these shops almost daily and knew the master workmen quite intimately. He secured most of his knowledge at first hand while his father would supplement his information.[1] Then the choice of a vocation was the result of years of observation and was based upon an intimate knowledge of the situation. The enormous multiplication of trades, the ever-increasing division of labor, together with the widening of the area in which a workman can sell his labor, have destroyed all possibility of either the modern child or his father knowing what occupations are best suited for him. Vocational guidance aims to create a definite organization which will perform a function previously carried on by the family.

I. Stages in the Development of Vocational Guidance

Formal vocational guidance in America is a product of only the last fifteen years. It began almost contemporaneously in New York and Boston,[2] but the main stream of influence has spread from Boston. Professor Frank Parsons of Boston University, a prolific writer upon social questions, became interested in the problem, and began talking with children who were either at work or who were about to begin. His activity ripened very naturally into the establishment of a vocational bureau attached to the Civic Service House of Boston. To this Bureau, Professor Parsons gave his last years before his death in 1908.[3] His

[1] See Franklin's *Autobiography*.

[2] A. H. Leake, *Industrial Education*, p. 155, states that organizations for vocational guidance had their inception in New York.

[3] Prof. Parsons' book, *Choosing a Vocation*, was published posthumously in 1909.

work was taken up and carried on by Mr. Meyer Bloom-field, who for some years was the most prominent and active worker in the movement.

1. The Guidance of the Individual child. Professor Parsons began by personally advising a few boys and girls. Flesh and blood children were asking for advice, and the advice had to be adapted to their particular needs. Parsons and his followers found that to do this effectively, they must investigate the child's past record and form a first-hand opinion of his capacities. Once the child was at work, the advisor or "counsellor" followed him up and found out how the child was progressing and why. The entire basis was one of friendship between counsellor and child, and was more amiable than scientific. In this stage, the counsellors were largely volunteers, and anyone capable of teaching a settlement class was considered capable of serving as a vocational adviser.

Vocational guidance in most places has today not proceeded beyond this primary stage. It concerns itself largely with individual cases and does not treat the problem *en masse*. In some cities, however, a second stage has been reached.

2. The Treatment of Vocational Guidance as a Community Problem. As vocational guidance progresses in a community, more and more children come to be affected by it. This increase may be due either to their voluntary request for counsel, or to the institution of counsellors in the public schools who are to guide students about to enter industry. The problem now becomes not merely how to place Johnnie or Susie in a good job, but how to take care of a hundred or a thousand boys and girls. The large numbers compel those in charge of vocational guidance to find out just how many children are wanted in the various industries and what are the advantages of each. From the collected trade experience of children who have been advised, a body of data is gradually built up.

The most prominent feature of this stage is the municipal survey. This is designed to cover some or all of the chief industries of the city to determine just what vocational opportunities they offer. These surveys are conducted by various bodies; sometimes by unofficial local societies, sometimes by organizations such as the Russell Sage Foundation, or the National Society for the Promotion of Industrial Education, and sometimes by municipal and state agencies. Often they are part of a general survey of the educational conditions of the locality.

Some forty surveys of varying degrees of elaborateness, which have been made during the last five years, have come to the author's knowledge.[1] Undoubtedly the most important of these are the Richmond Survey of 1915, the Minneapolis Survey of 1916 and the studies of Evansville, Indianapolis, and Richmond, Indiana, of 1917. The last three were coöperated in by the National Society for the Promotion of Industrial Education. These investigations laid a basis of facts upon which counsellors and educators could build their policy. In this respect the second stage is really the beginning of scientific vocational guidance.

3. Vocational Guidance as a Shop Policy. Within the last few years, the discovery of the amount of labor turn-

[1] Boston, Somerville, Holyoke, Waltham and Worchester, Mass.; Bridgeport and Hartford, Conn.; Buffalo, N. Y. City, Poughkeepsie, Rochester, Syracuse and Troy, N. Y.; Jersey City, N. J.; Duquesne, Ia.; Pittsburgh, Philadelphia, Scranton and Wilkesbarre, Pa.; Richmond, Va.; Louisville, Ky.; Winston-Salem, N. C.; Little Rock, Ark.; New Orleans, La.; Cincinnati, Cleveland, and Dayton, Ohio; Indianapolis, Richmond, Evansville, Terre Haute and Hammond, Ind.; Chicago, Peoria and Springfield, Ill.; Grand Rapids, Mich.; Duluth and Minneapolis, Minn.; Topeka, Kan.; Sioux City, Iowa.; Oakland, Calif.; Portland, Ore.; Seattle, Wash.

over, absenteeism and withheld effort, has caused hundreds
of plants to create functionalized employment departments.
These departments have taken hiring away from the shop
foremen and have centralized it.   The best conducted have
tried to test the ability of the applicants for work, to place
them in the proper positions, to follow them up in order
to see whether they are succeeding and to adjust any difficulties that may arise.   This constitutes the third stage of
vocational guidance.

II.   The Methods of Vocational Guidance

As vocational guidance has increased in importance, its
methods have naturally become more scientific.   Both the
children and industry itself demand accurate investigation.
The following discussion considers the attempts made by
vocational guidance to determine for what positions children are fitted and what positions are best fitted for children.

*1. Determination of the Positions for which the Child is
Best Fitted.*   The following principles have been advanced
as methods whereby the capacities of the child can be
ascertained.

*A. Determination upon the basis of the child's in-
terests.*   This theory runs somewhat as follows: "If a
child is interested in an occupation, he will work hard
at it and ultimately master it.   The task then is simply to
guide his interests.   This can be done by letting him know
about various industries, and by stimulating him to think
about his future vocation."

This is evidently a *laissez-faire* theory of vocational
guidance and is a part of the modern movement in which
John Dewey and Madame Montessori, have been leaders.
This doctrine of interest should be examined from several
standpoints, however, before it is accepted.   (1) *Is interest
a real index to ability?*   Thorndike, after an investigation

of 100 college students, concluded that if a person is interested in a subject, he generally has ability in it.[1] This apparently conclusive study should not, however, be regarded as settling the matter at issue. The students' interests which were measured were in subjects that they had studied or were then studying. The students knew from first-hand contact whether or not they liked a given subject. Plainly this does not apply to the children about to choose a vocation. Their interest is based on desire, with little or no contact with the facts. Being prospective, not retrospective, it is clearly no index of their ability in the given industry.

(2) Is the interest of a child permanent or temporary? If it is permanent, the child can perhaps be allowed to make its choice. If temporary, grave dangers immediately arise.

Thorndike, in the study already mentioned, states that, "these facts unanimously witness to the importance of early interests. They are shown to be far from fickle and evanescent. On the contrary, the order of interests of twenty shows six-tenths of perfect resemblance to the order from 11 to 14, and has changed little more than the order of abilities has changed."[2]

This study is open to the immediate criticism that the statistics for the earlier years were based upon memory which is an untrustworthy source, since one is apt to underestimate changes and to overestimate permanence. But even if we should waive this criticism, the study would not prove that interests are permanent in the industrial field. Thorndike was measuring interest in school subjects which are broader classifications than specific jobs. The curriculum can at most be divided into only a score of general

[1] E. L. Thorndike, "The Permanence of Interests and their Relation to Abilities," *Popular Science Monthly*, vol. 81, pp. 449-456 (Nov., 1912)

[2] Thorndike, *op. cit.*, p. 455.

subjects, while industry has thousands of occupations. A boy may have a permanent interest in economics, yet that interest may lead him equally well into law, business, railroading, banking, teaching or politics. In the same way a boy might have a permanent interest in " factory work." Does that determine what particular industry he will enter? Moreover, does it determine the particular occupation he will assume in any one industry? The fact that " general " interests are permanent, may narrow the field, but it does not settle the choice. A child's preference for a concrete position, such as that of civil engineer or carpenter, is not necessarily permanent. There is indeed a very strong presumption that the interest of children in specific positions is anything but permanent. It is likely to change because the child himself is in the very process of change.

(3) Will the children be able to indulge their interests in industry as it is? Children are naturally interested in picturesque and striking occupations, but unfortunately there are only a few such. They are not interested in the routine tasks, but industry is chiefly composed of these. Most children desire positions which, in the nature of things, only a few of them can attain. The tendency of children to choose occupations which are impossible for all, save a small percentage finally to engage in, is shown by the following studies. Zeidler, in his investigation in the schools of Santa Clara County California, found that 122 boys out of 293 wanted to enter one of the five following occupations: machinist, mechanic, engineer, aviator and electrician, while only two of their fathers were so engaged.[1] Close study of over 1000 boys in Oakland, California, disclosed that 56.4% of them wanted to be one of

[1] Richard Zeidler, " Occupations of Fathers and Occupational Choices of Boys in Twenty-two Rural and Village Schools in Santa Clara County, California," *Manual Training*, May, 1916, pp. 674-80.

the following: engineer, lawyer, mechanic, farmer, architect, electrician, doctor, book-keeper and chef, yet only 12.4% of the parents of these boys were employed at these occupations.[1] Wood's study of 990 boys in St. Paul, Minn., lends further confirmation. 28% of the boys wanted to go into the professions, while only 5% of the parents were professional men. 14% of the boys wanted clerical jobs although only 6% of the parents were so employed.[2]

Conversely, those occupations where most of the fathers are employed, are those towards which the boys manifest the least interest. Zeidler's study showed that fifty-three fathers were either laborers, contractors, ministers, painters, or fruit packers, yet only three sons want to enter any of these occupations.[3] Sears' study showed that while 30% of the parents were engaged in the manufacturing trades, only 7% of the boys wished to enter them and that although 32% of the fathers were in business, but 14% of the sons wanted to enter this field.[4] The St. Paul investigation showed that whereas the trades employed 33% of the fathers, only 14% of the boys had chosen it, and that while 10% of the fathers were unskilled laborers, only 1% of the boys wanted to go into this class of occupation.[5]

Interest therefore seems to be insufficient as a sole method of vocational guidance. The truth is probably that while no child should preferably go into an industry unless he is interested in it, it is also true that he should not

[1] T. B. Sears, "Occupations of Fathers and Occupational Choices of 1039 Boys in Grades Seven and Eight of the Oakland Schools," *School and Society*, vol. i, pp. 750-56.

[2] Erville B. Woods, "The Social Waste of Unguided Personal Ability," *American Journal of Sociology*, vol. xix, p. 365 (Nov., 1913).

[3] Zeidler, *op. cit.*

[4] Sears, *op. cit.*, pp. 750-56.

[5] Woods, *op. cit.*, p. 365.

enter it just because he is interested. Advocates of vocational guidance must furthermore face a truth that they have hitherto found it more pleasant to ignore: namely, that a large part of the world's work is so dispiriting and dull that, were interest depended on, these positions would never be filled. They are filled at present, not by choice, but by economic pressure. Vocational guidance in itself will be insufficient to drain children off from these pursuits. Somehow they will still have to be recruited.

B. Determination by Self Analysis. Few would advocate this as the sole method of vocational guidance, but it has its place as a part of the system. It is really an inventory of the individual's assets and liabilities. Parsons, indeed, made self-analysis the basis of his method, and required those who came to him for guidance to make a written analysis of themselves by following an outline that he had prepared. This outline was exceedingly elaborate, containing over four hundred questions.[1] Obviously it would require a capacity for patient accurate introspection that few adults and practically no juveniles possess. Hollingworth has found that the individual tends to overestimate himself upon desirable traits and under-estimate his possession of undesirable ones.[2] Furthermore, such abstract qualities as energy, honesty, truthfulness, industry, *etc.*, that Parsons tried to evaluate, are prerequisites for all industries, nay for life itself; they do not determine which of a number of industries one should enter.

C. Determination by the Impartial Judgment of Others. Men are hired by others, they are not employed merely because they want to work at a particular job. Employers

---

[1] Frank Parsons, *Choosing a Vocation*, pp. 26-44.

[2] H. L. Hollingworth, *Vocational Psychology*, pp. 151-155.

have used the most diverse methods of selecting men.   Most of them say that they use their "knowledge of human nature" to make proper choices.   Few could tell what they mean by "human nature."   It generally means that they employ those that make a good impression on them. Terman, in a San Diego examination, found that many candidates having a good personal appearance, were of a low degree of intelligence.[1]   A good or bad impression may be and often is caused by details that have no real connection with the applicants' power of filling the position satisfactorily.   A sallow skin, a retreating forehead, and close-set eyes, are traits that the vast majority of business men would stamp as undesirable, yet there is not one iota of proof to indicate that they are any index of a man's true worth. Phrenology has long since been exploded by scientists, but many so-called "practical" men still cling to it.[2]   Nor is the ability or inability to impress an employer by short conversations, general dress, and bearing, an index of ability. The methods of employment have all too frequently been, in the past, a mixture of guess-work and false science.

One very distinct fault with this method of employment has been that judgment has been passed by one man only. Individual judgments are notoriously open to error.   Group judgments are much more reliable.[3]   In the personal examination, undoubtedly a better selection of men would be obtained if several persons passed judgment on the men and rated them as regards certain concrete characteristics. From these individual judgments, a composite rating could

---

[1] L. H. Terman, "A Trial of Mental and Pedagogical Tests in a Civil Service Examination for Policemen and Firemen," *Journal of Applied Psychology*, vol. i, pp. 17-19 (March, 1917).

[2] *E. g.*, the wide attention that is being paid by business men to Dr. Katherine Blackford's methods of analyzing character.

[3] See Hollingworth, *op. cit.*, pp. 133-142.

be made which would tend to eliminate many individual errors. Exactly such a system was worked out for the rating of officers during the war by the committee on classification and personnel of the War Department.

D. Determination by Means of Psychological and Trade Tests. Individual judgments are faulty and take the time of high-salaried officials. Group judgments are expensive. How much easier it apparently is to turn over the applicant to a psychological laboratory and ask for a quantitive measurement of his qualities! The tests do not take long and there is a numerical precision about the results that is highly impressive. The question is: are these tests an index of ability? If so, how far?

A variety of tests has been used. They may be divided into two main groups, (1) general intelligence tests, and (2) specific abilities tests. Typical of the first group are the revised Benet-Simon tests, the Terman, Thorndike, Woodworth and Wells tests and the army general intelligence tests.[1] These intelligence tests have developed far beyond the crude forms of the original Benet-Simon test so that not only can the definitely feeble-minded be identified but all others can be classified into various groups. The general intelligence of a fairly large sample is shown to conform to the normal probability curve. A firm desirous of hiring high-grade men will find its choice greatly assisted by the use of these tests.[2] Positions may also be classified into groups according to the amount of intelligence required of those who work at them. Then men with grade A intelligence, can be employed at grade A jobs, those of grade B

[1] See Terman, *The Measurement of General Intelligence*; Yoakum and Yerkes, *Army Mental Tests.*

[2] See W. D. Scott, "The Selection of Employees by means of Quantitative Determinations," *Annals, American Academy Political and Social Science*, May, 1916, pp. 182-193.

at grade B positions and the men of the lowest intelligence at the least skilled jobs. Care should be taken, however, that the classification be not made minute and not more than four or five groups should be separated at first. While this method is applicable among groups, it does not afford a basis for apportioning positions within any one of these groups.

The question may then be asked: does experimental psychology afford a means for determining the specific capacity for specific occupations? Certain tests such as those for color-blindness, for such occupations as engineers, motormen and flagmen, can be given and the defectives weeded out. The discovery of specific aptitudes, however, is much more difficult. Applicants for switch-board work can be tested for auditory acuity, and, if below standard, refused employment, while Seashore has developed tests to test natural singing ability.[1]

Hollingworth classifies the methods of testing specific abilities as follows:[2] (1) By use of the vocational miniature. An example of this is testing "hello" girls on a toy switch-board. Hollingworth and Muensterberg both believed that this was not a fair test. What is essential to the test is not the similarity of external mechanism, but the internal similarity of the mental attitude. (2) By sampling. This is the taking of an actual part of the work that must be performed in a specific job and trying the candidate out on it. As Hollingworth points out, this is not essentially psychological. Furthermore, to make it a fair test, a large number of samples must be chosen. No judgment can be

---

[1] See G. M. Whipple, "The Use of Mental Tests in Vocational Guidance," *Annals, American Academy*, May, 1916, pp. 193-204.

[2] H. L. Hollingworth, "Specialized Vocational Tests and Methods," *School and Society*, vol. i, pp. 918-922 (June 26, 1915); also chapter v of his *Vocational Psychology*.

given as the result of a trial upon one piece of work.   (3) By analogy.   This is the testing of the subject under certain situations that are supposed to be analogous to those which the worker will face in a given job.   Under this head come: (a) Muensterberg's famous test for sea-captains by the quickness and accuracy shown in rating cards, (b) his test for motormen by the use of a crank in connection with a strip of paper, and (c) the test for telephone girls by canceling letters from a newspaper page.   The great difficulty here is in getting tests which are really analogous to the situation which confronts the worker in the specific industry.   Breese, of Cincinnati, applied Muensterberg's test for sea-captains and his result showed that according to the tests, women should make the best marine officers.   It may be that it is so, but the more probable supposition is that the test was not a real measurement of all the qualities needed.   (4) By miscellaneous empirical tests.   This method consists in starting out with no one *a priori* test, but using a number of tests and then correlating them with the later progress of those tested in the industry itself.   The tests which actually are an index of ability can thus be secured and those that are not, can be discarded.   This method has been adopted by Mrs. Helen T. Woolley in her investigations in Cincinnati.   Through the coöperation of the Board of Education and the Schmidlapp Bureau, Mrs. Woolley and her staff of investigators are placed in charge of the issuance and reissuance of working permits.   The children are given mental and physical tests on their going to work and their later industrial history is checked up.   The results will determine what correlation exists between the various tests and industrial success or failure, *etc.*   The work has probably not been in operation sufficiently long to permit complete correlation, but preliminary studies have been

made.[1]   It is this last method, which has been followed by
Lough in the testing of typists is beginning to be used in
trade tests by such men as Dr. Link, and which seems to promise most.   Positive correlations will be worked out, it
is to be hoped, which will establish the adequacy of some
tests and the inadequacy of others.

A word of caution is perhaps needed concerning the present development of psychological tests as a method of determining vocational bent.   General intelligence can perhaps
be roughly determined, but only slight headway has been
made in the determination of specific aptitudes.   Experimental psychology gives some promise that in the future it
will be able to do this, but it has little concrete accomplishment.   The claims of the vigorous advertisers of psychological tests, both within and without college ranks, should
be most carefully scanned, for their boasts are beyond their
deeds.

E. By Testing the Worker Out on Actual Jobs.   This
theory is based on the belief that it is impossible to determine in advance for what a child is best fitted.   If psychological tests, and interest and character analyses are inadequate, what can be done?   Plainly, try the child out in some
position and see what success he has.   If he fails at it, his
failure should be studied and he should be guided into
other positions in the light of the characteristics that he
has displayed.   If he succeeds, the characteristics that he
shows may aid in determining whether he should be guided
into a better job, or continued for a term in his original
position.

[1] See Helen T. Woolley and Charlotte R. Fischer, *Mental and Physical
Measurements of Working Children*, vol. xviii of Psychological Mono-
graphs; Helen T. Woolley, "Charting Childhood in Cincinnati," *The
Survey*, vol. xxx, pp. 601-606 (Aug. 9, 1913) also "The Issuing of
Working Permits and its Bearing on other Educational Problems,"
School and Society, vol. i, pp. 726-733.

This is not the old hit-or-miss method of letting the child find out for himself for what he is best fitted. In this plan, the child is supervised and followed up and not left to shift for himself.

F. Conclusion. While no one of these methods is sufficient in itself, none of them is inconsistent with any other. It is not a question of choosing between one of these methods and the rest. They are not substitutes for one another, but are complements.

A boy may be psychologically adapted for a position, but if he is not interested in it he will prove to be an inefficient worker. He may be both interested and pass a high psychological test, yet be dishonest and untruthful and, therefore, incompetent. He may have a high moral record, be keenly interested in the position and pass the psychological censor, and still make a dismal failure on the actual job itself. Human capacities are too complex to be evaluated by a single scale of measurement.

Probably a combination of nearly all of these methods should be used. A child's interest in the general field of occupations should be stimulated in a critical manner. He should be encouraged to analyze his own capacities and find out his strong and weak points. Psychological tests can separate people into rough groups as respects their general intelligence, and if positions be classified correspondingly the field of choice can be limited. It may well be that future developments will enable the psychologists to assign individuals to specific tasks, but their science does not permit them legitimately to claim the power to do so now. Finally, since man is essentially changing and his personality is not fixed, the record on the job should be carefully watched. If he improves, he should be promoted. If he does poorly, the causes of his failure should be noted and he should be assigned to work at which he can be more efficient.

III. Determining What Jobs are Fitted for Children

It is not only necessary to examine children in order to determine what they are fitted for, but it is equally necessary to examine industry to determine whether children should be allowed to enter it. A' child should be as careful in choosing an industry, as an employer is in choosing the child. An analysis of industry is therefore a necessary part in any democratic system of vocational guidance.

A. Investigations already made. Many such investigations have already been made in this country. Not only have the city surveys conducted by the National Society for the Promotion of Industrial Education accumulated a mass of material concerning specific trades but many surveys have been made of individual industries as well. A list of the more important of these studies is given below [1] as well

[1] See the Richmond Survey, *Bulletin 162, U. S. Bureau of Labor Statistics*; The Minneapolis Survey, published both by the *National Society for the Promotion of Industrial Education* as *Bulletin 21* and by the *U. S. Bureau of Labor Statistics as Bulletin 199*. The Richmond, Indiana, the Evansville and the Indianapolis Surveys are published as *Bulletins 18, 19 and 21 respectively, of the Indiana State Board of Education.* See also *Survey of Printing Trades of Cincinnati*, by the Cincinnati Chamber of Commerce; R. J. Leonard, *Some Facts concerning the People, Industries, and Schools of Hammond, Indiana*, 165 pp. (1915); Anne Davis, *Occupations and Industries open to Children Between Fourteen and Sixteen Years of Age*, published by the Chicago Board of Education, 1914; Arthur D. Dean, *Education of Workers in the Shoe Industry*; Frederick J. Allen, *The Shoe Industry as a Vocation.* See also the following volumes on industrial conditions in Cleveland, Ohio, published by the Russell Sage Foundation, F. L. Shaw, *The Building Trades*; R. R. Lutz, *The Metal Trades*; Bertha M. Stevens, *Boys and Girls in Commercial Work*; R. R. Lutz, *Wage Earning and Education.*

as a list of the investigations made particularly for women.[1] These studies however are for the shelves of the research student or for the vocational adviser and not for the children who are to be guided; the children need shorter and more popular pamphlets, similar to those issued by the Boston Vocational Bureau on a number of trades.

B. Type of investigations needed. Unquestionably the great need is now for a series of short, accurate and terse descriptions of the various industries which will give the child a clear comprehension of the economic, hygienic, educational, and social prospects of each industry.[2]

The economic aspects should include: (1) The size of the industry,—number of plants and employees. (2) Whether it is localized or diffused. (3) Is it growing or decreasing and at what rate? (4) Is it overcrowded or is there a scarcity of high-class workmen? (5) What are the hours of work? (6) What are the wages for the various kinds of work? (7) How computed? Time or piece work? (8) How much unemployment is there?— seasonal fluctuations, casual employment, *etc.*?

[1] See Lorinda Perry, *Millinery as a Trade for Women*; Mary Van Kleeck, *A Seasonal Industry—A Study of the Millinery Industry in New York City*; Van Kleeck, *Women in the Bookbinding Trade*; Van Kleeck, *Artificial Flower Makers*; May Allinson, *Dress Making as a Trade for Women in Massachusetts*, *Bulletin 193, U. S. Bureau of Labor Statistics; Fourth Annual Report of New York State Factory Investigating Commission*, vol. iv,, containing studies by R. J. Leonard, *An Investigation of the Paper Box Industry to Determine the Possibility of Vocational Training*, pp. 1243-1347, and by Anna C. Phillips, *An Investigation of the Candy Industry, etc.*, pp. 1363-1406; I. P. O'Leary, *Department Store Occupations*; Edna Bryner, *The Garment Trades*; Edna Bryner, *Dress Making and Millinery*; Alliance Employment Bureau, *Inquiry into Trades for Factory Workers*; Women's Educational and Industrial Union, *The Public Schools and Women in Office-Service.*

[2] See as a model the admirable handbooks of the London Apprenticeship and Skilled Employment Association, *Trades for London Boys and How to Enter Them* (1912); *Trades for London Girls and How to Enter Them* (1914).

The description of the hygienic and safety conditions should include: (1) What is the death rate for that trade? The morbidity rate? How do these compare with other trades? (2) What particular dangers are there in the industry? (3) Accident rate; what percentage are fatal; what per cent serious; what are slight? If no accurate figures can be obtained, a general estimate of the dangers could be given. (4) Is the work out of doors or indoors? (5) Does the worker sit, stand, or move about? (6) Degree of eye-strain? (7) What rest-periods are allowed. How long is the noon hour, *etc*. (8) Conditions of ventilation and temperature; hot, cold, medium, variable or constant, degree of moisture, circulation. (9) Nervous strain and fatigue. This involves a statement of the speed required of the worker and how specialized and repetitious are the tasks. (10) Is the industry noisy? Disagreeable odors? Is the industry stimulating or enervating?

The survey of the educational possibilities of the industry should cover: (1) How great is the division of labor? (2) Relative proportion of skilled, low-skilled, and unskilled labor? (3) Are new processes being invented? If so, what is their influence upon the division of labor and the amount of skilled labor required? (4) Are untrained beginners wanted in the trade? (5) What is the average age of entrance to the trade? (6) What age is preferable? (7) Wages at entrance? Do they increase? If so, how much and how rapidly? (8) Is there opportunity to learn more than one branch of work? (9) Is there a possibility of changing from one department to another? (10) What are the possibilities for promotion? (11) What kinds of skill are required in the different occupations within the industry? (*i. e.*, how much general knowledge, industrial and economic intelligence, specialized technical knowledge, manipulative skill?).

To answer these questions, some detailed job analysis is needed. The various surveys have accumulated a mass of information which can be adapted and supplemented to meet local conditions. The job analyses which the United States Bureau of Labor Statistics prepared for the Federal Employment Service for some twenty industries give information on many of these topics.

The social questions which should be asked of an industry are every whit as important, though very often neglected. Especially important to consider are: (1) The moral dangers of the industry, exposure of messenger and news boys, waitresses, sales-girls, theatre ushers, *etc.* (2) Racial composition of the trade; what races chiefly predominate in the particular industry? (3) What is the attitude of employers toward unionism; whether sympathetic, unconcerned, or antagonistic? (4) Degree of unionism existing; name of unions and headquarters, importance of the unions. (5) Policies of the unions. This should cover a brief statement of the policy towards extrance to a trade, whether it is "closed" by means of apprenticeship rules or high initiation fee, or "open" to all workers; policy of union as respects industrial or craft organization, collective bargaining, *etc.*

Not only should the industry be investigated, but local vocational authorities should gather information about individual employers. The possibility of promotion, working conditions in the particular plant, whether welfare work exists and if so, whether it is a substitute for an increase in wages, *etc.*, might well be studied and recorded. Particularly bad employers might indeed be placed upon a "black list," or good employers upon a "white list."

Such a thorough investigation of industry would give the child a clear picture of the advantages and disadvantages of each trade. One of the great dangers of vocational guidance is that it may become inspirational rather than in-formational. An allied danger is the implanting in the child of individualistic ideas of success alone, and the neglect of the social agencies through which the child can better his position. This is illustrated by a recent book on vocational guidance which emphasized the necessity of copying Patrick Henry, Andrew Carnegie, Hugh Chalmers, Henry Clews, Albert J. Beveridge and John D. Rockefeller, but did not once mention trade-unionism!

IV. Problems of Vocational Guidance

1. What Agencies Should Administer Vocational Guidance. It is of course quite clear that the school has a large part to play in any program of vocational guidance. The school should know the aptitudes and interests of the child better than any other agency and it can furnish him with information about the industries and help to form his choice.

But only in the rarest of cases can the school find him a job, or follow him up at his work after he has once begun. Once he has left its doors, its contact with him ceases and the youth is left to get a job in the same fashion as an adult.

In the main, he must depend either upon tramping the streets looking for a position or upon the services of private employment agencies. This is bad enough for a man, but it is still worse for a child. Such a method or rather lack of method not only results in a great waste of time and exorbitant fees, but also in no attempt being made to fit the youth into his proper niche. Whether he places himself, or is placed by one of an innumerable number of private agencies, the number of positions from which he has to choose is necessarily limited. The private agencies, moreover, are more anxious to place him than to place him correctly, since what they are concerned with is the fee.

Not only does this result in an almost complete lack of

proper placement, but it effectively prevents follow-up work. Neither the school nor any other agency can coördinate the large number of private employment agencies and thus keep in touch with the boy while he is at work, help him while there, and assist him to new positions. He is inevitably lost sight of, and there is no one permanent record of his industrial experience and no one body in continuous touch with him.

It is plainly necessary that there should be some one central agency which should: (1) have the exclusive task of finding work for juveniles under a given age, preferably 21; (2) be run for service, not for profit. Private philanthropic agencies, such as the Alliance Employment Bureau in New York, are clearly inadequate. The only possible agency to meet these needs would be a system of public employment offices, which would not be merely one of a number of juvenile placement agencies, but would have an absolute monopoly of the field. This bureau would not only place the child in his first position, but every time the child left one job and sought another, he would be compelled to clear through the bureau. This would keep the bureau constantly in touch with what the boy was doing and with his home address. The boy's record would show how he was progressing in industry and follow-up work could easily be administered.

The removal of the profit motive would in itself abolish one cause of improper placing, but the public bureau should beware of following the same principles in placing juveniles as in finding employment for adults. While a public employment office does not measure its success by the amount of fees received, it frequently does regard the number of positions filled as the crucial test. This is perhaps a proper test for adults, but not for children. Children need not only to be placed, but to be placed correctly. If an employment office is anxious to make placements, it is likely to send children to jobs at which they should never work. The National Labor Exchanges in Great Britain made this mistake during the first years of their work.

So different are the problems of juveniles, that every public employment office of sufficient size should have a separate juvenile division to care solely for minors. The British employment system has such a division and it has done very effective work,[1] as has the Indiana State Employment Service in this country. The Federal Employment Service, in the latter part of 1918, also created such a staff bureau and tried to get its local branches to create such functionalized divisions.

Juvenile placement work of this sort should of course be thoroughly coördinated with both school and industry. The school can do the preparatory work of information and guidance and turn the child over to the employment office for placement. The employment office on the other hand, can study the industries and enlist their coöperation in receiving the boys and giving them an opportunity for advancement. Both employers and workmen should be enlisted in the support of the work and joint boards, similar to the community labor boards created during the war, would be of great benefit.

2. When Should Vocational Guidance Begin. We have seen that the schools should always do preparatory work in vocational guidance before turning the child over to the employment office. But when should they begin this preparation? Vocational guidance is today almost entirely confined to the high school and rarely exists in the lower grades save in the form of some casual instruction. This

[1] See Arthur Greenwood, *Juvenile Labor Exchanges and After-Care*; Bruno Lasker, *The British System of Labor Exchanges*, pp. 39-44; U. S. Bureau of Labor Statistics, *Bulletin No. 206*.

means that the vast majority of children do not receive this guidance, and in order that they may, it must be introduced into the elementary schools. This has been done in certain Cincinnati schools.[1]

3. How Much Assistance is Vocational Guidance for Children under 16? The fact that the vast majority of children under 16 go into routine jobs which require little or no intelligence has already been fully shown. Employers will not hire boys and girls of this age for responsible positions. What can vocational guidance do for this class of children? It cannot recommend those occupations which children now enter, nor can it secure better positions for them because they are not wanted. Its hands are tied. Modern industry makes it impossible for most children of this age to develop at work; they can only degenerate. There is little choice between good and bad jobs; the child can as a rule choose only between a number of evils. Keen students of vocational guidance have observed this: Mrs. Helen T. Wooley after her investigation in Cincinnati, declared: "There is no work open to them (14-16-year-old children) worth advising them to take."[2] Dr. E. L. Talbert concluded as a result of his Chicago study that: "Little service can be rendered by the vocational adviser if children leave school before the age of sixteen years."[3] Mrs. Alice Barrows Fernandez made a thorough investigation in New York City and expressed her conclusions in even stronger language: "The only thing which vocational guidance could

[1] A. F. Goodwin, "Vocational Guidance in Cincinnati," in *Bloomfield's Readings in Vocational Guidance.*

[2] Helen T. Wooley, "Charting Childhood in Cincinnati," *The Survey*, vol. xxx, p. 605 (August 9, 1913).

[3] E. L. Talbert, "Opportunities in School and Industry for Children of the Stockyard District," in Bloomfield's *Readings in Vocational Guidance*, p. 432.

contribute to the problem was that there was no possibility for vocational guidance." [1]

Vocational guidance by itself is, therefore, almost power-less to better the immediate condition of the child. If they could stay out of industry until they were 16, however, it would give them not only more knowledge but a more mature physique and mind.

[1] *Bull. No. 9, Publications of the Educational Association of the City of New York,* p. 9.

CHAPTER XIII

THE SMITH-HUGHES ACT OF 1917

Providing Federal Aid to Vocational Education [1]

IN 1917, the Smith-Hughes Act, providing federal aid
to the states for vocational education, passed Congress and
became a law.   The passage of this act was the fruition of
a long legislative campaign to secure federal aid for this
purpose.   Somewhat similar bills had been introduced in
several preceding Congresses, and in 1912 the Page bill had
passed the Senate but had been defeated in the House.   In
1914, upon the recommendation of Congress, a commission
on National Aid to Vocational Education was appointed
by the President.   This commission reported favorably and
submitted a bill to Congress which was introduced in the
Senate by the same state.   This bill was vigorously supported by the American Federation of Labor, the National
Society for the Promotion of Industrial Education, and by
large industrial interests.   It was passed by the Senate in
1916 and, with slight modification, by the House in
February 1917, and went into effect on July 1st of that
year. [2]

The act provides that every dollar allotted by the Federal

---

[1] This chapter has appeared in the *Political Science Quarterly* for
December, 1920.

[2] Public, No. 347, 64th Congress.   For an analysis and interpretation
of the law, see "What is the Smith-Hughes Bill?" *Bulletin 28, of the
National Society for the Promotion of Industrial Education* and
Bulletin 2 of the Federal Board for Vocational Education.

Government shall be met with an additional dollar appropriated by the state or locality. The money allowed by the national government and duplicated by the states must be spent only for the salaries of teachers of trade and home economics subjects and of teachers and directors of agricultural subjects, and in preparing teachers for these subjects. The state or local community must provide, maintain and equip the buildings where the subjects are taught, while the federal government will permit a small portion of the funds for teacher training to be used in selecting and placing the vocational teachers.

The amount appropriated for the varying purposes by years is given below:

FEDERAL AID FOR VOCATIONAL EDUCATION

Fiscal year ending June 30th	Total	Agriculture: For salaries of teachers, supervisors and directors	Trade, home economics and industry: For salaries of teachers	Teacher training: For salaries of teachers and maintenance of teacher training	For Federal Board for Vocational Education
1917–18 . .	$1,860,000	$548,000	$566,000	$546,000	$200,000
1918–19 . .	2,512,000	784,000	796,000	732,000	200,000
1919–20 . .	3,182,300	1,024,000	1,034,000	924,000	200,000
1920–21 . .	3,836,000	1,268,000	1,278,000	1,090,000	200,000
1921–22 . .	4,329,000	1,514,000	1,525,000	1,090,000	200,000
1922–23 . .	4,823,000	1,761,000	1,772,000	1,090,000	200,000
1923–24 . .	5,318,000	2,009,000	2,019,000	1,090,000	200,000
1924–25 . .	6,380,000	2,534,000	2,556,000	1,090,000	200,000
1925–26 . .	7,367,000	3,027,000	3,050,000	1,090,000	200,000
Annually thereafter.	7,367,000	3,027,000	3,050,000	1,090,000	200,000

It will be noted that the appropriations increase annually from 1917-18 when only $1,860,000 was available to 1925-26 when nearly $7,500,000 will be available. The amount appropriated for the administrative expenses of the Federal Board remains constant at $200,000 throughout the period.

While teacher training reaches its maximum of $1,090,000 in 1920-21 and does not increase thereafter, the other two branches of work increase annually until 1925-26 when they each will have approximately $3,000,000 from the Federal Government. Since every federal dollar must be met with at least an additional dollar, as much as $14,000,000 may be available for vocational education in 1925-26, as a direct result of this legislation.

The types of schools which can receive aid from the Federal Government should be carefully noted. As has been said, they must be publicly controlled, and supervised, and designed to meet the needs of children over 14, in order to fit them for useful employment, but they must be of less than college grade. Within these general requirements the schools were required to conform to the following regulations together with such others as the Federal Board might set up.

1. Schools for Agricultural Subjects. Proper methods of teaching agriculture have not yet been agreed upon by educators and the act was purposely somewhat vague in laying down standards in this field, providing merely that supervised practice in agriculture, on a farm provided by the school or some other farm, should be given for at least six months per year and that the teachers and directors should have the minimum qualifications determined by the state and approved by the Federal Board.

2. Schools for Trade, Home Economics and Industrial Subjects. (a) At least one-third of the money appropriated to any state should be devoted to part-time (continuation) schools or classes for workers between 14 and 18 years of age. These continuation schools should provide for not less than one hundred and forty-four hours of class-room instruction per year and could teach such subjects as would "enlarge the civic and vocational intelligence" of the worker. (b) That schools of classes instructing persons not yet entered upon employment should devote not less than half of their instruction to practical work "on a useful or productive basis." The total time spent for instruction was not to be less than thirty hours a week for a minimum of nine months of the year. This type of trade school was really designed as a unit trade school where the child would be taught one particular trade. (c) In cities and towns of less than 25,000, the unit trade-school plan for those not yet entered upon employment could be modified with the approval of the Federal Board to meet the needs of the particular locality. This was designed so that the basic principles of a number of trades could be taught in the smaller cities instead of those of one only, as is the case in cities of over 25,000. (d) Evening industrial schools should not admit anyone under 16 years of age, and should confine their instruction to that which is "supplemental to the daily employment." (e) All teachers in these schools or classes should have the minimum qualifications for teachers of such subjects as determined upon by the state and approved by the Federal Board.

3. Schools for Teacher Training. Since teacher-training for vocational subjects was an almost wholly unexplored field, the act granted to the Federal Board the power of laying down general standards, but specified: (a) That the teacher training should be given only to those who had had adequate vocational experience in the line of work they were preparing to teach. The general principle that competent workmen should be trained to teach their trade knowledge rather than that teachers be given trade experience was thereby established. This was undoubtedly a wise act, and it should insure a more solid content to the vocational work

than could ever have been obtained by the other method.
(b) To prevent the undue slighting of any subject, it was
specified that not less than 20% nor more than 60% of the
quota of any state for training teachers should be spent for
agriculture, for the trades and industries, and for home
economics.

The funds apportioned among the states by Congress
were not left to be distributed according to their whims or
the demand for "pork," but upon the basis of population, as
evidenced by the last preceding census, according to the following system: Each state was granted a minimum appropriation of $5000 annually for the salaries of teachers and
directors of agricultural subjects, the same amount for the
salaries of teachers of home economics, trade and industrial
subjects, and the same for the maintenance of teacher-training for these subjects, or $15,000 in all.   The amount ap-
propriated each year for teachers and directors of agricultural subjects was to be divided among the states in the
proportion which their rural population[1] formed of the
total rural population of the Continental United States.
The amount appropriated for the salaries of teachers of
home economics, trade and industrial subjects was to be
divided among the states in the proportion which their
urban population[2] formed of the total urban population
of the Continental United States.   The sums appropriated
for the maintenance of teacher training for these subjects
was distributed on the basis of the proportion which the
total population of each state formed of the total population
of the Continental United States.

There was a very real opposition on the part of the advocates of the bill to placing the administration of the act

[1] Localities under 2500.
[2] Localities over 2500 people.

under the Bureau of Education or where control could be exercised by the "school men." The Smith-Hughes Bill consequently originally provided for an interdepartmental board of five cabinet officers,[1] as the agency to administer the act. This was wisely amended so that three independent members who were to be appointed directly by the President would serve with the four ex-officio members.[2] The cabinet members have been so busy with the affairs of their own departments that the actual conduct of affairs has largely fallen upon the three appointees to the board.

The Federal Board was given wide powers and was the agency created to evolve national standards and minimums of vocational education. It was given the authority to withhold allotments to any state when it believed that the federal moneys, or their state equivalent were not being expended for the purposes of, or under the conditions laid down by the act. A state board had the right of appeal from the decision of the Federal Board to Congress, but unless specifically upheld, the sums in question were to revert to the Treasury.

In addition to its administrative powers, the Board was authorized to conduct investigations and make researches into the various phases of vocational education and its administration, and to publish its findings. Since it was provided with liberal funds for its purposes, it was made the center for research in the field as well as for the formulation of policies.

In order that a state might receive the benefits of the act, the legislature was compelled to create a state board of not less than three members, to administer the act within

[1] This was to consist of the Postmaster-General and the Secretaries of the Interior, Agriculture, Commerce and Labor.

[2] Secretaries of Commerce, Agriculture and Labor, and the Commissioner of Education.

the state and to coöperate with the Federal Board. This board could be either the state board of education or a separate body. Since many legislatures were not meeting in 1917 or had closed their sessions before the act was passed or at least was generally known, the governors of these states were authorized to accept the act temporarily and to create a board to administer it, pending action by the state legislature in the first sixty days of its next session.

Any state could defer accepting any of the three funds provided, but after June 30, 1920, in order for a state to accept federal funds for teachers' salaries in agriculture and trades, industries and home economics, respectively, it was compelled to take advantage of (and match equally) the minimum sums appropriated for teacher training in these two branches of subjects.

Although the act was passed in February, 1917, the pressure of war conditions was so great that the President did not appoint the three members of the board till July 17th.[1] Charles A. Prosser,[2] was appointed Director (or executive officer) of the Board in August. A series of meetings with representatives of the states was held in the same month, at which the act was explained and general policies formulated.

The tasks of the Board were increased by the war-time responsibilities that they assumed. Emergency training for conscripted men, conducted chiefly in the evening, was promoted by it and approximately 19,000 men were given some training in radio classes, and 16,000 in mechanical trades. In addition to this, the Smith-Sears Act, passed in April,

---

[1] They were Arthur E. Holden, to represent Labor; Charles E. Greathouse, to represent Agriculture; and James P. Munroe, to represent Manufacturing and Commerce. C. E. Mackintosh has since replaced Mr. Greathouse.

[2] Since resigned.

1918, placed the Federal Board in charge of the vocational
education of the disabled soldiers and sailors, and appropriated $2,000,000 to be used by the Board for this purpose.
$14,000,000 more was appropriated for this purpose by
Congress in the summer of 1919 and large appropriations
in 1920. The board has therefore concentrated its attention on problems for which it was not originally created.[1]

By June 30, 1919, the act had been accepted by legislatures of all the states save that Rhode Island did not accept
the federal aid for agriculture. Due to the newness of the
act, practically one-half of the allotments were not utilized
by the states during the first year (June 30, 1917-June 30,
1918) and one-third were not utilized in the second year
as is shown by the following table:[2]

AMOUNTS OF FEDERAL AID GRANT EXPENDED AND UNEXPENDED BY THE
STATES, FOR THE FISCAL YEARS, 1917-18, 1918-19

Purpose	1917-18			1918-19		
	Amount sent to States	Amount expended by States	Amount unexpended by States	Amount sent to States	Amount expended by States	Amount unexpended by States
Agriculture...	$547,027	$273,587	$273,440	$783,000	$526,000	$257,000
Trade, Industry and Home Economics..	364,444	365,469	198,975	794,000	610,000	184,000
Teacher Training	544,144	196,727	347,417	730,000	426,000	304,000
Total.....	$1,655,615	$835,783	$819,832	$2,307,000	$1,561,000	$745,000
Per cent....	100.0	50.5	49.5	100.0	67.7	32.3

[1] The administration of this work has been upon a national and not
upon a federal basis.

[2] Compiled from data given in the *Second Annual Report of the
Federal Board for Vocational Education*, pp. 110-112; and *Third Annual
Report*, p. 210.

The unexpended balances are to be deducted from the next year's allotments to the respective states.

It was feared in many quarters that the opportunity given the states to set up separate boards from the state boards of education would cause the so-called "dual system" of control to be fastened upon the country. This system had been advocated in 1914 and at later sessions of the Illinois legislature by Mr. E. J. Cooley and by the Chicago Commercial Club, and had been opposed by labor unions and civic bodies who feared that the vocational school would thus be taken out of the hands of the educators and placed in the control of the manufacturers.

In 31 states the state boards of education were made the boards for vocational education and unit control was thereby continued. For eight of the remaining states there had previously been no state board of education that could have assumed the duties, while one (Wisconsin) already had a separate board of vocational education. Omitting Wisconsin and Colorado, (where the state board of agriculture was designated to act for the state), an analysis of the remaining fifteen states indicates that control is still exercised by the educators and has not been ceded to the employing interests. In six of these boards all the members are educators;[1] two of them are composed exclusively of educators and state officials;[2] on two more the educators are overwhelmingly in the majority;[3] while on all of the remaining five[4] they are represented, and the farming and labor interests are also represented, so that control cannot be exercised by the employers.

[1] Alabama, Kentucky, Michigan, Mississippi, North Carolina and South Dakota.

[2] Illinois and Nebraska.

[3] Ohio and Oklahoma.

[4] Georgia, Iowa, Maine, New Hampshire and Oregon.

While it is possible that later appointments may change the complexion of some of these boards, for the present at least, there need be no fear that the large industrial interests will dictate the policy of industrial education that is to be pursued.

At the time of the passage of the act, seven states [1] had systems of state aid to localities for vocational education. In five of these states [2] the addition of federal aid was met by merely continuing the previous state appropriations, while in two,[3] additional sums were appropriated. In certain of these states the state contributes an equal share to that of the federal government and requires the locality to contribute at least an equal amount. Here each of the three agencies bear one-third of the expense, and the federal aid is doubled by the state and by the localities. In other states, the share of the locality is merged with that of the state in meeting the federal appropriation.

A different sort of a problem faced the legislatures of the remaining forty-one states, which had previously had no system of state aid to localities for vocational education. Should the state itself appropriate the money to match the federal grant; should it throw the burden upon the localities, or should the two bear it jointly? Twenty-five states [4] or over half the remaining number, made appropriations equal to or greater than the federal allotments. Localities

[1] Connecticut, Indiana, Massachusetts, New Jersey, New York, Pennsylvania and Wisconsin. Virginia had a law providing for such a system but no funds for this purpose had been provided by the legislature.

[2] Indiana, Massachusetts, New York, Pennsylvania and Wisconsin.

[3] Connecticut and New Jersey.

[4] Alabama, Arizona, California, Colorado, Delaware, Florida, Idaho, Illinois, Kansas, Maine, Minnesota, Missouri, Montana, Nebraska, Nevada, New Hampshire, New Mexico, North Carolina, Ohio, Oregon, South Carolina, Tennessee, Utah, Vermont and Virginia.

of course could make additional appropriations and in many cases were expected to do so. In the sixteen remaining states,[1] appropriations were made by the legislatures which were not equal to the federal allotments and the localities were expected to make up the remainder. In Mississippi, Oklahoma and Texas particularly the intention seems strong to have the localities (if they will), rather than the states, assume the brunt of duplicating the federal allotments.[2]

It will be seen from the foregoing analysis that the federal appropriations have not resulted in replacing funds previously appropriated by states or localities for vocational education. To illustrate: (1) Let us suppose that the localities of a state have been spending $50,000 annually for vocational work. The state's allotment from the federal fund is $25,000. In the first year, the state or its localities cannot reduce their expenditures and have the difference made up by the federal funds. The $25,000 of federal money must be added to the $50,000 of the state or locality.

(2) Indeed what has generally happened in the states which have appropriated funds equal to the federal grants, has been as follows: Whereas the localities of a state may have been spending $20,000 a year for proper vocational education projects and the state nothing, the federal grant of $25,000 is met by a state appropriation of an equal amount and $50,000 is thus added to the amount hitherto expended. Even where the state has not duplicated the federal funds, they have generally made a net addition to the general cause. Localities, moreover, have in many cases increased their previous appropriation.

[1] Arkansas (until 1921), Georgia, Kentucky, Iowa, Louisiana, Maryland, Michigan, Mississippi, North Dakota, Oklahoma, Rhode Island, South Dakota, Texas, Washington, West Virginia, Wyoming.

[2] Thus in Oklahoma, the state appropriation amounted to about 5% of the federal allotment and in Mississippi, to about 10%.

The federal grants mean consequently not only a net addition to the funds for vocational education but in the majority of cases have called forth at least an equal additional appropriation from the states or localities. Several states have indeed already appropriated far more than is legally required and doubtless many others will follow their example in the future.

The Board has been slowly working out standards of vocational education upon which to base its policy in granting or refusing aid. Training in agriculture and home economics subjects is still in such chaotic condition that the Board has not found it possible to lay down standards for the fields other than indicating that the supervised home project should be used as much as possible in agricultural work.

Perhaps the most important issue in vocational education is as to whether the training given shall be confined solely to the trade at which the student works or whether it shall also prepare him for other trades, if he needs such preparation, and educate his general faculties as well. As has been mentioned previously, night-schools receiving federal aid must confine themselves to those things connected with the occupation the student follows. Continuation schools may be (a) supplementary to the young workers' trade, (b) a preparation for other industries or (c) a medium of giving general civic training. All of these subjects may indeed be given as courses in the same school and be taken by the boys and girls.

It is, however, probably not unfair to the Federal Board of Vocational Education to state that its influence is more on the side of the narrow supplementary training than upon the broader aspects. Any such conception of industrial education fails of course to take account of the fact that it is manifestly improper to train boys and girls only for the occupations at which they are engaged, when most of these occupations are ones that should never be filled by the children.

The work of the various types of schools must conform to a certain standard of efficiency before the Federal Board will grant aid.   To determine this, the Board relies upon the reports made by the state boards and inspection by its own agents who operate from the headquarters of the five districts into which the country is divided for the purpose of administration.[1]   During the second fiscal year which ended June 30, 1919, 1931 schools applied for Federal Aid and of these, 1789, or 92.6%, were approved and 142, or 7.4%, were rejected.[2]

In the year ending June 30, 1919, approximately 195,000 pupils were enrolled in the vocational courses; 121,000 of whom were males and 74,000 females.   Some 18,000 of these were enrolled in agricultural subjects; 19,000 in all day trades or industrial schools; 73,000 in continuation schools[3] (51,000 of these being in general continuation schools and 22,000 in trade or industrial continuation schools); 44,000 in the evening industrial schools, and 41,000 in home economics schools.[4]   In addition to this, 7400 students had received teacher training during the year.   As has been pointed out in Chapter XI, as a result of the act seventeen states have now passed compulsory continuation school laws.   The use of the federal aid system is

[1] New York City, Atlanta, Ga., Indianapolis, Ind., Kansas City, Mo., San Francisco, Cal.

[2] *Third Annual Report of the Federal Board for Vocational Education*, 1919, p. 229.

[3] 40,000 of these were in the continuation schools of Pennsylvania, and 9,000 in those of Massachusetts.

[4] Compiled from data given in the *Third Annual Report of the Federal Board for Vocational Education*, 1919, p. 220.

a particularly happy administrative device since it:[1] (1) assists the poorer states, (2) ensures a certain national minimum standard, (3) ensures relatively economical expenditure of federal funds, since the localities are compelled to contribute at least an equal amount, (4) grants initiative and autonomy to the states, (5) solves constitutional objections to federal action, since a state only accepts the system of its own free will, (6) centralizes research, and (7) integrates the educational system within the states.

[1] For a description and analysis of the newly created system of federal aid see my articles, " The Development of a System of Federal Grants in Aid," *Political Science Quarterly*, vol. xxxv, pp. 255-272; 522-545 (June and December, 1920).

CHAPTER XIV

ECONOMIC EFFECTS OF INDUSTRIAL EDUCATION

1. Some Claims as to the Wage Value of Industrial Education. Many ardent advocates of industrial education have unfortunately approached this question with the zeal of the propagandist rather than with the clearness and patience of the scientist. The Commission on National Aid to Vocational Education for instance estimated that by vocational education the average earning power would be increased approximately 25 cents per day "which would make a total increase in wages of $6,250,000 per day and $1,875,000,000 per year."[1] This estimate was based upon a study of the records of 839 graduates of the Baron de Hirsch Trade School of N. Y. City, together with a study of 12 graduates of the Beverly, Mass., Coöperative School.[2]

Mr. James M. Dodge in 1903 tried to prove that industrial education resulted in greatly increased earning power. He cited statistics to prove that while the average unskilled worker reached his maximum weekly wage of $10.20 at approximately twenty-one, the shop-trained worker reached a maximum of $15.80 at twenty-four, while the average trade-school graduate at the age of thirty-two was receiving $25. a week and his earning curve was still rising.[3] These

---

[1] *Report of the Commission on National Aid to Vocational Education*, 63rd Congress, 2nd Session, House Doc. 1004, vol. i, p. 21.

[2] *Ibid.*, vol. i, pp. 94-97.

[3] J. M. Dodge, *Transactions of American Society of Mechanical Engineers*, vol. xxv, pp. 40-48, see also, *Fourth Report N. Y. Factory Investigating Commission*, vol. iii, pp. 1418-1422.

statistics were used by many others besides Mr. Dodge to prove the great economic advantages of industrial education. They were, however, based upon a study of the employment records of only two corporations. We do not know whether those plants were typical of industry as a whole or how many cases they included. Miss Marshall,[1] Dr. Kingsbury,[2] and Professor Ellis[3] have likewise claimed that greatly enhanced earnings were the consequence of industrial education. Mr. Wesley A. O'Leary has made perhaps the most scientific effort to determine the economic effects of industrial education. He compared the wages of 201 workmen before and after they studied in trade schools, and tried to discover whether their wages increased at a faster rate after their school training than before.[4] He found that the difference was exceedingly slight.

The wage increases cited by the Federal Commission, by Mr. Dodge, and by others deserve close scrutiny before they are accepted as establishing the high monetary value of vocational education. In the first place they cover too few cases to be accepted as indicating general tendencies. Secondly, the increase in the wages of trade-school graduates may be explained by their inherent ability and energy, as well as by their training. Only a selected group will be willing to go to the trouble of acquiring such an education. Would not these have received wage increases even had they not studied at the trade school? Finally, the supporters of

[1] Florence M. Marshall, "The Public School and the Girl Wage Earner," *Charities and the Commons*, vol. xix, p. 849, Oct. 5, 1907.

[2] Susan M. Kingsbury, "What is Ahead for the Untrained Child in Industry," *Charities and the Commons*, vol. xix, p. 813 (Oct. 5, 1907).

[3] A. Caswell Ellis, "The Money Value of Education," *Bull. Bureau of Education*, 1917, no. 22, pp. 20-41.

[4] Wesley A. O'Leary, "The Wage Value of Vocational Training," *Fourth Annual Report N. Y. Factory Investigating Commission*, pp. 1411-1460, esp. pp. 1440-1450.

industrial education are guilty of bad logic, when they declare that, because the wages of those who have received industrial training have increased, therefore, under a universal system of industrial education, the wages of all would increase equally. As Professor Taussig cogently remarks, " Computations are sometimes made of the profitableness of trade training. It is figured out that the return in enhanced wages, compared with the expense of education, amounts to a magnificent profit on the investment. But it is forgotten that if a multitude get the training, the wages will be much less enhanced, conceivably not enhanced at all." [1]

2. Methods by which Wages can be Increased. In general there are at least four ways of raising wages: (a) By increasing the efficiency of any given wage group as a whole. This raises the productivity of the so-called " marginal " man within the group and consequently the general level of the group's wages. (b) By increasing the efficiency of individual workers. They are thus made abler than their fellows and consequently will receive higher wages for their difference in skill. (c) By decreasing the barriers between non-competing groups and establishing more nearly equal economic opportunity. In part this merely levels wages between groups, lowering those at present born into the higher groups and raising those in the lower. Whether any general movement in this direction would increase the total amount paid in wages is uncertain. But one indubitable effect would be the better apportionment of men to tasks according to their abilities. Many incompetents in the upper grades who are now employed only because of their monopolistic position would be replaced by men from the lower grades of labor. The resulting gain

[1] F. W. Taussig, *Quarterly Journal of Economics*, vol. xxx, p. 437.

in efficiency would be marked. (d) By strengthening the
bargaining power of labor. Where laborers are unorgan-
ized they are to a certain extent in the hands of the employer.[1] Their organization in labor unions and the institution of collective bargaining places them on more even
terms.

*3. Effect of Specific Methods of Industrial Education
upon Wages.* Turning now to the specific effects of industrial education, perhaps the first point to be realized is
that the various systems of industrial education will have different effects. The question is, therefore, not, what will
be the economic consequences of industrial education in
general?, but rather, what will be the consequences of
vocational guidance, of the trade school, of the corporation
school, and of the continuation school?

(1) Vocational guidance alone will not produce far-
reaching economic readjustments. It will undoubtedly make
for a somewhat better adjustment to positions and, through
a study of the opportunities of the several industries, will
abolish friction within a non-competing group. By itself,
however, it will not abolish or greatly lessen non-competing
groups themselves or mitigate the friction between groups.
As long as children are forced to leave school at 14 because
of economic necessity, they will be forced inevitably into the
ranks of the unskilled and, unless other means are provided,
they will remain there. They will rear large families who
in turn will be compelled to leave school at an early age.
and who will be condemned to the same class of labor at

[1] There is of course a vast literature concerning the weaker bargaining
power of labor. I venture to suggest a few works that are especially
valuable on this topic: Seager, *Principles of Economics*, pp. 537-538;
Commons and Andrews, *Principles of Labor Legislation*, p. 116; Sidney
and Beatrice Webb, *Industrial Democracy*, esp. " The Higgling of the
Market," pp. 654-702.

which their parents were employed. The upper grades of
labor, on the other hand, will be recruited in the main from
those classes who can afford to keep their children in school.
Because of their monopolistic position, therefore, the latter
will be able to get a greater return for the same amount
of effort expended.

Nor will the efficiency of labor, either individually or as
a group, be appreciably increased. Vocational guidance is
not vocational training. The worker will be guided to a
job for which he is perhaps better adapted than for most
other positions, but his ability to perform his work will not
be enhanced by vocational guidance itself.

(2) The effect of the all-day trade school would be to
increase the efficiency and, all other things being equal, the
wages of the aristocracy of manual labor. The productivity
of the skilled workmen would be raised appreciably. Since
attendance at such a school must be limited to a group somewhat strongly entrenched economically, it could not benefit
the members of the lower economic groups. As has been
pointed out, it would not enable the unskilled or semi-skilled
laborer to better his position. Hence it would still per-
petuate the existence of the non-competing groups and
would indeed increase the difficulty of passage from one to
another.

(3) The corporation school for apprentices would have
effects similar to the trade school save that there might be a
tendency to lessen the sharpness of the distinction between
the various industrial groups. Promising boys of unskilled
and low-paid fathers might be trained for higher positions
than would be the case were they compelled to receive their
training at an all-day trade school. The training given the
workmen at the unskilled or semi-skilled positions would, so
far as it went, increase productivity and hence presumably
wages. Were corporation schools to become the quite

universal method of training, (however, their effect might well be to decrease the strength of the labor unions and in consequence ultimately to lower wages.   For if education is controlled by the employers, organization on the part of the workmen becomes increasingly difficult.)

(4) The economic effects of the continuation school would be much more thoroughgoing.   Not only would the general efficiency of all classes be increased and their wages consequently raised, but the men in the lower grades of labor would be given an opportunity to rise to the higher.   By making it possible for boys and girls to study while working, large numbers of those at present in the lowest grades of labor would be enabled to enter both the semi-skilled and skilled groups. Non-competing groups amongst manual workers would largely cease to exist, and there would be an assortment of labor according to inherent abilities rather than according to monopolistic advantages.

The probable effects of the continuation school may therefore be summarized under four heads: (a) A general increase in productivity resulting in a consequent rise in the wages. (b) A further increase in wages for those who were lifted from the unskilled to the skilled and semi-skilled groups. (c) A decrease in the wages for those in the upper groups who had hitherto enjoyed the advantages of limited numbers. (d) A further increase in the wages of those still occupying the unskilled positions.   Since their numbers would be lessened by the drafting off of a part of their former members, the marginal man would be more productive than he had been under the old conditions of the labor supply.   The wages in this group would consequently rise above their former level.

These effects would be complete were the continuation school training superimposed upon a broad public school training.   For the continuation school in order to attain

a maximum of social efficiency, must be preceded by a prolonged and thorough training of the child. Were all the
children to be released from school at the age of 12 and
then given compulsory continuation school work, the results would not be as satisfactory as they would be were the
children not released until they were 14. Nor would as
favorable results be obtained when the continuation school
work began at 14, as when the compulsory attendance laws
were raised to 16 and the continuation school began work
then. The continuation school, in order to succeed, must
have mature rather than immature students.

4. *Some Additional Effects of Industrial Education.*
There are two further probable effects of a general system
of industrial education that are worthy of notice: (1) the
lessening of unemployment and (2) the increased use of
machinery. (1) Were the worker better trained, he might
well take a greater interest in his work and be less liable to
throw up his job through sheer ennui. Moreover, once
unemployed, he would find it easier to secure work because
his general training would fit him for positions which
otherwise he would find it difficult, if not impossible, to fill.
Personal dislocation as a cause of unemployment would
be lessened and perhaps even removed.

(2) Moreover, labor-saving machinery would probably
be introduced. As we have seen, the wages of the unskilled
would increase if, by means of continuation schools, passage
were made easy from one non-competing manual group to
another. Now it pays the employer to economize in the use
of well-paid workmen where it may not pay him with low-
paid labor. If labor is cheap, the employer tends to be satisfied either with no machinery at all or with antiquated
equipment. If wages are, therefore, increased, it then becomes uneconomical to waste this expensive labor and new

machinery is either invented to economize effort or the existing equipment is bettered.

The prevention of child labor at night in the glass factories of Illinois and Ohio was followed within five years (1900-1905) by an increase in output of 98%, while in New Jersey and Pennsylvania, where child labor was permitted, the increase was only 25%. This greater increase was largely caused by the removal of the cheap supply of child labor. Men were hired at higher wages for the positions formerly occupied by children, and manufacturers consequently introduced more efficient methods of glass blowing to economize the expenditure of high-priced labor.[1] The enactment of minimum wage laws in Australasia and the consequent increase in wages produced a similar effect. Mr. Ernest Aves, in his classic investigation, found that it had compelled the use of better machine methods.[2] Many other illustrations of the same general nature could be given.

Undoubtedly, therefore, an increase in the wages of the unskilled would mean a further development of machinery and automatic processes. Much of the present unskilled labor is so automatic that it could indeed easily be replaced by machinery. The result would be to decrease the field for unskilled labor, while it would at the same time increase the productivity of industry and still further enhance wages.[3]

[1] For a fuller statement of the development of machine methods caused by the elimination of child labor, see *Bull. 185, National Child Labor Committee*, p. 14; and *The Survey*, March 11, 1911, p. 976.

[2] See *Parliamentary Reports for 1908*, vol. 72, p. 167. To the question "has the minimum wage compelled the use of better machine methods," 68 manufacturers answer, "yes" and only 2 "no."

[3] That is, *ceteris paribus*. A counter movement, such as the suppression of labor organizations, might more than overcome this.

CHAPTER XV

THE ATTITUDE OF LABOR AND CAPITAL TOWARDS INDUSTRIAL EDUCATION

THIS chapter will trace the evolution of the opinions about industrial education which have been held by the various industrial groups, and will then analyze the present attitude of labor and capital upon a number of connected issues.

1. The Attitude of Labor. The laboring classes were at first decidedly suspicious of industrial education. They regarded it as merely a method by which the employers could train swarms of boys, inculcate them with anti-union doctrines, and then bring them into the factories to undermine wages and deprive union men of employment. It is this fear of lowering the standard rate which leads many unionists today to distrust industrial education.

A decade and a half ago when the trade school was regarded as the most practicable plan of industrial education, the unions generally charged these schools with being " scab hatcheries." Though these charges were widely circulated, they were rarely accompanied with specific proof of such action on the part of any school. There have probably not been more than three schools which have taken an open anti-union policy and have sought to train boys to be used as strike-breakers. These were: (1) the New York Trade School. Soon after this school was founded, in the early eighties, it furnished strike breakers in a local strike. Since then, so far as is known, this action has not been re-

peated either by it, or by any other school in New York.
(2) The Winona Technical Institute of Indianapolis,
Indiana. This school was founded in 1904 by friends of
the Winona religious movement and by manufacturing interests. Various manufacturers' organizations furnished
$50,000 worth of equipment and gave approximately
$15,000 a year to its support. The school was thus chiefly
supported by the manufacturers' organizations and it was
largely directed by them. Forty-one of the fifty directors
were manufacturers while only seven were ministers, and
the policy was consequently shaped by the employing interests. The teachers were recruited from the trades and
were nominated by the National Association of Manufacturers. Needless to say, the school was aggressively anti-union
in its attitude; the students were taught to abhor trade
unionism and to believe in individual bargaining. When
these students went into the trades however they soon joined
the unions, and the purpose of the manufacturers was
defeated. The school became embroiled in financial difficulties and was placed under new management in 1909.
Since then it has not been anti-union in its policy. (3) A
school for molders in Chicago during the nineties. This
school was run by the employers in the molding trade and
its students were used by the directors of the school to break
strikes. This school has however also failed.

While open hostility to the unions was practised by only
a few schools, it is nevertheless true that most of the
schools were distinctly unsympathetic towards collective
bargaining and their covert influence was anti-union. There
is probably not a school in the country today that is openly
hostile to the unions or one that has within recent years
supplied strike breakers. Of course, many schools are controlled by men who do not believe in trade unionism and
these schools, therefore, probably discourage the union side

of the case from being advanced but, at least, they do not take sides openly with the employers, or furnish strike breakers.

Distrustful of privately endowed and managed schools, the labor unions have made some progress in establishing schools under their own direction. In 1903, the American Federation of Labor appointed a committee to consider the manual training and technical training given by the unions themselves. This committee reported that " the subject of manual training and technical education to be given by trade-unions is of such a general character that this convention could not very well recommend any plan or policy that would apply equally to all unions on account of the diversity of conditions and difference in skill required." [1] Though committees were appointed in 1904 and again in 1905, they never reported.

Trade union schools were established among others by the Printing Pressmens Union in 1912, by the Chicago Carpenters Union in 1907, and by the New York Typographical workers in 1909. The International Typographical Union established a correspondence course in 1907 which has given instruction to many thousand printers. The task of training workers was of course too heavy for the limited financial and educational resources of the unions to bear.

In 1907, Professor Charles R. Richards, then secretary of the newly-formed National Society for the Promotion of Industrial Education, addressed the American Federation of Labor and asked for its co-operation. He assured the union men that the new movement did not intend to play into the hands of the employers, and that industrial education would greatly benefit labor by giving to it the training which had been absent since the downfall of apprenticeship. As a

[1] *Report of Committee on Industrial Education of the A. F. of L.,* published as Senate Document No. 93, 62nd Congress, 2nd Session, p. 21.

result of his address the convention instructed the committee on education to study the matter.   In 1908 the convention passed a resolution declaring that

there are two groups with opposite methods and seeking antagonistic ends now advocating industrial education in the United States.   One of these groups is composed largely of the non-union employees of the country who advance industrial education as a special privilege under conditions that educate the student or apprentice to non-union sympathies, and prepare him as a skilled worker for scab labor and strike breaking purposes, thus using the children of the workers against the interest of their organized fathers and brothers.   This group also favors the training of the student or apprentice for skill in only one industrial process, thus making the graduate a skilled worker in only a very limited sense and rendering him helpless if lack of employment comes in his single subdivision of a craft.

The other group is composed of great educators, enlightened representatives of organized labor, and persons engaged in genuine social service who advocate industrial education as a common right, to be open to all children on equal terms, to be provided by general taxation and kept under the control of the whole people with a method or system of education that will make the apprentice graduate a skilled craftsman in all the branches of his trade.[1]

The convention further declared that "organized labor has the largest personal and the highest public interest in the subject of industrial education and should enlist its ablest men in behalf of the best system under the conditions that will promote the interests of the workers and the general welfare."[2]

A committee of fifteen was appointed to investigate the matter and a preliminary report was made to the 1909 con-

[1] Senate Document No. 936, *op. cit.*, p. 22.
[2] *Ibid.*, p. 22.

vention. The committee was carried over to the 1910 convention and it induced the United States Bureau of Labor to undertake a survey of the existing facilities for industrial education.

A report of this committee on industrial education, drafted largely by Charles H. Winslow and John Mitchell, is one of the most remarkable documents in the history of industrial education. It was adopted in its final form by the convention of 1911. The committee placed itself squarely on record in favor of industrial education and declared that:

If the American workman is to maintain the high standard of efficiency, the boys and girls of the country must have an opportunity to acquire educated hands and brains, such as may enable them to earn a living in a self-selected vocation and acquire an intelligent understanding of the duties of good citizenship. No better investment can be made by taxpayers than to give every youth an opportunity to secure such an education. Such an opportunity is not now within the reach of the great majority of the children of the wage workers. The present system is inadequate and unsatisfactory. Only a small fraction of the children who enter the lower grades continue until they finish the high school course. The prime causes for withdrawal are, first, a lack of interest on the part of the pupils and, secondly, on the part of the parents and a dissatisfaction that the schools do not offer instruction of a more practical character. The pupils become tired of the work they have in hand and see nothing more inviting in the grades ahead. They are conscious of powers, passions and tastes which the school does not recognize. They long to grasp things with their own hands and test the strength of materials and the magnitude of forces.

Owing to past methods and influences, false views and absurd notions possess the minds of too many of our youth, which cause them to shun work at the trades and to seek the office or store as much more genteel and fitting. This notion will be entirely eradicated if industrial training becomes a part of our school system. And in consequence of this system of training he will advance greatly in general intelligence as well as technical skill and in mental and moral worth. He will be a better citizen and a better man and will be more valuable to society and to the country.[1] [The committee further declared that] The 90 per cent who are going into manual occupations have the same right to the best preparation for their life's work that the state can give them as has the 10 per cent who go into the professions.[2]

The committee did not confine itself to a general indorsement of industrial education but made a specific declaration of policy. Some of the more important points in its program were:

(1) Industrial education should not displace any of the present general education but should be added to it. Up to the age of 14, the pupil's time should be devoted to general education; after that, industrial education can begin, but not before.

(2) Industrial education should be controlled and directed by the public, not by private institutes or corporations.

(3) Supplemental technical education for those already employed in the trades should be provided by means of continuation schools.

(4) Schools should be established whereby children between fourteen and sixteen might be taught the principles of trades.

(5) The training given in these schools should be thorough and not merely prepare the worker for a specialized machine position.

[1] Senate Document No. 936, *op. cit.*, p. 112.
[2] *Ibid.*, p. 19.

(6) While the student might be employed upon productive work, emphasis should be " placed upon education rather than upon product."

(7) The teachers of industrial subjects should have practical experience and should be recruited from the trades themselves.

(8) A system of vocational guidance should be established to determine the child's aptitudes.

(9) The curriculum should include civic and social subjects as well as trade technique.   As the report stated, " we want men as well as mechanics."

(10) Trade-unions should not only establish schools of their own wherever possible, but should agitate for the creation of a system of industrial education conforming to the standards laid down.

Through this report, the A. F. of L. came to support industrial education enthusiastically with a definite program to fight for.   The report was of really epoch-making significance because it caused the labor forces of the country to use their influence for a constructive program of vocational education, instead of confining their efforts to the negative and sterile policy of opposition.

This action of the general federation spread slowly back to the unions themselves and the old hostility to vocational education began to disappear.   Many state federations began to agitate for the adoption of industrial education.   Mr. Gompers again pledged the support of labor at the 1914 convention of the National Society for the Promotion of Industrial Education and used all his influence to secure the passage of the Smith-Hughes Bill through Congress.   Indeed, it is doubtful whether that act, giving federal aid to state projects for vocational education, could have been enacted had it not been for the active support of the labor leaders.   We have already pointed out that this act provided that one of the members of the Federal Board should represent labor.   Mr. Arthur E. Holder, a prominent leader of the A. F. of L., was appointed to this position and he has been very influential in framing the Board's policies on various problems.

Since the passage of the act, the A. F. of L. has still further defined its position.   The 1917 convention adopted a resolution urging all affiliated unions to press for the acceptance of the Smith-Hughes Act by the states.[1]   The resolution declared however that it was necessary to prevent the system of industrial education from being perverted to the purposes of exploitation.   It declared that the best safeguard against this was to give organized labor equal representation with the employers on all state and local boards created to administer industrial education.   The resolution also stated that no separate system of control should be set up but that the administration of industrial education should be unified with all other educational work.   Other important features of the report were the statements that:

(1) Vocational and pre-vocational training shall be for educational purposes only and under no circumstances shall it be commercialized through the manufacture of products for sale. (2) In all courses of study—the privileges and obligations of intelligent leadership must be taught more vigorously and effectively than has been done in the traditional civics.   (3) At least in all vocational and industrial courses, an unemasculated industrial history must be taught, which will include an accurate account of the organization of the workers and of the results thereof and will also include a summary of all legislation, both State and Federal, affecting the industries taught.

These resolutions quite clearly show that organized labor

---

[1] For text of resolution adopted see *Proceedings 1917 Convention of A. F. of L.*, pp. 391-93.

did not feel that the battle was won with the mere passage of the Smith-Hughes Act but that it was resolved to democratize the system of industrial training to be established.

Of especial note is their insistence that vocational training should include not only trade instruction, but an understanding of the history of industry, the necessity for collective action, the relation of the state to industry, and the duties of citizenship.

2. The Attitude of the Employers.   Employers early welcomed and supported the trade-school, both because they believed that it would provide a means of trade-training, and because they believed that it would remove preparation for the trades from the potential or actual control of the unions.   The various associations of employers, most notably the National Association of Manufacturers, claimed that the unions through their limitation of apprentices were hostile to industrial education.   The employers therefore advocated both crushing the power of the unions over apprenticeship and building up a system of industrial education.   The committees on Industrial Education of the National Association of Manufacturers, during the first few years, devoted nearly all their spare time to the denunciation of the inequities of the union apprenticeship regulations with a minimum of constructive suggestion.[1]

The trade school was the type that early met with the greatest favor on the part of the manufacturers.   The

[1] Thus the Committee on Industrial Education of the N. A. M. when informed of the intention of trying to get organized labor interested in industrial education, declared that "to invite labor leaders affiliated with the American Federation of Labor to become members of the Society (the National Society for the Promotion of Industrial Education) would be tantamount to inviting the devil and all his imps to participate in a movement for the promotion of the Christian Religion as taught by the lowly Nazarene while on earth!"   "Report of Committee on Industrial Education," *Proceedings 14th Annual Convention, National Association of Manufacturers,* 1909, p. 2.

annual conventions of the National Association of Manufacturers from 1905 to 1908 endorsed the trade school but seemed to feel that the communities should depend for their creation upon the donations of philanthropists rather than upon the use of public funds.

The National Association of Manufacturers also urged that industrial training should be begun at as early an age as possible. Thus Mr. J. W. Van Cleave, President of the Association, declared that the training should commence " just as soon as the boy can hold tools in his hand or say at the age of nine or ten. Give an hour every school day under a competent instructor to the use of tools through all the primary grades. Make this instruction compulsory on every boy." [1] Such a plan would of course have meant that some of the curriculum for those under 14 would have been inevitably displaced.

Shortly after 1910, Mr. H. E. Miles of Wisconsin was made chairman of the Committee on Industrial Education of the National Association of Manufacturers and a series of reports was made under his guidance of a more progressive nature. The 1911 report [2] states that the trade school was incompetent to solve the problem and that the Munich and Wisconsin system of compulsory continuation schools for those over 14 in industry should be universally adopted. To that end, federal and state aid was urged. The convention as a whole resolved that " we favor the establishment in every community of continuation schools wherein the children of 14 to 18 years of age now in the industries shall be instructed in the science and art of their respective industries and in citizenship." [3]

[1] J. W. Van Cleave, "Let Us Send the Whole Boy to School," *Bulletin of the National Association of Manufacturers*, p. 4.

[2] Reprinted as *Bulletin No. 22 of the National Association of Manufacturers*.

[3] *Ibid.*, p. 15.

The 1912 report[1] again pointed out the superiorities of the continuation over the trades school as the core of any system of industrial education. New features were the recommendations: (1) that no deduction of wages should be made for the time during which the juvenile worker attended the continuation school (this time was to be not less than one-half day per week); (2) that so far as possible the teachers of industrial subjects should be recruited from the trades; (3) that the administration of industrial education in each state and locality should be under the direction of a special board composed of practical men, and not under the regular school boards; (4) that a revision of the apprenticeship laws should be made along the lines of the Wisconsin legislation with provision for specific indenturing, state supervision of the contract, and the requirement that the whole trade must be taught. The Convention passed a resolution embodying these points.[2]

The 1913 report[3] again stated that the continuation schools furnish the broad base upon which a system of industrial education should be built and that the trade school was merely the apex of the pyramid. The report declared that " we of the United States have tried for thirty odd years to build the apex of our pyramid before laying its foundation and small indeed has been our accomplishment." [4]

The convention passed a resolution declaring that " state and local boards of control should be created (either as now bodies or re-organizations of former bodies) consisting principally of employers and employees from the vocations." [5]

---

[1] Published as *Bulletin No. 28 of the National Association of Manufacturers*.

[2] *Ibid.,* p. 38.

[3] Published as *Bulletin No. 34 of the N. A. M.*

[4] *Ibid.,* p. 3.

[5] *Ibid.,* p. 24.

(a) *Control.* Despite the fact that for the present, the dual system of administration seems to be defeated, it is probable that it will not be long before many employers will demand that separate boards be created to administer vocational education within the respective states. The attempt by the Illinois Manufacturers Association and the Chicago Commercial Club to accomplish this purpose through the Cooley Bill cannot be viewed as an isolated occurrence. When once the novelty has worn off the various state systems of industrial education, it seems inevitable, in many states at least, that the employers will demand that more "practical" men be added to the controlling boards. A moderate admixture of this class would indeed be of distinct advantage and would probably be approved of by the unions, provided that they too were granted equal representation with the employers.

The preponderance of such interests, however, or the creation of specialized boards, would undoubtedly be opposed by organized labor with all the vigor at its command. That some such contest is likely to occur is evident. In this contest, labor will have the advantage of the *status quo* and will not be compelled to wage an offensive struggle, but can instead merely defend the existing system.

(b) *Content of Courses.* Here again in the light of what has happened, as well as of the logic of the situation, we may expect spirited opposition between the two groups of interests. The employer wants to have his "hands" trained to become better and more docile workmen. Organized labor, of course, does want to train better workmen within certain limits, but it also wants these workmen to be given a training in and an appreciation of the industrial and political background of their work, and also a preparation which will enable them to co-operate more effectively with their fellows to better the condition of their class as a whole. The first part of this program would be regarded by the more militant type of employer as unnecessary while the second would be considered as an innovation to be resisted at all costs.

(c) *The Number to be Trained for Particular Trades.* Just as this question was perhaps the chief point of conflict between labor and capital on the regulation of apprenticeship, so may it be the rock upon which they will split in the administration of industrial education. All grades of labor have not as yet been reduced by the machine process to one interchangeable group. There are still classes of labor that are somewhat distinct from the unskilled. This skilled group enjoys higher real wages than the unskilled largely because of its monopolistic position and the limitation of its supply caused by the fact that the children of the unskilled and poorer paid classes are largely debarred from learning a trade. To be sure, the distinction between these classes is not sharp and is more and more tending to be obliterated by the development of machinery. It is, however, still existent. Furthermore, a large proportion of the A. F. of L. membership and a still larger proportion of the " elder statesmen " who direct its policies belong to this aristocracy of labor.

Now, in so far as the new system of industrial education will permit the unskilled to pass into the upper ranks of labor, the monopolistic advantages of the skilled trades will be destroyed. The real wages of the unskilled will be raised by the decrease in their numbers, while the real wages of the skilled will be lowered until an equality of reward for equal effort and ability between the two groups is reached. Beneficial as this would be for the general public, it would be foolish to believe, unless a new wave of solidarity sweeps over the world of labor, that this will be quietly acquiesced in by the still powerful skilled trades. For them at least, it will mean a real deprivation of advantages they have hitherto possessed.

Mr. Gompers's cryptic statement before the National Society for the Promotion of Industrial Education that " Industrial education must maintain a fair and proper apportionment of the supply of labor power to the demand for labor power in every line of work " [1] and similar statements will be cited by the spokesmen of the skilled trades as a ground for their opposition. The very fact that *their* wages are being lowered will be regarded as proof positive that there is an over-supply of labor being trained for that trade. The result may well be that the skilled trades will try to have just enough men trained to maintain their wages.

On the other hand, there is the danger that so many will by trained for particular occupations that an actual glut will ensue and a large number will be rendered idle or compelled to follow other trades. The determination of how many men should be trained for the various trades is indeed not an easy matter. It calls not only for much careful study of the actual conditions of each trade but for a well thought out policy as well. An approach to this problem is outlined in the concluding chapter.

(d) *Payment of Child's Wages While Attending Continuation School.* Much difficulty has been encountered in enforcing the various compulsory continuation school laws for young workers, by the action of many employers, who either deduct the time spent in school from the child's wages, or discharge him outright. This of course puts the employers who do pay the children wages for the school-time

---

[1] *The Attitude of the American Federation of Labor Towards Industrial Education,* p. 5.

at a distinct disadvantage. Where the child is not paid for attendance, he tends to lose interest in the school-work, while if he is discharged both he and his parents become embittered. A movement is under way to compel the employer to pay the children for the time spent in school. The majority of employers will probably oppose this measure while organized labor will, in general, favor it. If such an act is passed, it will probably lead to a lowering of the hourly wage in order to make up for the time spent in school. This however would at least establish a substantial uniformity of practice which would be far preferable to the present conflicting policies, with their inevitable accompaniment of dissatisfaction.

CHAPTER XVI

A PROGRAM

WE return to the same point from which we started. How can we, in our complex industrial society, devise a system which will fulfill all the functions of the old-time apprenticeship and at the same time improve upon its less favorable aspects. Certainly it cannot be done primarily by trying to breathe new life into the decaying system of formal apprenticeship itself. Apprenticeship can never revive appreciably under modern industry with all of its impersonality, its division of labor, the ephemerality of the relationship between worker and employer, and its basic motive of profit. Rather must our efforts be turned towards bringing a number of factors into harmony, so that children may be at once protected from the undue burdens of industrial life and enabled to develop themselves. If then, we try to gather together the threads of the discussion and to determine just what policy should be adopted for the future, is it not apparent that at least the following steps should be taken?

1. Raise the Age of Compulsory Full-Time Education to 16 Years. The years that a child spends from 14 to 16 in industry today are worse than wasted. He is not ready for industry at 14 and, if he works, he can only do so in blind-alley trades and then only intermittently. Vocational guidance is impossible for the 14-year-old child since there are few occupations into which he can conscientiously be guided which will accept him. Continuation schools, while valuable as an alleviatory measure, can only better the situation to an inappreciable degree. The only effective way to protect the manhood of our youth from being degraded by the work they are now engaged in is to prohibit them from working. The children who leave school at 14 or 15 cannot be called educated, since few of them have finished the grammar grades. They are too scantily equipped to face life and need further protection and development. Certain states have made tentative beginnings at raising the age and educational requirements for compulsory school attendance above 14, and the time seems ripe to raise our national educational minimum to 16 years.

2. Provide Scholarships to Compensate Parents of Poor Children for Loss of Earning Power. To require children to attend school until 16 and to make no financial provision for their support would be to throw an unjustifiable burden upon the already overtaxed shoulders of the poor. Free tuition is not enough to ensure free education. The poor would suffer greatly if deprived of even the meager earnings of their children for two years. In order to protect needy parents from this economic disability, they should be granted scholarships of from 50 to 75% of what the child would be able to earn were he at work. Scholarships of that nature have been successfully administered by the Henry Street Settlement in New York and by the White Williams Foundation of Philadelphia. These scholarships, however, should probably always be somewhat less than what the child would be able to earn, in order that the parent may feel some responsibility. They should be carefully administered and be given only to the needy, while contact with the family should be maintained while the child is in school. The school is the logical instrumentality to administer these scholarships, and a new type of social worker is clearly needed to be attached to the schools for this purpose.

Perhaps a combination of family visitor, school nurse, and teacher is needed to coördinate these various functions.

3. Revise the School Curriculum for the Two Added Years. It would be inconsistent to require two years more of school and at the same time to maintain the existing curriculum with all its faults. The curriculum should be revised so as to give general information and education in these last two years and at the same time give the child some prevocational work, preferably in the form of manual training. It should be general and preparatory in nature, keeping the child away from undue early specialization, and be such as would permit him to enter any one of a number of trades or industries.

4. Create an Adequate System of Vocational Guidance and Supervision of the Young Worker. During the 14-16 year old periods the schools should inform the child about the opportunities in various industries and should try to develop his interests. Guidance, however, is useless without placement and follow-up work, and for that reason we need the re-establishment of a nation-wide system of public employment offices, equipped with a special juvenile division, which will coöperate with the schools and try to place the child in proper positions. Despite the decision of the Supreme Court in the Washington case, it seems necessary, moreover, that these public employment offices be given the exclusive monopoly of placing at least juvenile workers.

The juvenile branches of these public employment offices should of course keep in close touch with the shop and should follow up the work of the child on the job and guide him further as may be necessary.[1] If he is required

[1] For an account of the English experience, see Arthur Greenwood, *Juvenile Labor Exchanges and After-Care.*

to clear through them every time that he seeks a new job, a permanent record can be kept and his progress followed much more effectively. Such bureaus, moreover, would be able to try out on a wider scale the experimentation on mental and physical tests now being conducted by Mrs. Wooley in Cincinnati, and, by correlating them with actual success in industry, should be able to work out approximately accurate criteria of ability.

5. Establish Compulsory Continuation Schools for Children Between 16 and 18 in all American Communities. With the raising of the compulsory school age from 14 to 16, the ages for compulsory continuation school attendance should also be moved up two years. Attendance at these should be for not less than 8 hours per week for the period of from 16 to 18 years. If a child is unemployed during these years, he should be compelled to attend school full-time until he finds another position. This would at once protect the child from the perils surrounding idleness and deter him from throwing up positions at the slightest excuse. The curriculum of these continuation schools should include trade extension, trade preparatory and general subjects. By means of the continuation school, therefore. society would be enabled to keep its supervision over the boy for a still longer period.

6. Prohibit the Entrance into Certain "Blind-Alley" Trades for Children under 18. Certain kinds of labor are disastrous for youth and since a 16 year old child cannot be depended upon to choose wisely, the state should protect the child and itself from the consequences of the ignorance, helplessness and carelessness of the individual. Among the jobs which should be barred are the street trades, such as those of messenger boy, newsboy and bootblack and for girls, chambermaid work in hotels and boarding houses, *etc.*

7. Establish Voluntary Schools for Those Over 18 to be Conducted during Off-Hours and During Periods of Unemployment. Opportunity for education should be provided for those over 18 who wish to study further. These classes may be held at night, or better still, on Saturdays. The subjects taught should include not only an expansion of the trade extension and trade preparation training given in the compulsory continuation schools, but subjects of a general and cultural nature as well. As Mr. and Mrs. Sydney Webb suggest, there should be opportunity for the unemployed adults to study trades while idle, and thus be better prepared to obtain and hold positions.

8. Create a Limited Number of Trade-Schools. The rôle of the trade-school is but a minor one. A few such schools would be very valuable in training men, already experienced in industry, to become especially skilled or to train them for foremanship. Scholarship arrangements by which plants would send some of their promising men to the trade-schools would be a most effective method of co-operation.

9. Every Industrial Enterprise of Moderate Size should Establish a Training Department and an Industrial Relations Division, Charged with Real Powers. The worker needs to be guided and directed at his work. This cannot be left solely to the foremen, since they are already overburdened by the myriad of tasks that are heaped upon them. The creation of a functionalized training department, heading up under a general industrial relations division, would furnish a definite instrumentality whereby new men might be "broken in" with a minimum of loss and the efficiency of the older hands raised.[1] This would also permit of the

[1] For an outline of suggested organization, see my article " Plant Administration of Labor," *Journal of Political Economy*, July, 1919, pp. 544-560.

changing of men from position to position, and the adoption of scientific methods of promotion. Such a department would train workers for specific positions and give the specialized production training that no school system can impart.

10. Organize each Industry and Secure Collective Action in Training the Workers. It has been pointed out that when the burden of training workmen rests solely upon the individual firm, concerns are deterred from training lest other employers should "steal" the men once they have been trained, while many others are so small that they cannot afford an adequate training department. The employers and employees of an industry organized in a joint body,[1] similar to the Whitley councils in England, could take steps to meet the situation by (a) pledging themselves not to entice apprentices from the plant that trained them, (b) carrying on trade investigations and publishing courses of study to assist individual plants in their training program, (c) creating and supporting schools or preferably training departments within plants, whereby the training given the workmen of the smaller plants may be pooled, (d) computing, with the assistance of governmental authorities, the number of learners needed annually in the industry as a whole,[2] and (e) advising the educational authorities concerning the vocational education given under the public school system.

11. Enact and Enforce Legislation Providing for the

---

[1] The employers and unions in the book and job printing trades are beginning to take joint action on the control and supervision of apprenticeship.

[2] For an excellent discussion of the proper method of computing the number of skilled workers needed, together with the necessary mathematical formulae see C. P. Sanger, "The Fair Number of Apprentices to a Trade," *Economic Journal*, vol. v, pp. 613-36.

Registration and Supervision of Formal Apprenticeship by the States.   State action however is needed to supplement action by the industries as well as to provide general direction should the industries refuse to adopt collective measures.   The Wisconsin apprenticeship law might well be followed by all the industrial states, and thus make apprenticeship a definite and supervised contract to be carried out by both parties.   Legislation without proper administration, however, is useless and a specialized agency should be created to follow up the apprentice problem and see that the contracts were respected.   Such a system, by making the conditions definite, might well lead, as in Wisconsin, to a moderate recrudescence of apprenticeship.

12. Confide the Administration of the System of Vocational Education in the Main to the Same Body that Administers other Branches of Education.   In order to protect society, it is necessary that the public system of vocational education should be directed by the same body that directs general education but it is essential that both workers and employers should have advisory committees to advise the educational authorities on the needs of industry and the best means of coördinating school and shop.

13. Increase the Salaries of Teachers of Industrial and Vocational Subjects Sufficiently to Attract Skilled Craftsmen to the Teaching Profession.   The principle that skilled workmen should be given teacher-training and then used as teachers of vocational subjects is fundamentally sound. Skilled workmen, however, will never leave their trades for the low salaries now being paid, and in consequence the ranks of the teachers are being filled by a large percentage of mediocre workmen or by failures.   This plainly will produce a travesty upon industrial education unless competent teachers are secured.   They can only be secured by providing adequate rewards.

14. Develop Other Agencies beside the State to Assist in Providing Supplementary Vocational Training. It has been indicated that industrial education should not be solely a governmental affair. The government, to be sure, is the only agency that can create a compulsory national minimum of education, and the main part of the program must necessarily be confided to it. But other groups can and should supplement the efforts of the government. The unions might well assist in developing craftsmanship among their members, while the employers should continue to develop the corporation schools and training departments, and individuals might endow specialized trade schools. Joint industrial councils would also be of assistance. All groups can assist and all should do so. More indeed will be accomplished if there are several bodies approaching the situation from different viewpoints, and the result will be an enrichment of experience that would be lacking under purely governmental activity.

15. Have System Administered from the Standpoint of Social as well as Industrial Efficiency. Apprenticeship was an institution designed to turn out good men as well as good workmen. Any modern revival that confines its attention purely to the immediately practical aspects neglects, therefore, a significant part of the old system. This neglect should not be tolerated in any plan devised. It is as important for society to have good citizens as it is for industry to have efficient workmen. It is as important for the individual to know how to live as it is for him to know how to make a living. The curriculum of any such system of industrial education should, therefore, include such subjects as civics, hygiene, physical training, practical economics, industrial history and literature, as well as more immediately utilitarian subjects.

16. Provide Funds for this System from the Social Surplus. The carrying out of such a program will necessarily involve an additional annual expenditure of many million dollars. An immediate extension of the existing system of federal aid is, therefore, a necessity. These funds should be secured by means of income, excess profits and inheritance taxes derived from the social surplus that the present economic system produces. Such a use of the surplus would be most productive, for it would be developing the human resources of the country and would bring out latent talent that would otherwise be unused.

17. Create a Federal Department of Education to Administer the System. It seems improbable that the Federal Board for Vocational Education can continue to administer the system of vocational education as it develops. Boards are not the best organs of administration. It seems clear that education deserves to be administered by a federal department, whose secretary would be a member of the cabinet. Vocational education should form one branch of this department.

BIBLIOGRAPHICAL NOTE

A complete bibliography on apprenticeship and industrial education would be out of place in a work of this compass. For those, however, who wish to go further into the various topics, the following works will be found helpful.

1. THE ENGLISH BACKGROUND OF APPRENTICESHIP:

Dunlop, J. C. and Denman, R. D., *English Apprenticeship and Child Labour.*

Scott, Jonathan F., *Historical Essays in Apprenticeship and Vocational Education.*

2. THE HISTORICAL DEVELOPMENT OF APPRENTICESHIP IN AMERICA:

Seybold, Robert F., *Apprenticeship and Apprenticeship Education in Colonial New England and New York.*

Sartorius von Waltershausen, A., *Die Arbeits-Verfassung der Englischen Kolonien in Nord-Amerika,* Strassburg, 1894.

Geiser, Karl F., *Redemptioners and Indentured Servants in Pennsylvania.*

Ballagh, J. C., *White Servitude in Virginia.*

McCormac, E. L., *White Servitude in Maryland.*

New York Historical Societies Collections, vols. xviii and xlii containing indentures of apprentices.

Luther, Seth, *Address to the Workingmen of New England.*

Otey, *Beginnings of Child Labor Legislation in Certain States,* vol. vii of the *Report on Conditions of Women and Child Wage-Earners.*

Commons, John R. and Associates, *Documentary History of American Industrial Society,* 10 vols.

——, *History of Labor in the United States,* 2 vols.

Lescohier, Don D., *The Knights of St. Crispin.*

Whitney, James, *Apprenticeship,* Philadelphia, 1871.

Report of Massachusetts Committee on Relations of Apprentices to Employers.

Wright, Carrol D., "Apprenticeship and its Relation to Industrial Education," U. S. Bureau of Education, *Bulletin No. 6,* 1908.

Douglas, Paul H., "The Recrudescence of Apprenticeship in Wisconsin," *School and Society,* Jan. 5, 1918, pp. 22-23.

3. THE PRESENT CONDITION OF CHILDREN IN INDUSTRY:

Report of the Commission on National Aid to Vocational Education, House Doc. 1004, 63rd Congress, 2nd Session, 2 vols.

Thorndike, E. L., "The Elimination of Pupils from Schools," United States Bureau of Education, *Bull. No. 4,* 1908.

Strayer, George D., "Age and Grade Census of Schools and Colleges," United States Bureau of Education, *Bull. No. 5,* 1911.

Report on Condition of Women and Child Wage-Earners in the United States, 19 vols., Senate Doc. 645, 61st Congress, 2nd Session.

Barrows, Alice P., "Report of Vocational Guidance Survey," *Bull. No. 9,* Public Education Association of the City of New York.

Report Massachusetts Commission on Industrial and Technical Education (1906).

Atherton, Sarah H., *Survey of Wage-Earning Girls below 16 years of age in Wilkesbarre, Pa.,* published by the National Consumers' League.

Talbert, Ernest L., *Opportunities in School and Industry for Children of the Stockyards District.*

Davis, Anne, *Finding Employment for Children Who Leave the Grade Schools to go to Work.*

Hiatt, J. S., *The Child, The School, and The Job.*

4. THE AMOUNT AND CHARACTER OF SKILL REQUIRED IN MODERN INDUSTRY:

de Rousiers, Paul, *The Labour Question in Britain.*

Thirteenth Annual Report United States Bureau of Labor, "Report on Hand and Machine Labor."

Taylor, Frederick W., *Shop Management.*

Drury, Horace B., *Scientific Management.*

The Present State of the Art of Industrial Management, Report of Committee on Administration of National Society of Mechanical Engineers (1912), reprinted in C. B. Thompson's *Scientific Management,* pp. 153-174.

"Vocational Education Survey of Richmond, Va., *Bull. 162,* U. S. Bureau of Labor Statistics.

"Vocational Education Survey of Minneapolis, Minn.," *Bull. 199,* U. S. Bureau of Labor Statistics.

"Vocational Education Surveys of Richmond, Evansville, and Indianapolis, Indiana," Indiana State Board of Education, *Bulletins Nos. 18, 19 and 21.*

5. THE STATUS OF WOMEN IN INDUSTRY:

Report on the Condition of Women and Child Wage-Earners (19 vols.) referred to above.

Abbott, Edith, *Women in Industry.*
Hedges, Anna C., *The Wage-Worth of School Training.*
References to the studies by Van Kleeck, O'Leary, Bryner,
Allinson, Perry, Butler, Leonard, and Phillips on specific trades
can be found in the footnotes of Chapter VI.

6. The General Aspects of Industrial Education:

Eighth Annual Report U. S. Bureau of Labor (1892) on Industrial
Education.
Seventeenth Annual Report U. S. Bureau of Labor (1902) on Trade
and Technical Education.
"Trade and Technical Education in the United States," *Bull. 54,*
U. S. Bureau of Labor (1904).
Twenty-fifth Annual Report U. S. Bureau of Labor (1910) on
Industrial Education.
Bulletins of the National Society for the Promotion of Industrial
Education, now the National Society for Vocational Education.
Persons, Harlow, S., *Industrial Education.*
Leake, A. H., *Industrial Education.*
Snedden, David, *The Problem of Vocational Education.*
Gillette, J. M., *Vocational Education.*
Federal Board for Vocational Education, *Bull. 17,* Trade and
Industrial Education.
Hill, David S., *An Introduction to Vocational Education.*

7. The Trade School:

*The Report of the Massachusetts Commission on Technical and
Industrial Education* (1906).
Dean, Arthur D., *The Worker and the State.*

8. Evening and Correspondence Schools:

Annual Reports Commissioner of Education.
Jones, Arthur J., "The Continuation School in the United States,"
U. S. Bureau of Education, *Bull. No. 1,* 1907.
Van Kleeck, Mary, *Working Girls in Evening Schools.*

9. Corporation Schools and Training Departments:

Publications of the National Association of Corporation Schools.
Bulletins of the United States Training Service.
Miles, H. E., "The Vestibule School," *The Survey,* March 6, 1920,
pp. 700-706.
Beatty, A. J., *The Corporation School.*
Kelley, Roy W., *Training Industrial Workers.*

10. Coöperative and Part-Time Continuation Schools:

Park, C. W., "The Coöperative System of Education," U. S. Bureau
of Education, *Bull. No. 37,* 1916.

McCann, M. R., " The Fitchburg Plan of Coöperative Education," Bureau of Education, *Bull. No. 50, 1913.*

Kerchensteiner, Georg, *Three Lectures on Vocational Training.*

Carris, Lewis H., " Part-Time Compulsory School Attendance Laws," read before National Society for Vocational Education, Feb. 21, 1920.

Federal Board for Vocational Education, *Bull. 19,* " Part-time Trade Industrial Education."

11. VOCATIONAL GUIDANCE:

Brewer, John M., *The Vocational Guidance Movement.*

Bloomfield, Meyer, *Youth, School and Vocation.*

——, " The School and the Start in Life," U. S. Bureau of Education, *Bull. No. 4, 1914.*

——, *Readings in Vocational and Moral Guidance.*

Davis, J. B., *Vocational and Moral Guidance.*

Wooley, Mary T., " Charting Childhood in Cincinnati," *The Survey* vol. xxx, pp. 601-606 (August 9, 1913).

——, " The Issuing of Working Permits and its Bearing on Other School Problems," *School and Society,* vol. i, pp. 726-733 (May 22, 1915).

Link, Henry C., *Employment Psychology.*

12. FEDERAL AID FOR VOCATIONAL EDUCATION :

Report of Commission on National Aid to Vocational Education, 2 vols., House Doc. 1004, 63rd Congress, 2nd Session.

" What is the Smith-Hughes Act? " *Bull. No. 28* of the National Society for the Promotion of Industrial Education.

Federal Board for Vocational Education, *Bull. No. 2,* " Statement of Policies."

First, Second, and Third Annual Reports of the Federal Board for Vocational Education.

Douglas, Paul H., " The Development of a System of Federal Grants-in-Aid," *Political Science Quarterly,* vol. xxxv, pp. 255-272, 522-545 (June and December, 1920).

13. THE ATTITUDE OF LABOR AND CAPITAL TOWARDS APPRENTICESHIP AND INDUSTRIAL EDUCATION :

In addition to the historical references given, see:

Bemis, Edward W., " The Relations of Trade-Unions to Apprentices," *Quarterly Journal of Economics,* vol. xvi, pp. 76-93.

Motley, J. M., "Apprenticeship in American Trade Unions," *Johns Hopkins University Studies.*

Weyl and Sakolski, " Conditions of Entrance to the Principal Trades," U. S. Bureau of Labor, *Bull. No. 67.*

Sikes, George C., "Old and New Conditions of Apprenticeship in Building Trades," *Journal of Political Economy*, voL ii, pp. 408.

Wolfe, French E., "Conditions of Entrance to American Trade Unions," *Johns Hopkins University Studies.*

Ashworth, John H., "The Helper in American Trades-Unions," *Johns Hopkins University Studies.*

Report of Committee on Industrial Education of the American Federation of Labor, published as Senate Document No. 936, 62nd Congress, 2nd Session.

Bulletins National Association of Manufacturers.

Sanger, C. P., "The Fair Number of Apprentices to a Trade," *Economic Journal*, voL v, pp. 613-36 (1895).

14. ECONOMIC ASPECTS OF INDUSTRIAL EDUCATION:

Dodge, J. M., *Transactions American Society Mechanical Engineers*, voL xxv, pp. 40-48.

O'Leary, Wesley A., "The Wage Value of Vocational Training," *Fourth Annual Report New York Factory Investigation Commission*, pp. 1411-1460.

Ellis, A. Caswell, "The Money Value of Education," U. S. Bureau of Education, *Bull.* No. *22*, 1917.

Taussig, Frank W., "Minimum Wages for Women," *Quarterly Journal of Economics*, vol. xxx, pp. 411-443.

The footnotes to the various chapters will also serve as a guide to the investigator. There are several bibliographies which will open up a wider field, and among these may be mentioned:

Richards, Charles R., "Selected Bibliography on Industrial Education" (1907), published as *Bull. No. 2* of the National Society for the Promotion of Industrial Education.

"Selected Bibliography on Industrial Education" in the *Twenty-fifth Annual Report of the U. S. Bureau of Labor* (1911), pp. 519-539.

"Bibliography of Industrial, Vocational and Trade Education," U. S. Bureau of Education, *Bull. No. 22* (1913).

Brewer, John M., and Kelley, Roy W., *A Selected and Critical Bibliography of Vocational Guidance* (1917), Harvard University Press.

INDEX

A

Accidents, 125-126

Age of compulsory education advocated, 331, 332; at which children leave school, 85-88

Agriculture, 26, 27, 28, 38-39, 138

American Federation of Labor, attitude towards apprenticeship 281; advocacy of Smith-Hughes bill, 293; general policy towards industrial education, 315-323

Americanization classes, 218

Apprenticeship, definition, 11-12; English background, 25, 26; extent, 12-16; functions, 19-20, 41-47; 49-52; indentured servants and, 28-29; colonial, 39-52; legal theories, 12, 22-23-29; effect of factory system upon, 54-56, 56-58, 60-62, 73-74; 82-84; and trades unions, 61-67, 69-73; 75; in Wisconsin, 78-80; for women, 48-49; schools, 212-218, 222-228

Artificers, Statute of, 25-26

Arts and Crafts Movement, 122

Atherton, Sarah, 93

Ayres, L. P., 86, 88n., 199n
314

B

Ballagh, J. C., 33f, 38

77, 291

334-335

8

112, 116

C

Canadian Commission on Technical Education, 242

Chapin, R. C., 90
551]

Chicago City Club, investigation

Club, 301, 327
of Workingmen, 64, 65, 66

Child labor, 55, 56-59, 60-61, 85, 99-105, 105-109

Classes, unskilled workers, 218

Clerical force, 168-170; training of, 222

Cygnaeus, 176

Clothing industry, 112, 114, 142-150

Commons, J. R., 37

Continuation Schools, compared with co-operative schools, 244-246; early advocacy of, 252-253; Ohio, 253-254; Wisconsin, 254-255; New York, 255-256; New Jersey, 256; Massachusetts, 256-259; Indiana, 259-260, Pennsylvania, 260-262; results of Smith-Hughes act upon, 262; digest of recent laws, 263-265; advantages of, 265-268; economic effects, 312-3; suggested, 334

Cooley, E. J., 301

Coöperative schools, comparison with continuation schools, 244-250; origin of, 246-248; where practised, 247-251; evaluation of, 265-266
234
schools, 212-218, 223-

Correspondence schools, 239-43

Cotton industry, 56-59, 100, 112, 114, 151

D

David Ranken School, 189, 194, 196, 199

Davis, Anne, 98

Dean, Arthur D., 191

Debtors, 31-32, 42
345

Dewey, John, 273
Division of labor, 55-56, 86-87
Dodge, J. M., 307-308
Douglas Commission, 90, 96, 190-191
Domestic service, 139-142
"Dual" control, 301-302, 327
Dunlap, O. J., 23n.

E

Eastman, Crystal, 125-126
Economic effects of vocational
  education, 307-314
Eddis, William, 38
Ellis, A. Caswell, 308
Emergency Fleet Corporation, 116, 117
Employment bureaus, for juveniles, 288-290, 333-334
Evening schools, 229-230; private, 231-235; public, 235-239

F

Factory system, 52-56, 56-60, 62, 64, 75-76
Federal Aid, for vocational education, 293-298; response of states to, 300-304, 305; advantages of, 306
Federal Board for Vocational Education, creation, 294-295; powers, 298-299; activities, 299-302, 304-305
Federal Employment Service, 287, 290, 233
Federation of Organized Trades and Labor Unions, 75
Fitchburg coöperative school, 248-249
Flexner, Abraham, 17
Food industries, 112, 115, 132, 133, 152-154
Ford Automobile Works, 110
Foremanship, 120-122, 130-131, 211-212

G

Gallatin, Albert, 57
General Electric Co., 219, 226, 227
German, trade schools, 191-192; continuation schools, 24, 252
Gompers, Samuel, 321, 329
Green, Duff, 61
Guilds, English, 25-26; French, 23; Oriental, 16; American, 50

Glass blowing, 64, 70: child labor in, 314

H

Handicraft, 51-52
Hat workers, 61, 63
Health, of workers, 126, 127, 128
Henderschott, F. C., 225
Hoe and Co., 213
Hirsch, Baron de (Trade School), 188, 307
Holder, Arthur E., 299n, 322
Housekeeping, 170-173

I

Immigration, colonial, 27-28, 30-33; new and old, 76-77
Indenture, 12, 78
Indentured servants, 27, 39
Industrial Revolution, 53-55
Industrial schools, 207-210
Interest, as method of vocational
  guidance, 273-277
Iron-Molders Union, 63, 65

J

Job analysis, 287
Jones, A. J., 252

K

Kirchensteiner, Georg, 191-192, 252
Knights of St. Crispin, 64

L .

Labor-saving machinery, 313-314
Legal theories, of apprenticeship, 11, 12, 22-23, 29
Length, of apprenticeship, 13, 14, 23, 40-41, 49, 51, 60, 66, 67
Life occupations, of manual training graduates, 185
Link, H. C., 220, 282
Localization of industry, 198-199
Luther, Seth, 54, 58

M

Machine, building, 111; using, 112-117, repairing, 117-119
Mandatory and permissive continuation schools, 253-265
Manhattan Trade School, 195
Manual Training, 176-186; origin, 176-177; beginnings in America, 177-180; growth, 180-184; inadequacy of, 184-186

Maryland, indentured service in,
   27, 31, 33, 34, 35, 36, 38; child
   labor in, 101-103, 105
Master, 14-15, 34-35, 50-51
Miles. H. E., 193, 205, 324
Millinery, 144-146
Mitchell, John, 319
More, L. B., 90-91
Motley, J. M., 70

N

National Association of Corporation Schools, 214-216, 223
National Association of Manufacturers, 293, 316, 323, 326
National Society for Vocational
   Education (National Society for
   the Promotion of Industrial Education), 252, 293, 317, 272
New England, apprentices and apprenticeship education, 42-43, 43-
   45; early trades, 39-40; factory
   system 53-54; child labor 57-59
New York, apprenticeship and indentured service in, 40-41, 46;
   apprentice law of, 1871, 67-69
New York Trade School, 187, 315
Non-competing groups, 129-130,
   266-268, 310-313

O

Ogburn W. F., 93,95
O'Leary, W. A., 308

P

Parsons, Frank, 270, 277
Pennsylvania, apprenticeship and
   indentured service in, 28, 36, 40-
   41, 46
Permissive and mandatory con-
   tinuation schools, 253-265
Persons, C. E., 134
Poor law, English, 26; colonial,
   42-43; 19th Century, 59
Poverty, 88-95
Private schools, early, 56, 230;
   trade, 187-189, 192, 200-202;
   plant, 211-228; evening, 231-235;
   correspondence, 240-243
Professions, 17, 138
Program, proposed, 331-339
Prince, Lucinda W., 167-168
Prosser, C. A., 299
Psychological tests, 279-282
Public Schools, free, 44, 46-47, 86,
   87, 210, 331-332; manual training,

178-180, 182-186; trade, 189, 190,
   193, 335; technical high, 202-205;
   industrial, 207-210; evening, 230,
   235-239; co-operative, 246-251;
   continuation, 252-268, 334; agricultural, 295
Pupil-teacher system, 18

R

Railway schools, 213, 214, 217
Recording and Computing Mach-
   ines Co. 221
Richards, C. R., 317
Russell Sage Foundation, 199, 272

S

Sale of product, 195-198
Salaries of vocational teachers, 337
Salesmanship, 163-168, 222
Schneider, Herman, 246-248
Scholarships for children of poor,
   332, 333
School, age at which children
   leave, 85-88; reasons for leaving,
   88-96
Scientific Management, 120-122
Shipbuilding, 116-117
Shoe-makers, 50, 53, 62, 64, 150
Skill, in modern industry, 111-112,
   112-122; 160-162
Slater, Samuel, 53, 59
Slavery, and apprenticeship, 20-22;
   and indentured service, 36, 37-39
Smith, Adam, 12-13, 109
Smith-Hughes Act, 292-306: effect
   on continuation schools 262-265
South, indentured service in, 27-
   28, 30-31, 32-33, 33-39
Specialization, 109-110, 112-116,
   123-125
Steinmetz, C. P., 224
Strayer, G. D., 88
Streightoff, F. H., 91
Strikes, 70, 71
Supply of labor, what is a proper?,
   328-329
Surveys, of industries, 284-288; of
   schools, 272

T

Tabor Manufacturing Co., 121
Talbert, E. L., 291
Taussig, F. W., 309
Taylor, F. W., 120n, 121n, 211
Teacher-training, 296-297: 337

Technical high schools, 202-205
Textile industry, 112, 114, 150-152
Thorndike, E. L., 86-88, 273-274
Trade preparatory schools, 205-207
Trades-Unions, early attitude towards apprentices, 60-62; attempts to regulate apprenticeship, 62-67, 69-70; effect of restrictions, 70-73; attitude towards vocational education, 315-323
Trade schools, 187, 190-192; private charitable, 187-189; private commercial, 200-202; public, 189-190; German, 191-192; relative merits of, 193-200
Trade tests, 281-282
Training departments, 212, 219-221, 222-228
Turnover, of juvenile labor, 100-106
Typographers, 61, 62, 63, 66, 70, 73, 74
Typothetae, United, 326

U

Unemployment of juveniles, 105-108; effect of vocational training upon, 313
United Shoe Machinery Co., 117-118

Unskilled labor, 86, 109-122, 160-162

V

Van Cleave, J. W., 324
Van Kleeck, Mary, 160, 239, 285n.
Vestibule schools, 220-221
Vocational guidance, aim, 269-270; development of, 270-273; methods of, 273-288; problems of, 288-292, 333-334

W

Wages, of juvenile labor, 99-100; and the standard of living, 90-94; effect of vocational education upon, 307-310; 310-313; payment to children while attending continuation schools, 329-330
Williamson Free school, 187-188, 194
Winona Technical Institute, 316
Winslow, C. H., 319
Women, in industry, 138-170
Woodbury, R. M., 104, 106
Woods, Erville B., 276
Woodward, C. M., 177, 180
Wooley, Helen T., 281, 291, 334

Y

Y. M. C. A., 231-233
Y. W. C. A., 233

Printed in the United States
141250LV00003B/39/A